CW00847720

CONTENTS

COMMITMENT AND CONTROVERSY: LIVING IN TWO WORLDS.

COMMITMENT AND CONTROVERSY: LIVING IN TWO WORLDS.

COLLECTED ESSAYS AND BLOGS

Jeremy Rosen

ISBN: 151233443X
ISBN 13: 9781512334432
Library of Congress Control Number: 2015908717
CreateSpace Independent Publishing Platform
North Charleston, South Carolina

INTRODUCTION

"Better the criticisms of a friend than the kisses of an enemy."

Proverbs 27.6.

This book is a collection of writings I have submitted as columns and blogs over the past ten years. They vary in style and quality. Some are written as an immediate response to events or requests. Others are more considered. Some are serious, others written with tongue in cheek. But they all reflect the fact that I live in two worlds, admire a lot of what goes on in them both and yet deplore a great deal too.

I have always felt myself to be a maverick and have enjoyed tilting at windmills. There is an antinomian, anti-establishment streak in me despite my having occupied positions of authority in education and the rabbinate. Even when I think I have absolutely no effect on the world around me, I still feel impelled to criticize whatever I believe is morally wrong, though Lord knows I am no perfect example myself.

As a lifelong teacher I also aim to instruct and to open minds to alternative theories and points of view. I have always relished debate and disagreement and like to think it has prevented me from being intellectually and religiously close-minded. But I also want to entertain and I hope that whether my readers agree or not, they will still find these pieces of interest and challenge. They reflect the complexity of my loyalties and bêtes noir both as a committed Jew and as a citizen of the world. I never expect to be agreed with by everyone and am always pleasantly surprised when I discover that others share my views and biases.

Some of my writings are aimed at a universal audience, others primarily at Jews like me struggling to find a balance in the world we inhabit. We are sometimes hyper-sensitive, overly defensive and we over react. But at root I believe that we are all created in the Image of God, metaphorically of course. And that our aim in life is to be a kind, considerate and supportive as we can to everyone else we come into contact with whether they reciprocate or not.

This collection has been supported by my old school friend Joe Dwek MBE who was also the Head of my House and often sprang to my defense when he thought my father, my Headmaster, was treating me unfairly. The truth is that I probably deserved it. Years later he was supportive too as a Governor of Carmel College. We went through some good and some tough times together.

I am eternally grateful for everything my parents gave me and for the love and support of my wife, my family and my friends.

Jeremy Rosen New York 2015

PART 1

JEWISH LIFE

JUDAISM LIVES

Often attributed to Ernest Bloch is the thought that it is anti-Semitism that, for all its perniciousness, has preserved the Jews. Of course, if that were true, our position in the world would be very different today. After all (according to the *Encyclopedia Judaica*), Jews accounted for about 1 percent of the population of the Roman Empire at a time when, under the emperor Augustus, the empire's total population was around fifty-six million. And in medieval times, Jews again accounted for 1 percent of the Western world. Populations fluctuated, indeed, because of natural disasters, plagues, and wars. But by logic and right, we should be at least 1 percent of the Middle Eastern and Western world's population now. In fact we are a small fraction of that.

During these thousands of years, of course, Jews were not only being killed in vast numbers; they were also constantly converting to other religions, whether by force or simply to survive. Some converted because they actually believed in the alternatives (or perhaps came to after the fact). So if it was anti-Semitism that was keeping us alive, then frankly, it did a lousy job.

The truth is that proponents of such a madcap theory are invariably those Jews who want to find a reason for Jewish survival other than a profound commitment to Jewish civilization and religion. So they seek alternative theories to explain Judaism's persistence. Defining Judaism through historical, tragic, or other forms of "feeling Jewish" avoids it having to impinge on their daily lives. It's like claiming you can love someone without any sense of obligation. You can't argue with it, but it does seem trivial.

External threats do often bring out the best in us, but also the worst. The late Israeli diplomat and rabbi Yaakov Herzog often liked to say that were it not for the eternal threat, the internal divisions in Israeli society would have torn it apart long ago. I would add that the average left-wing secular Israeli has more in common with the average left-wing secular Arab than he or she has with Orthodox Jews. Indeed, soon after the establishment of the State of Israel, the Israeli Communist Party merged with the Arab Communists, while Ben-Gurion, the secular, and Begin, the traditional, were at armed loggerheads. This may be even truer now that both the right-wing and the Orthodox populations of Israel have grown exponentially.

In the Jewish world today, there is a perpetual motion of subsidized seminars, conferences, books, and articles all trying to find ways of keeping the Jewish people together so long as one doesn't have to live a traditional Jewish life. Yet it seems to me so obvious that it is the very behaviorism that is the distinguishing mark of the Jewish religion that has been the real reason for our survival against all the odds. This doesn't mean you have to be traditional to be Jewish, or that without tradition one cannot remain a Jew. But if you seek a way to perpetuate any tradition, you can only do it by living it.

Rabbi Marc Angel's Institute for Jewish Ideas and Ideals makes an important contribution to "sane Judaism" (www.Jewishideas.org). Its recent publication *Conversations* [1] focuses on why so many synagogues fail to inspire. The message one gets is that there are no shortcuts. Every panacea has been tried: change the music, change the words, change the style. And after all that has been tried for over a century in the United States, apart from the odd minor spike, it has had no significant overall effect on synagogue attendance. Quite the opposite is the case. Because, as with anything you want to take seriously, there are no simple fixes, only serious commitment. Jews vary in the way they like to pray, but the common denominator of those who are involved is that they are committed to act (in whichever way they decide works for them).

1 Conversation, Winter 2009 Orthodoxy and Religious Leadership

An article by James Loeffler appeared in *Mosaic* magazine bemoaning the collapse of secular Jewish culture in the United States (http://mosaicmagazine.com/essay/2014/05/the-death-of-jewish-culture/). He refers to the "death" of two institutions dedicated to Jewish culture in America, Makor and the National Foundation for Jewish Culture, saying that both of them failed the test of relevance. If the cause of Jewish culture cannot sustain a modest physical presence in New York City, the symbolic center of American Jewish life, then it would seem to have exhausted its *raison d'être*. Indeed, the time may have come to acknowledge the truth: the project of Jewish culture is dead.

Loeffler concedes that Jewish film festivals, klezmer, new Jewish museums, Jewish artists and composers making Jewish art and music, and Jewish titles enjoy a reliable body of readers and buyers, but notes, Jewish culture means something other than simply the sum total of works of art or other artifacts, of whatever quality, made by individuals who happen to be Jews. Nor is Jewish culture merely the sum total of such works made by Jews on explicitly Jewish themes. It refers instead to a self-consciously modern, public culture, rooted in the unique civilization that gave it birth and formed its voice, and expressive of a thick, expansive, and holistic identity.

I happen to think that what Loeffler says goes for the United States but not for Israel, where secular culture is indeed alive and flourishing precisely because it is the default although it too is increasingly using religious themes, poetry and music. But there Israeli identity works under different parameters than in the Diaspora, where it is marginal.

There have always been institutions, movements, and ideologies (and music) that have had mass appeal. But others have focused on quality, intensity, and depth. Judaism is not a mass movement to be reduced to minimal basic concepts. It's a way of life. You either live it or lose it. That is what is meant by the term used in the Bible, "a kingdom of priests." You have to take it seriously for yourself, not rely on others to do it for you or indeed to define you.

Many of us might not agree with ultra-Orthodoxy, either religiously, politically, or sociologically. We might even feel profoundly alienated from many of its followers for the way they dress and the way they behave. But it cannot be denied that they have come up with the best answer to Hitler. They have rebounded from the cataclysm that the ultimate anti-Semite forced upon them. They are growing all the time. And that is because they do not just care, they act. This does not mean we should not be critical of their failures. Whether they are the moral failings of some of their members or the inability of its leadership to face up to some of its most serious problems. There are enormous challenges within and without. But their commitment to a Jewish way of life, even if excessive on occasion, has to be admired.

JEWISH STATE

Modern Western states are slowly adapting to the idea that no one religion should monopolize its affairs. All religions within them should be treated with equality and respect. Too often modern states fail not in the theory as much as the practice. There is a powerful reactionary move in parts of Europe and the Middle East to drag everyone backward toward medievalism by tolerating no-go areas controlled by fanatical religious authorities. Even what is laughably called "mild" Islam in Turkey is failing to protect its secular and other religious minorities.

A state that defines itself as a religious state rarely gives absolutely equal standing to all its citizens. The only safeguard is if religion plays no formal part in the running of the state and its legislature, full stop. It may play even a dominant cultural role, but legislatively it must be defanged.

There are hybrids. Israel is an example of a hybrid. It is officially secular and democratic and gives equal rights to all its citizens regardless of religion. But it does also give preference to Judaism as a religion and to people of Jewish origin. This inevitably has consequences for secular Jews as well as other religions. The compromise worked for many for a while. But it is not working now if most secular Jews, most Christians, and most Arabs feel the state is not protecting or validating them sufficiently. How can it make sense that a Jewish secular couple have to go to Cyprus to get married without religion?

What is the solution? Recently Israel has allowed Muslim recruits to its army to swear on the Koran. Arab Israelis have equal civil and legal rights, yet it is also true that because they are regarded (sometimes very unfairly) as not fully loyal, they are often discriminated against, not by law as much as convention. On the other hand, to equate this with the discrimination of apartheid, in which state-legislated discrimination was the rule and interracial sex was a crime, is of course just the dishonest polemic of the prejudiced. Nevertheless, there is a problem that needs to be addressed. How?

Many Israeli intellectuals seem still caught up in an outdated debate about their identity caused both by their secularism and their left-wing ideology. It's as if they still live in the nineteenth century. In 2014 there was a fascinating debate about what kind of state Israel should be as two secular Israelis battled it out in the pages of *Haaretz*. Shlomo Sand, a secular Israeli professor at Tel Aviv University, is notorious for his banal theory that Jews today have no connection whatsoever with the Land of Israel because they are all descended from non-Jewish Khazars who converted a thousand years ago in the Caucasus. No unbiased academic has taken this seriously ever since Arthur Koestler first floated it in 1976 in his *Thirteenth Tribe*.

But Sand has a smattering of a point in challenging the concept of a Jewish nation as opposed to religion. In his latest book, *How and When I Stopped Being Jewish*, he says he wants to be an Israeli but not a Jew. Of course he is welcome and entitled, and I would say "good riddance." But that will not solve the problem of Jews who want to live in a state that supports Jewish values (however one wants to define them). Sand's arguments have sparked a lively response from other secular Israelis.

Vladimir Shumsky has argued in *Haaretz* that most Israelis, both Jews and Palestinians, feel a Jewish or a Palestinian national identity. This national identity is connected in both cases to a wider community beyond the borders of the state: Jews with world Jewry, and Arab Palestinians with world Islam or Christianity. To substitute a culturally neutral "Israeli nationalism" for this reality makes no sense to those who care about their Judaism or Islam. The only way Israel can truly be a more equitable state of all its citizens is not by eliminating identities but by negotiating rights for both national groups in an Israeli federation, he argues. Plausible, but it evades the question of the relationship between Israeli Palestinians and Palestinian Palestinians within the state.

Secular Israelis and religious Jews can now, if they choose, live safely in many countries outside the State of Israel. Yet many from both camps insist that they have as much right to live in Israel as any other religio-ethnic group that has qualified for a seat in the United Nations such as the separate parts of ex-Yugoslavia. Religious Israelis argue furthermore that whereas a secular Israeli could live the same lifestyle anywhere else in the free world, only in a Jewish state could a religious Jew live where Shabbat is Shabbat and public work stops on Jewish festivals. If there are states for Christians and Muslims, where their religions are state supported and enforced, what moral argument could possibly deny Jews a similar right?

What does the term "Zionism" add to a Judaism that wishes to express itself within a Jewish state? Is it anything more than Jewish nationalism? Before Zionism was created in the nineteenth century, what was the nature of Judaism's relationship to the land? Was it not simply the wish to live within a community of practicing Jews on its historical territory? Did that require a political movement? There was no political movement when thousands of Jews moved to Safed under the Ottomans in the sixteenth century. So why add this controversial notion of Zionism to Jewish proactive dynamism? And why not recognize secular Jews in the way, once upon a time, both Jewish commonwealths did, by including everyone, religious or not?

Zionism is a product of a specific, historic moment in time. It achieved its goal quite miraculously. However if now Israel declares itself to be a Jewish State, Zionism as an ideology becomes redundant. Judaism has been around for thousands of years. Trying to conflate a nineteenth-century nationalist ideology with a millennial religious tradition just cannot work. It's like trying to fit a fat man into a thin man's diving suit. Not only but it gives anti Semites of all sorts an acceptable outlet for their antipathy whereby they hope to avoid the claim that they are anti-Semitic. They are just anti Zionist, they say.

This is why many Israeli politicians now realize that if Israel is to be a Jewish state as opposed to a state for Jews, it must define itself as a Jewish state and support Jewish identity within its mission. The Palestinians should indeed also have a Palestinian state of their own that will define itself in any way it sees fit. Palestinian Israelis and Jewish Israelis, be they secular or religious, should be free to choose which state they want to live in and make whatever adjustments or compromises will be required. This is the fair solution in theory. Sadly, we know it's not that simple.

Given the unlikelihood of reaching an agreed solution with the Palestinians for two states (although I still hope against hope it happens), a single federal state looks like a possibility. Alternatively one might envision a variation of the Ottoman rule. A government bureaucracy ran the country, and each religion, or millet, was responsible for its own affairs. That would be the ideal solution if only the external threat was removed. But it won't be as long as militant Islam exists and so long as militant Judaism wants to defend itself with maximal demands. Or as long as both sides have political leaders with limited imagination and no stomach for risk taking.

Therefore, sadly I see no solution. There is only an unsatisfactory status quo, both externally and internally. That being so, I would argue that we have an obligation to make a regrettable occupation as livable, as fair, and as ethical as we possibly can. But ask politicians to achieve that (anywhere) and you're dreaming!

MARRYING OUT

Recently I have been asked once again to intervene in situations where a young Jew wants to marry a non-Jew. It is such a difficult position to be in. Love is a beautiful emotion, and on the other hand, marriage is such a complex, difficult, and challenging state. Of course both are immensely rewarding when they work. Being Jewish is very important to me, and so is being human. But when faced with this very common situation, inevitable in an open society, what can I do? What can I say? I have been facing this problem ever since I entered the rabbinate forty-five years ago.

In my youthful arrogance, I used to reply to parents that if all they showed of Judaism to their children was a social club with hardly any positive Jewish experience, then why shouldn't their children want to join a bigger social club? After all, I had seen in the Jewish school I attended how so many parents wanted the school to inoculate their children so that they would not marry out, but heaven forefend they should come home and want to be more observant.

But things are more nuanced in reality. I have come across young men from very observant homes who married out. Someone I knew from a Chasidic family fell for a woman in a bar in Moscow, and that was that: married with kids. Another was trapped by pregnancy into an inappropriate marriage. So often circumstances or accidents determined the course of a person's life: where he or she went to university or work, or who happened to know someone who knew someone.

There were other exceptional circumstances. I have met young men and women who were physically or mentally challenged, with little chance of finding a Jewish partner, yet had been fortunate to find someone on the outside who was willing to take care of them and perhaps love them too. Wouldn't I want a Jewish paraplegic to find solace with a nice non-Jewish lady? It is not as though we are dealing with different species.

The sympathetic, universal me wants to say that we must not treat such occurrences as the end of the road. The days are gone when parents sat in mourning for a child who married out, as if he or she had died. One must stay close to one's flesh and blood, regardless of what decisions they make. After all divorce is common. Many marriages tend to last less than they did. The child could return home or make a more appropriate choice the second or even third time around. If one retains a sympathetic connection, this might impact on the children who, ironically or unfairly, in the case of a Jewish woman marrying out, remain Jewish. Although it is true that statistically the children of mixed marriages are far less likely to be positively committed Jews, there are exceptions.

I might want to point out the examples I know of personally in which the non-Jewish partner not only converted but became a far better and more learned and committed Jew than the majority of born Jews I have met. One could argue that incorporating other talent and new genes into the pool might be beneficial. I could point to the biblical Ruth, the Judean and Maccabee kings who brought non-Jewish women into the fold.

But then another reality enters the debate. Without any doubt, marrying out weakens the bonds with one's religion and community. One side may be totally unreceptive or even antagonistic to the sensibilities and history of the other. This will all be disguised or avoided in the romance of love and the honeymoon period. Both parties will want to spend time with their families celebrating conflicting occasions. How will the children be raised? They will flit between conflicting cultures and values. Which of their parents' different families, religions, and cultures will prevail? They will hear very different and confusing messages. The dominant, majority culture will usually win, especially if it is more permissive. And if one parent dies, where and how will the remaining parent bring up the children?

What of the status of the children? If they are not accepted as Jewish by most of the Jewish people, what if one day they want to marry a Jew and find they cannot? Yes, it may sometimes work, but more often than not it doesn't, or it leads inevitably to the loss of the Jewish component.

As a result of Jews from wealthy families marrying out, I have often seen fortunes that might have benefitted Jewish charities fall into the hands of those who had no interest in supporting Jewish causes. We Jews are so few and our history so fraught, our support so limited, losing millions through murder or forced assimilation, that we cannot look dispassionately on those who leave our ranks.

Sadly these arguments and warnings tend to fall on deaf ears when love and passion have taken hold. We fancy that "love conquers all," and it might for a while. But too often when these issues emerge it's invariably too late. However sympathetic a rabbi is, his role after all is to defend Judaism. It is understandable that most parents will want to defend and protect their children. They will find it hard to stand firm because in the end money is usually the only weapon in their arsenal, and experience tells me they will rarely use it. If leadership regards marrying out as just another mild hazard of modernity, are we not failing our communities in withdrawing what few inhibitory factors are left in our heavily acculturated Diaspora communities where over 50 percent marry out and leave? So it falls to the rabbi to raise the problems.

I have always taken a lenient and inclusive approach to the less committed. I have justified this by saying that the majority of Orthodox rabbis take such a rigid and uncompromising line that I know they have driven many away whom they might have salvaged. Surely someone needs to offer an alternative approach, just as Shamai and Hillel presented different ways of defending the faith. Yet the fact is that for every ten converts I have seen welcomed into the fold through easy conversions or sympathetic exceptions, perhaps only two have stayed the course.

In New York I have encountered another phenomenon. In this most pro-Jewish of cities outside of Israel, there are thousands of nice Jewish boys who swear they cannot find a nice Jewish girl. And there are thousands of nice Jewish girls who claim they cannot find nice Jewish boys. Why? It doesn't make sense! Neither does claiming that all Jewish girls are materialist nags and all Jewish males are spoiled mamma's boys. They can't both be right. My own eyes and experience tell me they are not! But where there is no social pressure to marry, and when the availability of immediate gratification is so prevalent, it seems inevitable that without inhibition, without social pressure, we will continue to see the majority disappear while the minority put up the barriers, survive as committed Jews, and indeed expand.

Some are willing to suggest open, easy conversion. But unless the conversion is acceptable across the Jewish spectrum, it will create just as many problems. And to be acceptable, it must be genuine. Most authorities will require a standard of observance that even the Jewish partner is not prepared for.

Logic says, "Fight for one's standards!" Emotion says, "Be kind." My religion encourages me to be sympathetic and supportive as much as it insists on adherence to the letter of the law and discipline. As a parent, I wouldn't want to lose my children, no matter what mistakes they made. Yet if I care for the future of the Jewish people, I know that, except in a few and rare occasions, the Jewish people will lose. And still I side with Hillel, who in the Talmud, when faced with dubious applicants for conversion, gave them the benefit of the doubt.

NOT MY BIBLE

I am not among those who consider it a religious crime to live outside Israel. After all, since the days of the Babylonian Exile (actually even earlier, the Judean kings established an Israelite garrison and temple at Elephantine), large numbers of us have lived beyond our ancestral borders. But I do believe in the idea of *galut*, exile. And by that I mean the profound sense that one is fundamentally at odds with the prevailing culture. Sadly, one can often feel a sense of *galut* within present-day Israel's borders, where so many seem to want to imitate the very worst aspects of Western pop culture.

In America I have recently been feeling it more than ever. Even though for Jews in the Diaspora I cannot think of a better place to live in peace and harmony, you only need to read *FDR and the Jews* by Richard Breitman and Allan J. Lichtman to realize how vehemently we were hated and excluded even in the United States.

One of the most popular television shows in the United States in recent times is the History Channel's *The Bible*. It is watched more than the trashiest reality shows, the banal talent competitions, and the series about zombies and vampires (all good reason for banning television from any sane household).

My issue is not that the part that deals with our Bible is badly researched and full of anomalies and anachronisms. It is when it gets to the New Testament that I realize why anti-Semitism is still so prevalent and persistent all around the world and why I often feel so culturally alienated. The current rise of anti-Semitism is driven by neo-fascist thugs of various religions, and none. But it is the subtle undercurrent of negativity prevalent in more cultured sectors of western life, perpetuated by holy texts that gives a patina of justification for the antipathy.

I am among those who think Saint Paul invented Christianity. Pauline and later Christianity developed a series of myths based on earlier popular ideas rather than on a specific, living human being. There is nothing wrong with that in itself, unless it leads to torturing and killing those who do not agree with you. We too have our earlier Canaanite horror stories. Both Christianity and Islam wanted to supersede what came before. To do this they had to show how their religion was so much better. And to hammer it home they had to present the Jews as primitive, hypocritical, corrupt betrayers of truth. This would be something the new religion was going to put right. The very distinction between Old Testament and New Testament that make up the Christian Bible is a clear statement that we "primitives" are now out of date and out of touch.

I don't know which is worse: the Christians degrading the significance of the Old Testament, or the Muslims claiming that the text was distorted and the narrative twisted by the Jews. Certainly Maimonides was ambivalent. He said that a Jew could take an oath by Allah and Islam was not idolatry, but you could not teach Torah to a Muslim because he did not respect our holy text. On the other hand, while he thought Christianity was idolatry, you could study Torah with them because they did respect the same texts.

In the Christian world, for thousands of years Jews have been cursed and pursued for the "crime" of rejecting Jesus and the greater crime of causing his death. In some quarters we are still blamed for "killing God," ridiculous as such a claim might sound to you and me. As for the myth of Jesus being accused of heresy, you will not find anywhere in Jewish law any hint that it is heresy to say "I am the King of the Jews," "I am the Son of God," or indeed to claim, "I am God." One might think you are a lunatic, but hardly a rational heretic. If trying to make Judaism more popular and humane were a crime, then the great Hillel who lived a generation before would have been in trouble. So would all the many faith healers who abounded at that time.

And if the crime were a political one, like saying "I am the President, or King of the Jews," if the Romans had an issue with that, we certainly didn't. The proof of the pudding would lie in achieving the goal of actually getting appointed and then seeing off the Romans. Otherwise he'd be no greater a threat than bonnie Prince Charlie was to the English monarchy. It is possible that factions within the Jewish community supported Roman rule and had an interest in suppressing opposition, but then why do none of the New Testament texts say so? The whole narrative is so improbable and unhistorical.

The directors of TV series *The Bible* protested that they were not propagating hatred of Jews by having the Jewish priests accuse Jesus of heresy and handing him over to the Romans. But the series inevitably propagated the "official version" of the emergence of a new, clean, honest religion to replace a corrupt, petty, hypocritical one identified with Jews today. This message was hammered home visually by having the Jews wear a modern, immediately identifiable tallit. There were also not very subtle messages of Jews as the bad guys, the evil moneychangers in the Temple, reminiscent of Wall Street. They were in fact simply currency exchangers providing a service to pilgrims to cash in their local traveler's checks to pay for accommodation at the King David Hotel or a quick sacrifice to atone for whatever. But it is now a cliché to accuse Jews of being predatory moneylenders.

I cannot condemn Christians in what is predominantly a Christian country for propagating their myths. Every few years another similar version hits the big screen or the little one. But can you blame me for feeling a cultural dissonance? There are still plenty of crazy missionaries out there, and others, apparently sane, telling us Jews we will not get to heaven unless we repent.

Perhaps those who identify with Jesus might secretly think I'm one of the devil's squad? How else can you explain the persistence of that other myth that around 12 million Jews control the billions of others in this planet? It can't be logic. It must be myth. Who, pray, is responsible for that? Oh yes, they'll tell you, it is our entire fault!

Alienated in the United States, I can also be alienated in Israel. The values of Rehov Shenkin in Tel Aviv are as remote from mine as Christianity is in another direction. The aggression of right-wing extremists is the beginning of the road that eventually leads to murderous jihadis. Midnight mass in a Jerusalem church is hardly a Jewish experience. And yes, Jews whirling chickens around their heads in atonement before Yom Kippur are as remote as Ganesh drinking milk. In Israel one can choose where one goes. Yet Israel, because Judaism determines the public calendar, is still the only place on earth where Jews can feel culturally at home and not be aware of the prevalence of competing theologies and myths.

DIVORCE

It is not always easy being a Jewish woman. It is fine if you have a loving, caring husband, or if you are financially independent, if you can juggle the demands of motherhood and work and have the strength of character to ignore the constant snubs of male chauvinism. But sometimes it can be overwhelming.

The difficulties some Jewish women experience in acquiring their religious divorce, the Get (without which they cannot re-marry), are entirely the result of the refusal of current- day Orthodox authorities to use tools that Jewish law itself allows, to correct the imbalance that gives men the upper hand.

I have just seen a film called *Gett: The Trial of Vivienne Amsalem*, an Israeli French production. It is about an unhappy wife, mother of four children, desperate to escape a loveless marriage in which her Moroccan Israeli husband adamantly refuses either to understand her unhappiness or to grant her a get (Lord knows where the extra *t* in "get" came from). He is simply insensitive to her human needs and cannot understand what she is going through. Her agony extends over a five-year period in which she has to face caricatures of insensitive, hard-line rabbis, hypocritical Moroccan neighbors and relatives, two-faced friends, and incompetent legal experts: a grotesque cast of Fellini-like unsympathetic freaks. The film is so biased and unfair (the acting is excellent) that it will do nothing to advance the cause of those who want to see change.

I know better than most the limitations of Jewish divorce law, the male chauvinism of many rabbis, the incompetence of courts, and the abuses of the judiciary wherever they are. I have campaigned over the years consistently for changes in attitude and the application of Jewish law within the bounds of the system. But to see such a film that is a one-sided distortion containing factual errors, ignoring all the good that is done and offering the world a picture of traditional Judaism that is primitive and barbaric, simply made my heart sink and my hackles rise.

I have butted heads with religious authorities. I have often written about the problems of the *agunah,* a woman constrained under the law because a husband or brother-in-law refuses to release her to remarry, through blackmail or spite. Sometimes husbands have disappeared either violently or trying to escape their obligations. There are thankfully not as many cases as people think, but even if we were dealing with one, and the rabbis failed to solve it using Jewish law, I would still be offended and my sense of religious justice insulted.

Whatever my criticisms, most rabbis in Israel and abroad do a fair, sensitive, and reasonable job of ensuring that women get their bills of divorce without blackmail or delay. I have experienced this as often as I have the abuses. Most dayanim (judges) who sit on Jewish courts are humane, caring men. This goes for Ashkenazim and Sephardim (in this film the directors in their ignorance got terribly mixed up between the two). But even so, if there is just one court, one rabbi, one judge who acts like a boor in the face of a woman in distress, or if there is one sector of the Jewish world that still clings to male domination and expects female submission, I desperately want it to be challenged and pressure to be brought to stop this desecration and betrayal of Jewish moral values.

Nevertheless, upset as I am by this distorted picture of my religion, this film that I wouldn't give tuppence for, I am glad it is on general release. This is precisely why I value the freedom of the free world. Because we can go public, there can be redress. Because we can hold to ridicule the hypocrisies of those religious authorities who fail, we have a chance of getting them to see another point of view. If we lose that right, we have lost freedom.

Having been thus offended, I should, if I want to get people to recognize how offended I am, now go out to kill someone and firebomb a film studio to make my point in the hope that people will say, "There, there, poor Jeremy, we must not offend you or your religion. So we will say this is not a film about Judaism but rather about black bearded men who behave badly. And we will stop showing the film and withdraw it from public distribution." You can see where I am going with this. Why is it that the free world seems impervious to insulting Judaism or Christianity but bridles at anything that might give offense to some Muslims? Meanwhile, many Islamic societies are the source of anti-Semitism and Jew hatred. Why are they not cleaning their own stables if cleanliness is what they genuinely desire?

Whatever our Jewish obligations to immigrants of other religions are, and they are and must be broad and supportive, the one thing we must not compromise is our freedom to criticize and to hold to ridicule. That is an integral part of our civilization and culture that men like Voltaire, Ben Franklin, and Zola fought for. There is a difference between insulting people and insulting gross acts of violence and terror and their sources. But what is at the root of this issue is the demand of one religion that it be treated as exceptional.

This is why we must fight for women's equality and right to be free from unhappy marriages without blackmail. We should fight any attempt to allow religious courts to have the power to hold women back or to bring back blasphemy laws, because they will be used to prevent exposing the crimes of religious leaders who betray our moral values, just as libel laws are used to protect corrupt businessmen and politicians. Being publicly held to contempt by talk-show hosts and comedians is the only safeguard we have against financial corruption and religious fanaticism imposing itself upon us all.

Liberalism too is a religion that must be held to ridicule. And the pathetic cowardice of those who argue that using euphemisms will help solve a problem is precisely the kind of appeasement that has brought Europe to its present state of confusion. The more one gives in to bullies, the more one will be bullied. I hear pundits say that America, unlike Europe, in not publishing offensive cartoons, has found a balance between freedom of speech and offensive speech. That's hogwash. It is liberal hypocrisy and frankly defeatism. Liberalism too makes fun of traditional women who, for themselves, choose a more private way of life.

I believe our society requires that we can and should hold up to ridicule all religions, all ideologies when their members betray their ideals. Often that is the only way to get a reaction. Otherwise they retreat behind closed doors. Call a Chasid who steals "a Jewish thief," for that he is. Or say that a rabbi who abuses his position is a rabbinical abuser. That describes him to a tee. And if someone uses Islam or any religion as a justification to kill, he is a Muslim (or whatever other religion) killer. Morality hates hypocrisy no matter where it comes from. If there are those who fear prejudice and hatred, let them strive to remove the beam from their eyes too.

I want peace, tolerance, and freedom for women and men. But if we refuse to be honest with ourselves, there is not a chance. I knew in advance I would hate this film. But I went because I thought it would do my soul good and reinforce my sense of what justice should look like.

RUNAWAY GIRLS

A while back the story hit the news about two ultra-Orthodox 16 year old girls who had run away from their homes in Brooklyn in search of a more adventurous life. At the bus terminal in Manhattan they asked for tickets to take them as far away as possible and ended up in Phoenix Arizona. After a week of freedom and shopping they telephoned their teacher back in Brooklyn and said that they had just wanted to escape the claustrophobia of their community. Having had their fun they were now ready to return and resume their previous way of life.

What struck me as I read this was not that two girls had tried to escape a closed society (though the fact that they were girls, not boys, is very interesting) and not that they got hold of so much cash, but that this happens relatively rarely. The closed communities of the Orthodox world are the fastest-growing and exponentially exploding sectors of Jewish life today. Not for them questions about whether their grandchildren will remain Jewish. Not for them conferences about how to keep Judaism alive and deal with massive assimilation and marriage out. Throughout the Western world there are tightly knit, self-supporting, and closed communities where most families have ten to fifteen children and even if two per family were to drop out, they would be well ahead of the game played by those Jews who may have one and three-quarters children (always wondered how statisticians could come up with three-quarters of a child).

Whether or not you agree with their ideology, their dress, or their habits, the fact is that they are thriving, growing, spreading, and doing very nicely. They are totally dedicated to Jewish learning, Jewish practice, and the continuity of the Jewish people. And they are absolutely convinced that they are 100 percent right and everyone else is totally wrong. There is a lot to be said in favor, and there is also a case to be made against.

It is true that hardly a week goes by without yet another novel written, based apparently on firsthand experience, of a Charedi girl or boy who breaks away and starts a new life as a secular Jew. And hardly a week goes by without an article appearing in the *New York Times* that does not highlight the plight or otherwise of those who choose to leave what they feel is a suffocating environment. And sadly, it is true that not a week goes by without news of either some sort of abuse within these closed communities or their propensity to ignore the law mainly on financial matters and in particular misdirecting government funds. But very rarely do these books and articles place enough emphasis on the positive aspects of living within a supportive, protective environment, which is no small consideration in these times.

Of course the same could be said (mutatis mutandis, in other words, substituting different holy texts) about religious Muslims, Christians (from Mormons to the Amish and similar sects), and Hindus. Many of them live in closely knit communities, are mutually supportive, have lots of kids, retain their numbers, and are absolutely convinced that God speaks to them, that their holy texts are divine, and that they are absolutely right and everyone else is wrong. They must be doing something right for some people at least.

We live in a world of corrupt business practices, vacuous entertainment awards, pornography, drugs, depression, and dysfunction. It is reminiscent of the decline and fall of the Roman Empire, with its almost total lack of any value system other than the materialist. I want it, I deserve it, I'm going to get it at all costs and get away with whatever I can. It is hardly surprising that there will be groups of people who want something different, something deeper and more spiritually satisfying. Most human beings quite like being controlled, as Hitler discovered, particularly if they are convinced that they are the chosen. So belonging to controlling groups is not the unnatural state of human behavior. If anything, independent thinking is.

The story of the runaway girls illustrates several interesting points. One is that you cannot keep the lid on everyone. The human spirit defies all attempts to crush individuality. We were given minds of our own, and many of us rather like using them. There simply cannot be one system that works for every human being any more than there can be one spiritual system that works for all Jews or all Chasidim or all kabbalists or all Sephardim or all Ashkenazim. Yes, it is true there can be one constitution, and I believe that that is what Jewish law, Halacha, represents. But we all know too well that in practice Judaism is not about Halacha so much as about those who interpret it. Hence a rich man who drives to an Orthodox synagogue on Shabbat will be treated with respect and honor, but someone whose views differ from the norm, even if he walks all the way and does not use the eruv, will not.

It is understandable that people choose to cluster for protection, be it physical or cultural. It is right that communities should exist to propagate or maintain their specific ethos. The test of a humane system is how it deals with those who do not conform. It is easy to love your neighbor so long as he agrees with you. But Catholics massacred Huguenots and Shias destroyed Sunnis in even greater numbers than they did Jews. And some rabbis love to declare who is and who is not doomed, condemned as apostates, or, on the other hand, guaranteed a front-row seat in the world to come, as if they know how heaven actually works.

Those surprisingly few who do break away must be either desperate or in some way unusual. If I find it amazing that so few Orthodox Jews want to exit, I also find it surprising that in this story the particular community these girls came from seemed prepared to find some way of accommodating them. Of course this will have ruined their *shidduch* chances. Poor girls will have to end up marrying some Modern Orthodox boy, heaven forbid. But at least they will have been saved from a fate worse than death, living in Phoenix wearing trendy clothes!

The test of genuine spirituality does not lie in whether it creates closed communities or chooses to reject the values of the day, but rather on how it deals with those within who are not able to stay that way and those without who may share many of their values but not all of them. *Ahavat Yisrael*, love of one's fellow Jew, an essential principle of early Chasidism, really means something when he or she is different!

PROMISCUITY

One of the essential principles of Torah is that a person is responsible for his or her actions. This is the burden of the third of the Ten Commandments. There we are warned that if we do wrong, it will be "visited on sons, grandsons, and great-grandsons." The Hebrew phrase *poked avon* is often translated as "visiting the sins." But all translations are approximations. The phrase really means that there are consequences. What parents do, how they act, and what example they set all have consequences. This is not a legal statement because in Jewish law the official position comes in Deuteronomy 24:16. "Fathers are not punished for sons, neither are sons for their fathers. A person is punished for his own crime." But it is a call to accept responsibility for failure to teach values.

There has been a huge increase in sexually transmitted diseases. This epidemic is going unchecked because underfunding and government dithering have left clinics unable to cope, and our permissive liberal society is willing to tolerate sexual promiscuity. But as usual, someone has to be blamed, and being a world of political correctness, we must never blame the victims. So blaming others is surrogacy for our own failures. Everyone else is to blame for the fact that chlamydia is up 108 percent, syphilis 500 percent, and AIDS 203 percent.

Television and the gutter press readily make available at almost every hour programs and articles that implicitly if not explicitly encourage sex. Promiscuous behavior, nudity and pornography are universal commonplaces.

Escapades of loutish teenagers on holiday in Majorca or spring-break students in the United States are turned into popular programs and laddish girls and boys behaving like apes in heat are given publicity and accolades. If clubs and concerts are scenes of unbridled sex, it is hardly surprising that youngsters think it is normal to have multiple sex partners, handshake sex, hook up with anyone available and treat it as mundanely as going to the toilet.

My e-mail is swamped with spam, day after day, assuring me that penises can be doubled in size, breasts can be enlarged, sexual performance enhanced, and that pills will turn everyone into a champion stud. You might well think that nothing else matters, no other values exist in life but sex.

So what do we do? Pour more money into warning them? Are youngsters who degrade themselves to the level of animal coupling likely to be heedful of warnings about the dangers of sexually transmitted diseases any more than they give a damn about the dangers of smoking? Unlikely. If teenagers given equality in law and rights want to disfigure themselves with tattoos and body piercings, we won't be able to stop them disfiguring their internal organs with syphilis, chlamydia, and herpes.

Do I, as a taxpayer, have to pick up the bill? I guess I do, for sex maniacs, crazy drivers, smokers, druggies, alcoholics, and horse riders (who account for twice as many hospital admissions as motorbike riders). After all, it is the policy in most civilized countries to pay for varying amounts of medical support to citizens even when they are the engineers of their own misfortune.

However, I believe that we should tax the sex industry very heavily. I don't just mean porn shops and mags and porn movie companies, but clubs, pop concerts, and any program or event that indirectly or directly encourages sexual promiscuity. Revenue can be used to help deal with the ensuing damage (not to be spent on spin doctors).

But who will teach youngsters other values? Not state schools. The teachers unions all have their own self-serving interests. It is up to us to take care of our own homes. No, I don't want to live under a Taliban regime or have religious police inspecting our homes. Compulsion rarely works. It is up to me, you, the home, in a free and an open society, to teach and to exercise restraint and control.

Judaism is blessed with a healthy and positive attitude to sex so long as one is doing it within a framework of love and sanctity and responsibility, both religious and social. Our tradition is far more liberal and positive than many other religions with their monastic taboos and celibacy. For us, marriage and sex are positively commanded, not treated as a way out for those who fall short of the ideal standard of celibacy.

We do indeed have guidelines. But they are such that they insist on giving pleasure as much as limiting to whom and when we can. Biblical Judaism was certainly not censorious or prurient. Any such attitudes that crept into Judaism came in through and from other cultures and religions. And societies have gone through cycles of permissiveness to censoriousness. As the Talmud says, "When it comes to immorality, there are no guarantees." People do get into situations, and with the constant pressure, it is hardly surprising that so many of us succumb. But tolerance does not mean having no standards, no expectations, and it does not mean letting kids think that anything goes. I am more and more amazed at the permissiveness of so many parents. They will reap the whirlwind. And more and more young women will end up being unable to conceive because sexual diseases will ravage their bodies.

We are frail humans, and few of us can afford to throw stones or claim we have not slipped. But that does not mean we should not do our best to educate ourselves as well as the next generation to make the right and sensible decisions. Pretending all is well and ignoring the extent of the problem will benefit no one.

TORTURE

Can torture ever be acceptable? There is no word in the Bible that means "torture" the way we use it nowadays. Modern Hebrew uses the word *inui.* But that is used in the Bible to describe what we do to ourselves when we fast on Yom Kippur. Hardly a defiance of the Geneva Convention, unless being deprived of a Krispy Kreme is torture! It is also used to describe slavery in Egypt, and that might well have included torture, but not necessarily. The great Rabbi Lowe of Prague described the whole of exile as inui. And he is of course right given the physical and mental pain inflicted on so many Jews by religious and civil authorities under whom we were forced to endure the indignity of being treated as subhuman.

The Hebrew word for cruelty is *tza'ar*, or "pain," which is nearer to what we mean by "torture." Cruelty to animals, for instance, is *tza'ar baalei chayim.* Under no circumstances are we allowed to torment animals. Even to the point where we must feed animals dependent on us for food before we feed ourselves. Cruelty is banned as one of the seven Noachide commands, fundamental laws that apply to everyone.

There is another biblical word, *oness*, "compulsion," which is also the biblical word for rape. In Jewish law anything achieved as a result of compulsion is negated, invalid. This is why the forced converts to Christianity under the Inquisition or under the periods of Islamic oppression were held blameless and allowed to slip gently back into Jewish communities when the opportunity arose.

There is a Talmudic principle that says we do not rely on a person's own testimony against himself (in the absence of any other evidence). "A person cannot incriminate himself." Confessions under *oness*, duress, would not be acceptable. So under Jewish law, judicial torture would never be tolerated in the way that it was in European legal systems where ordeals were a common way of eliciting confessions. The only pressure brought to bear to clarify events in the absence of witnesses was the "oath." You might call it psychological pressure at a time when people really feared taking the Lord's name in vain, but this cannot compare to the way most Western systems worked until barely a few hundred years ago. In Britain they used to "hang, draw, and quarter." That meant hang the poor sod until nearly dead, then take him down and castrate him, and then slit his body down and across. If he still wasn't dead, they'd chop his head off. Doubtless they thought it fair punishment rather than torture. The gory torture chambers reconstituted for public entertainment were what they used to get confessions. Even the saintly Sir Thomas More used those methods to weed out heretics.

If torture was so common once, why is there no discussion in the Talmud on the merits of or the moral abhorrence of torture? After all, three thousand years ago life was cruel and vicious. Children were killed before their parents' eyes, and then the parents were blinded, if not killed themselves. Casual reading of the books of Samuel or Kings confirms that kings and their courts got up to all sorts of unsavory business, as indeed did the last of the Maccabee kings. However, only one example turns up of what we would call torture, and that was the case in 2 Samuel 12 where King David conquers the Ammonites and does some things that look like torture but we can't be sure. However, kings had certain exceptional rights that were extrajudicial. Besides, that was 2,900 years ago!

Anyway, we need to look at Torah legislation itself rather than at those who betrayed it. One reason that torture is not an issue is that biblical and Talmudic law is very definite about the immorality of any harm or damage done to a person. Whole chapters of the oral law are devoted to *chavala*, physical assault or damage to another human, and the necessary compensation.

I have seen it argued that the lex talionis ("an eye for an eye," etc.) is proof of sanctioned torture. That's rubbish on two counts. First, it is arguable whether "an eye for an eye" was ever taken literally in Jewish law, because on either side of it in the Torah, the laws talk about financial (not physical) compensation. Besides, when we discuss torture, we are not talking about a judicial system of clearly laid-down crimes and punishments. Torture is when a possibly innocent person is harmed physically, for either religious or political reasons.

One might argue that violence was once accepted because Jewish law accepted beating a husband who refused to give a divorce to his wife! But it was a judicial process and in a person's own hands to avoid it, and he could. Even so, Rabbeinu Tam, who lived in France in the twelfth century, effectively put an end to it, probably on the grounds that, being surrounded by a violent Christian society, he wanted to distance Judaism from anything vaguely similar. There is more than one Jewish woman alive today who regrets that decision!

Nowadays however, leaving aside the barbarians of ISIL and Boko Haram or any religious lunatic who thinks torturing a human being is the will of God, for whom no discussion is relevant, the argument in favor of torture in so-called civilized societies is usually confined to conditions where obtaining information may be a matter of life and death. It is simplistically put like this: You have someone who knows that a bomb will go off and kill thousands. Isn't it worth torturing him to save a catastrophe?

According to Jewish law, one may indeed even kill someone who represents a clear and present danger to on's life. The Talmudic principle is "If someone comes to kill you, get there first and kill him." This justifies a preemptive strike in self-defense. But torture is a different issue.

Once you tolerate the idea of torture, then every sadist or Nazi doctor will argue that, for the greater good of mankind, you can experiment on defenseless victims. See the film *The Constant Gardener* to get an idea what our modern civilization is still capable of. Judaism has never accepted the principle that "the end justifies the means." Every life is precious, and the Talmudic debate over the biblical case of Sheva Ben Bichri (Samuel II.20), who rebelled against King David, confirms that you may not, as a general rule, hand an innocent person over to certain death to save the lives of others.

Under torture a person will say whatever he thinks you want to hear. It is rarely reliable. There was the case of the Marrano Dr. Lopez who confessed under torture to plotting to kill Queen Elizabeth. He hadn't. And she felt so bad afterward she gave his widow a pension. And what about all those Russians who confessed to Stalin that they had been traitors when, on the contrary, they were loyal acolytes?

If someone really does have information, there are nowadays lots of chemical and psychological ways of getting him to talk, without having to torture or set the dogs upon him. I am bitterly disappointed that I cannot find important rabbinic response on torture. Neither can I recall hearing, or seeing in print, any major Orthodox rabbi denouncing it unequivocally and explicitly. Are we to bury our heads in the sand and think it's none of our business?

Torture deprives not only the victim but also the torturer of his humanity. No sensitive, ethical human can tolerate inflicting pain on another. It is our moral and religious obligation to speak out against it.

MEAH SHEARIM

I have fond memories of the years I spent studying in Meah Shearim in Jerusalem. That quaint quarter of Ottoman courtyards that housed ultra-Orthodox Jews was tucked away over a hill from the main city streets and down into a valley that once was the border between Jewish Jerusalem and Arab, by the border post known as the Mandelbaum Gate.

I recall it particularly fondly during Sukkot. Not only because every balcony, every spare space, is was packed with booths of all sizes, shapes and materials. Not only because of the way the markets and streets were full of tables of etrogim and lulavim and the way the aficionados examined in minute detail each leaf, frond, and fruit with microscopes and obsessive concern for the minutest of imperfections. But also because of the weeklong celebration of Simhat Beyt HaShoeva, an innovation attributed to the prophets that commemorates the processions in the Temple to pray for rain and pour out precious water over the altar in the hope that God would replenish it. The dancing and the amazing music one could hear there every night proved more than anything else that the image of Meah Shearim as a joyless black hole of fanaticism was far from reality. As is the myth that everyone there belongs to the extreme fanatical anti-Zionist Neturei Karta, refuses to pay taxes, and will not serve in the army.

In truth, down there I have met some of the most spiritual, sensitive and caring human beings anywhere, even the most tolerant. It is also true, as in any community, that there are lunatics, louts, bullies, and lascivious criminals.

Even in my day, now some fifty years ago, gangs of overzealous, hormonally aroused young men with no other outlet for their pheromones used to go wild at demonstrations against anything that offended them, from swimming pools to driving on the Sabbath. And to be fair, it was a form of blood sport in the Jerusalem of my day for young secular toughs to provoke as much as they could in the hope of a good punch-up and of course a feeling of moral superiority. Back then all religious authorities to a man publicly excoriated the aggression and condemned the violence. It didn't stop it, but it kept it in reasonable bounds.

They didn't call themselves Charedi in those days. They were simply the keepers of tradition. The modern term should distinguish between genuinely saintly men, those who really did and do "tremble" before God (that's where the word *charedi*, "trembling," comes from) and the black-dressed bearded hooligans who masquerade as ultra-Orthodox and brutalize anyone, male, female, or child, they can gain power over. Another problem is the fact that the revered rabbinical giants of our times, in their aged infirmity, are surrounded by secretaries and gatekeepers. This means that only what the gatekeepers feed gets through and only what they declare is his word is heard on the outside. Proxy political battles are fought, and all of this further undermines the power of authority and allows lesser men to wield it.

One result is that we are seeing increasing social (as opposed to military) violence in Israel, both in the Charedi community and beyond. I was terribly upset to see BBC report the way Charedi extremists attacked and trashed the car of a Charedi serving in the army when he came home to Meah Shearim for a visit. And the way ultra-Orthodox men attack religious girls and throw stones and feces at them on their way to school simply because their skirts are not down to the ground or their sleeves end at the elbow instead of the wrist. I know full well that the media need to find stories, and they particularly love to find the odd story of Jewish fanaticism so that they can say "see the Jews are just as bad as the others." Nevertheless, I am convinced that what those bullies really need is a dose of military service and discipline. And I believe it would do the religious world a power of good if these underemployed and underdisciplined young fanatics were put to some hard physical work.

I realize the army is not a cure-all. Among the National Religious fanatics there is a sort of movement called "Tag Mechir," literally "Price Tag." It seems to be made up of dysfunctional religious Zionist settler youth, and they simply attack, deface, slash, and burn any convenient Arab target every time something bad happens to Israelis, whether it comes from Palestinian sources or even the Israeli army taking down an illegal settlement. Most of them have served in the armed forces. And yet they have also attacked Druze men also serving in the Israeli armed forces simply because they were overheard speaking Arabic.

This need for violence, for a desire to take the law into one's own hands, is a growing disease that undermines the rule of law, morality, and religion. Things are getting worse in God's territory wherever you look. Once violence is allowed to sprout, it soon mushrooms. I fear the whole culture of Israeli discourse, the aggression, and the violence that was directed against the enemy outside is now being turned inward. Once again, I blame the leadership for not doing enough to stop it.

It is a sign of the times everywhere, of course. There are battles going on in the Amish community that resemble rivalries between Chasidic courts. In both cases they cut off opponents' beards, humiliate their women, vandalize each other's property, and knock off hats in public. I really feel for the Copts in Egypt. Since there are no Jews left there, they are the new scapegoat. The murderous political rivalry and pursuit of heresy between Shia and Sunni, indeed the campaigns against the Roma and vice versa in Europe, are all part of a similar fundamentalist and primitive way of thinking and behaving that lacks respect for difference and underpins all kinds of extremism.

In our modern world, there is a false assumption that anyone wearing black is automatically holy, that the outwardly pious ought always to be given the benefit of the doubt, for they are keeping tradition alive. In reality they are destroying tradition by causing alienation and portraying a mutation of religion that is morally corrupt. If we really care about our religion, we must bring pressure to bear on its religious leaders to stop such extreme behavior instead of encouraging it for political ends. And we should withhold support if they do not. A bully only stops when he is bullied back and true leadership accepts responsibility.

AUTHORITY

Cursing God, "Killelat HaShem" is the theme of a sad story in the Torah about the alienation of a son of a mixed marriage between an Israelite woman and an Egyptian man (Leviticus 24). It is a most serious infraction. But just as bad is the similar "Chillul HaShem," desecrating God's name, giving God a bad name, bringing religion into disrepute.

There are so many stories in the non-Jewish press of well-known and less well-known charismatic rabbis charged with inappropriate sexual behavior and often much, much worse. Such charges range from chief rabbis to dayanim (judges), from humble teachers to leaders of weird sects. There seems to be no country, no community without its stories of scandalous rabbinic behavior. You might have thought that only the Catholic priests and evangelical preachers had problems. But it seems that giving people authority over others, regardless of the religion or the situation, only leads to abuses of power.

A few years ago, such incidents would have been swept under the carpet. A notorious case of child molestation in Stamford Hill resulted in the accusers, the victims, being hounded out of town. A similar story played out in Brooklyn. And a Charedi rabbi in London who seduced and then turned on his victims was also exposed, though some of his supporters have refused to repudiate him, and his potential for evil remains within their community. Now I'm glad to say these cases are being brought out into the open. Websites such as Frum Follies by Yerachmiel Lopin or Failed Messiah have ensured that the perpetrators and those who cover up for them are outed and exposed.

Politics and religious politics and power play are indeed about power, manipulation, and dirty tricks. But ultra-religious Jewish life does also still suffer from an eastern European tendency to want to hide from secular authority and hush things up. There is a reflexive tendency to pretend these things don't happen and accept the premise that a beard automatically indicates sainthood.

The issue that intrigues me is why does religion—and I'm talking here very generally because this seems to be a pretty universal problem—with all its structures and safeguards, seem to suffer conspicuously from cases of sexual abuse? All authority is powerful. Is it a case of "power corrupts and absolute power corrupts absolutely"?

A recent biography of Khrushchev by William Taubman has him repeatedly excusing himself for Stalin's atrocities by claiming he could not challenge Stalin's power. Anyone who has read up on the subject will know full well that Khrushchev as the overlord of the Ukraine was a dab hand at terror himself. How many Germans argued that they were helpless in the face of Hitler's magnetic authority? Power and charisma are hypnotic. Which is one of the reasons one needs a free press and a democratic process to constantly challenge them.

Religious authority is just as powerful a tool as political. All the more so because it carries with it implied divine authority. If we rely on other human beings to tell us the will of God, they may actually come to believe that they know the will of God. Giving human beings, however saintly or learned, too much authority, distorts even self-perception. Some may actually come to believe them so explicitly that if they say black is white, the insecure or the credulous may persuade themselves that they are right. They have been conditioned to doubt their own capacity to think. Many are persuaded that they are inadequate, not learned enough and have no right to challenge them.

My concern and caveat apply to established religious communities, both Lithuanian and Chasidic. The earlier skepticism traditionally associated with Litvaks, Lithuanian Jews or nowadays "Yeshivish," as being more intellectual and disciplined is now seriously out of fashion. The authority of Chasidic rebbes has emerged as the new paradigm of orthodoxy. Equally the Baal Teshuva movements that bring Jews back to Judaism do great work, but they too are all based on this formula of charisma, religious certainty, and authority.

It is very attractive to be drawn into a community of the great and the good who can convince you that everyone else is wrong and only they and you are right. They control by insisting on a monopoly of truth and by imposing standards of conformity in dress and behavior that reinforce social cohesion. They may initially appear tolerant and open, but as they draw people in closer and stronger, the patterns of control soon emerge. I am not in any way against trying to bring Jews back to their faith—on the contrary. I only object to abuses. But the dangers are latent in all charismatic religious movements, and in all of them one comes across magnetic personalities who tend to believe their own publicity, go too far, and don't see where the boundaries should be drawn.

Charisma linked to religion is powerful stuff. I should know. My years as a headmaster and a rabbi taught me all about the potential for abuses of power.

This is why I believe it is so dangerous to accept religious authority without question. It is important for the health of Judaism that there are mavericks out there challenging. Of course I believe in Torah and am committed to it. But the Torah I believe in allows for questions. It encourages challenge based on text and ideas. The only necessary commitment is to Torah itself.

What the Torah stories of rebellion against Moses's authority all conclude is not that challenging is wrong. But you have to be very certain of the purity of your motives and ultimately to accept that there is a higher authority than you. No person is above the law. No authority can afford to do without a healthy dose of challenge and skepticism.

PILLS AND RELIGION

As children in Britain, we used to make fun of Americans with their bottles of vitamins and supplements: a pill for every hour of the day, every limb of the body, and every possible deficiency known to man and animal. The GIs who came over to rescue Europe seemed bigger and stronger and more handsome than the local infantrymen. Some thought it was because of the Bazooka bubblegum and soda they consumed. But perhaps the real secret was that they took all those fortifying pills. We were trained to think of going to a doctor and taking pills as a sign of weakness, of namby-pamby overindulgence. We were brought up on Arnold of Rugby's physically robust empire-building ideology. We thought that we were morally superior because we did not take pills.

British children of World War II had been forced to be basic. We had to eat our rationed, unappetizing food and not leave any on the plate because the poor Chinese were starving (how the tables have turned). We were urged to eat carrots for our eyesight and spinach for iron, bland local vegetables (swedes, turnips, and rhubarb), and (as soon as rationing ended) fruit. "An apple a day keeps the doctor away," we were told. We hated all that healthy stuff. All we wanted were "chips with everything."

After the war, returning sergeants major took jobs teaching physical education in our schools. I remember being yelled at often enough: "Rosen! Chin in, chest out, you lily-livered little weakling! You have sparrow's kneecaps for biceps!" We tried. But still the Americans won more competitions (perhaps because they had many more millions to choose from). They looked bigger and handsomer and took the girls. Later on, of course, it became obvious when I met Americans that they too had their fat and small and pimply and ugly.

But what has remained true is that America was indeed addicted to pills. Not just the vitamins but all kinds of horrid stuff, from steroids and artificial stimulants to Lance Armstrong's blood replacement and everything that now makes American sport as dirty and dishonest as the old East German sports teams. America is a society in which pills are the answer to everyone's problems. Pop a pill and it will all be better. Antibiotics became so popular that people ended up becoming resistant to them. And once you started popping one kind of stuff, you popped others.

Then the "pop it" mentality spread into other areas of instant solutions such as gurus, mystical healers, and kabbalists. Like snake-oil salesmen, they all had the answer. *How to Win Friends and Influence People* made Dale Carnegie the new god. Charles Atlas urged us to exercise, and we had home exercises and exercise machines, then gyms, and now spinning clubs. But it is so much easier to pop a diet pill or have an operation. And even reading became like taking pills, easy, quick instant *CliffsNotes* and a self-help culture that inevitably once more fell back on pills when nothing else worked. Timothy Leary brought us LSD, and American hippies made drug taking normal, and then came ecstasy and all the other ways of avoiding reality. Now even many of my Charedi friends are heavily into the game.

If you watch American television today, you might think that the most serious threat to our lives is erectile dysfunction, given the amount spent on advertising it. Drug companies dominate the commercials (or "messages" as they facetiously call them). Every American child seems to be on Ritalin. Israelis are imitating them. And adults need a pill to go to sleep, a pill to wake up, and another pill to keep going through the day. Only we older-generation Brits still cling to the belief that this pill business is a bit of con, a trick pulled by commercial enterprises in the United States to get us to part with our cash. But we are capitulating too.

The disease is not simply pills themselves, but the areas they have completely conquered, like John Wyndham's triffids. The pill changed our sex lives in the sixties with contraception; it enabled everyone to go at it like rabbits with Viagra. It's going to ensure that no one should ever go without an orgasm. And the morning-after pill that is now available to everyone (and frankly I am not against it if it means fewer abortions) will ensure that no one has to think before they act. Websites have now graduated from pornography to finding a one-night stand ("hookup," I believe they call it) in an area near you. Relationships? An optional extra. Every problem can be solved instantaneously without much effort.

No wonder we have become a species of addicts. From the cradle to the grave, we have been trained to take pills for everything. Morphine and opium have morphed into OxyContin, Vicodin, Percocet, Percodan, and Tramadol, to name the best known. In New York there is a pharmacy on every corner.

One of the most influential books in America today is a handbook of the American Psychiatric Association. It is officially called the *Diagnostic and Statistical Manual of Mental Disorders*, or *DSM*. The fifth edition has just been released. This is the bible of American psychiatry, a profession that for years advocated lobotomies and misdiagnosed and invented all kinds of mental states that might or might not have been the cause of every ill in American society. This often led to people being institutionalized or being persuaded that they had traumatic experiences, which then led to charges that ruined other lives. It had advocated the talking cure for years. But now it has decided that that takes too long and it is just cheaper to give out a pill. Ah yes, here we go again. So doctors can once again prescribe a quick-fix pill.

So far the fun; I may have needlessly insulted Americans, Britons, and Israelis. But to be serious, of course many pills in many situations are essential and quite miraculous. It's the abuse, the idea of an instantaneous solution without effort, quick and easy, that worries me for our future as a species. And religion, which should be a bulwark against this instant gratification, has borrowed and adapted the very mentality it excoriates as corrupt Western materialist paganism. It is all there among the black hats and the long black coats. The "wonder rabbi" solves our problems. And if not a magic cure, a drug will do. This of course is not new in our tradition, indeed in all religion. But it is getting surprisingly worse, not better. Superstition is a placebo too.

The instantaneous phenomenon is there among our less religious too, this desperate need for someone else to take responsibility, for something else to blame. Someone I know who is not Orthodox agreed to my suggestion that he put on tefillin every morning to start the day in a more spiritual, meditative frame of mind. He did for a while, and he said it helped. But then he made some terrible decisions, and his business plummeted. Off came the tefillin. He had expected the magic to work and it hadn't, so he blamed the pill.

As for me, I don't take pills. I try to eat healthily and carefully. And I exercise. If I want God to do His bit, I had better do mine!

WASHING HANDS

In my callow youth I used to think it excessive, as Jewish law requires, to wash and make a blessing so often. My stern grandfather insisted that I make use of a bowl he placed under my bed, together with a jug of water and a cup. The moment I woke up I had to wash my hands, *neigelvasser*, as it was called in Yiddish. My father, on the other hand, was more lenient, and he was satisfied if I walked the few paces to the bathroom.

Then after I went to the "loo," there was another wash and a blessing to thank the Almighty for my bodily functions performing normally with references to cavities to put things in and others to let things out and all of them working as they were intended. Well, of course they did, I thought. I can't exactly recall when I realized that it was, indeed, something to be very grateful for if all these intricate, complex, and malfunction-prone orifices really did function normally. Of course, as you get older you are reminded all the time of what a miracle it is, and the miracle gets bigger as each year passes.

The most obvious and regular wash in the Jewish tradition is before meals and also before praying. I do not believe that one of the primary intentions of Jewish ritual is hygiene or physical well-being. There are too many exceptions, and besides, you can adhere to the letter of many laws and still be an unhealthy, cigarette-smoking, overweight slob. Even if the Torah itself commands that we take good care of our bodies, it's like lots of laws that are [illegible] [illegible]garded in practice even by the most orthodox. I find these rituals significant spiritually rather than physically. But hygiene and physical well-being actually turn out to be very important elements in leading a religious Jewish life.

Washing hands has helped us, but it has even got us into serious trouble more than once, most notably during the Black Death. As Jews were expected to wash after going to the toilet and before meals, it is hardly surprising that they were less likely to be the victims of a disease that spread through unhygienic conditions. Because they were less likely to succumb, the rest of the population saw their seeming imperviousness to plagues (it was not true in fact, but prejudice was never interested in logic), and Jews were accused of spreading the disease and poisoning the wells.

If hygiene in itself is not the reason for our laws, it is connected. The consistent theme that underlies all Jewish ritual is, to take a phrase from Georgian literature, "only connect" to "think about the consequences." Thinking before acting can add a spiritual dimension to everything one does. It may be that avoiding certain foods has beneficial side effects or that abstaining from sex during a period lessens the likelihood of catching certain types of diseases, or that circumcision reduces susceptibility to certain types of infections. But the importance of such ritual activities has much more to do with sanctity than hygiene, as the great anthropologist Mary Douglas has often pointed out (most relevantly in *Purity and Danger*).

Adhering to Jewish ritual is, as the late Professor Yeshayahu Leibowitz loved to claim, simply an act of obedience and submission to a higher dictate. Perhaps it is, as the kabbalists believe, a supernatural matrix that links our actions to heaven where each action establishes a secret connection. Whatever the reason, in my youth I thought it a bind, and I bridled at the inconvenience to have to bother all the time over what I felt were petty restrictions.

Now I thank the Almighty for the understanding that maturity (of sorts) is giving me. Because I know myself how easy it is to say "What the heck" when you come out of the bathroom and just rub your hands against your trouser leg or dab a few drops from the faucet in a symbolic gesture. But actually washing hands properly, and being forced into a complex ritual each time one goes to the bathroom, and having to recite a serious blessing afterward, is terribly important on hygienic as well as religious grounds because it does indeed force you to stop and think.

I wouldn't want you to think I frequent "conveniences" like American senators or British MPs who prowl for nefarious ends. Heaven forefend. Neither do I stand around taking notes on those who walk past the sinks after relieving themselves in public conveniences to check if they wash. But I have noticed how often, or in fact how rarely, people actually do wash their hands after excusing themselves. I am just amazed that even in airport lounges or places of intellectual entertainment, such as concert halls and theaters, or at fancy restaurants (even kosher ones), the vast majority, and I repeat, the vast majority of well-brought-up Western men do NOT wash their hands after they handle certain parts of their anatomy that are best left unmentioned, even if the Good Lord created them too!

According to the medical journal *The Lancet*, tests taken at sophisticated bars (not the grubby boozers of the unwashed masses) have shown that the levels of bacteria from excreta to be found in shared bowls of peanuts and snacks are dangerously high. The same goes for the telephones we place close to our faces. Money is heavy with contaminants, and yet most of us don't wash each time we handle it. In our modern, health-conscious world, the majority of us are spreading our dirty stuff around without second thought. I know some people think we have become cleanliness freaks, and that's why so many allergies have proliferated in modern families.

How wonderful, therefore, that our ancient and, as some sadly suggest, old-fashioned, restrictive, narrow-minded, primitive religion requires us to wash our hands several times with a goodly measure of water, praise the Lord, and think after relieving ourselves. If hygiene were the only reason, then of course we would have to add soap and disinfectant and a lot more. And indeed I would heartily recommend that too. But at least if we adhere to the minimum traditional requirement when we come out of the toilet and shake someone's hand, we can do so with confidence, secure in the thought that we have done our bit to avoid passing something unhealthy on to our fellow creatures. Indeed, respect for God should lead to respect for humanity.

HAIR

Hair, whether facial or on one's head, makes a lot of statements about who a person is. In my youth, almost every male in England would go into a barbershop and ask for a "short back and sides." It was not until the era of the Beatles that anyone, apart from a few eccentrics, considered letting their hair grow into a floppy imitation of a juvenile sheepdog. Looking back at it now, one is amazed that anyone could have thought it to have been a protest against authority. But that was also the era when most middle-class males went to work in London wearing a bowler hat and carrying a furled umbrella.

Since then different hairstyles have proliferated. A baldpate no longer automatically suggests one might be ill or even an employee of the Israeli Secret Service. A Mohawk cut is no longer the preserve of the Mohawks. Punk rockers gave us every color and shape option, and hair gel has allowed every strand to go in a different direction. One's hairstyle tells us a great deal about the person. Dying one's hair, the norm for females and overage male lotharios, is now what anyone who wants to be different or try to look younger does.

The messages that hair sends are part of ancient human tradition (let alone among animals). Anthropologists have written about the way hair delineates different levels in what we like to call more primitive societies. In ancient Egypt priests shaved their heads. In many other societies, only the wealthy had the leisure and assistance to cut or shave their hair, so uncultivated beards became associated with the poor and barbarians. Beards were once forbidden in the British armed forces, except the navy (it was too difficult to shave on a rolling ship).

As we grew up, what were we to do about letting our facial hair grow? In my youth, dispensation was the norm as Jews working in city firms or chambers simply could not hold down their jobs if they looked scruffy. It was almost unheard of then for a Jew to be seen wearing either a beard or a *kipa* in any company or firm except his own. You might be a Jew at home, but you had to blend in on the street.

In my youth in England, if you went to an ordinary barber, you would automatically be shaved up way above the ears. I had to tell them to leave my sideburns in place and not to use a razor. Look at photos of, say, George Orwell, and you will see how upper-class Englishmen actually did shave their sideburns almost all the way up to mid-skull.

The Torah had commanded to avoid allowing a razor, a sharp blade, to touch the hair on the corners of our heads. Priests used to have additional restrictions, and it is pretty obvious that this was intended to contrast with the pagan traditions of priests being clean-shaven. Christianity itself reflects the cultural varieties from clean-shaven Catholics and tonsured monks to bearded Orthodox clerics and neophytes. The Talmud refers to special kinds of haircuts that the clean-shaven upper-class Greeks and Romans sported. Jews were forbidden to imitate "idol worshippers" unless they had to appear in diplomatic roles and did not want to undermine their suits by being hirsute.

In the past, by tradition Jewish males wore beards and covered their heads. Married women covered their heads out of modesty and also because that was what both Christian and Muslim societies expected of good wives. As modernity slowly affected Jewish communities, Jews were allowed to look like everyone else, and ways had to be found of looking more integrated. A distinction was made between shaving with a blade directly against the skin and shaving with a foil that intervened. If you think that was strange, and many did, what about the fact that instead of a woman covering her hair with a scarf or a hat, many rabbis allowed her to wear a wig? In some communities of Carpathian origin, women wear a hat on top of a wig on top of a shaven head. Both issues are still contentious, even in the most Orthodox of circles. All the more so since the vast majority of religious males in Judaism nowadays wear beards and sport ethnic black hats!

Chasidism made a virtue of looking different to everyone else. Before every festival, if you happen to be in a Charedi neighborhood, you will see freshly shaved male heads, zero all round except for where their *payot* sprout out of their upper temples. It's a two-sided variation of the Mohawk. Instead of the ridge, if you walk behind a Chasid you will see the snowy-white close-shaven back of the head peeping out from under the black hat and kipa. It looks as weird to me as a punk! But if people actually want to look different, isn't that what freedom is for? The only thing that worries me is when anyone preserves peculiarity for himself but refuses to countenance it in others.

In Israel one sees all sorts of weird haircuts. For some reason the secular love to sport last year's style as though it were still current—minipigtails and Mohican for example. But I guess that's because wherever you get one trend, there's always a countertrend. If the Charedi cut one way, the opposition has to find another. Compare Mormon haircuts or San Francisco old hippies.

I do see a value in dressing modestly, whether male or female. Modest attitudes in dress, speech, and conduct are important elements of our spiritual tradition. I resent that in the postwinter United States we are subjected to so much unsightly bare flesh wherever you look. I do not find it attractive any more than the flabby bare shoulders of ball gowns. To avoid this bodyism, strict Muslim women cover up almost entirely so that you are never certain if under the burka it's a male or a female. And I never understood why only Muslim women were expected to cover up and not Muslim men. But then religious worlds are still male dominated. Even in the Charedi world, where men are indeed expected to be modestly dressed as much as women, they still seem to think women are to blame for encouraging male sexual predators. The latest nonsense I have heard is that it is forbidden for girls to have dresses with zips down the back in case a randy male tries to unfasten them!

Nowadays our societies are less homogeneous. In some countries laws protect the rights of religious minorities to dress in accordance with their customs. In others, like France, they are restricted. But in Britain and the United States, Sikhs can cover their heads, wear beards, and carry daggers. Rastafarians display dreadlocks. And yet increasingly Jews are being told not wear a kipa or any other overt Jewish symbol in public for fear of being attacked by anti-Semites. Isn't it interesting that Chasidim, most vulnerable to being attacked, are most obviously Jewish, and yet most Chasidim are not particularly pro-Israel?

Being different for the sake of difference is, I suggest, a trivial pursuit. But being different to remind oneself of a higher calling, of a moral imperative, can be beneficial. In truth, "difference" is often just a matter of degree. You can make the point in a modest way without needing to shove it in someone else's face. After all, the Torah only commanded us to put fringes on our garments. It did not tell us to wear dhotis.

So shave your head, by all means, and leave your payot naked to view, but don't then turn up at nightclubs (as I am reliably informed happens from Tel Aviv to London to New York) as if you went through the wrong door by mistake. Either it is to identify and behave as a religious person or it is no more than a fashion statement, and a not very attractive one at that!

A REPLY TO ATHEISTS

What is an atheist? The usage I am used to—and clearly Richard Dawkins agrees with me—is that the idea of God is senseless. Atheists have a problem believing in God, and they disapprove of God-related religion. The believers, on the other hand, often use very weak arguments in their debates with them.

Atheists argue that religion is the cause of most violence in the world and has been for thousands of years. Not just killing people of other religions, but killing each other, Catholic and Protestant, Sunni and Shia. However, one could counterargue that the worst mass killers—Hitler, Stalin, Pol Pot, Mao—were not religious in any way that makes sense, unless you consider Nazism or Marxism a religion, in which case we mean different things.

It is not religion that is at fault, but rather people who use religion for their own ends, for power rather than God. There is absolutely no area of human activity I can think of, no ideal or dream, that has not been systematically plundered and destroyed by its most faithful adherents in the pursuit of power and triumph, whether it is football, politics, art, music, or tiddlywinks (I could tell you horror stories of corruption in the Cambridge University Tiddlywinks Club of 1963). When humans get involved, they fight over the pettiest of things, argue over minutiae, and turn everything into a power struggle where the original goals and dreams become distorted. Sadly, religion is the same. Power and money do bad things to almost every institution.

Religious people tend to argue that religious people are generally better and more moral and that religions have brought more good than evil to the world. It might be argued that way, but no one has yet done a survey to prove it. On the contrary, religious people seem just as good or bad as most other people of a similar social class. They argue that no one has yet come up with a better basic moral code for society than the so-called Ten Commandments. The atheists would counter again that the Ten Commandments did not do much to restrain Hitler.

I do believe that humans need a moral system that overrides human mental ingenuity. As Hobbes said, humans left to their own devices are nasty and brutish. And the more intelligent are capable of justifying almost anything (as it was once said of Bertrand Russell, "the higher the brow, the lower the loins"). But still the contribution of morality neither proves the existence of God, nor does it make up for the sins of religion, any more than do great works of architecture (built on the bodies of thousands), art, or music do.

If it were simply that atheists attacked religious abuse or credulity, I'd be with them almost all the way. The weakness of their position lies in the arrogance of claiming to know for certain what is not. Agnosticism is one thing. It is reasonable to say that one does not know anything about what people call God and has had no direct experience of anything spiritual or divine, that one imagines death to be the end, like finally falling asleep. But to say "I know there is absolutely nothing else in the universe beyond what I experience" is to arrogate the very omniscience they complain about in believers. If believers are guilty of wishful thinking, atheists are guilty of wishful doubting.

Imagine I said to you, "There is no such thing as love. I can understand physical attraction, the pleasure of sex and what goes on in the brain when we are stimulated, but love is myth. It does not make any sense, and it is responsible for countless deaths and agonies and tortures." You would laugh and say, "Well, clearly you have never been in love." Indeed, to someone who has never experienced God, it is as meaningless as trying to describe the taste of butter to someone who has never tasted it. Impossible, of course, but that doesn't mean butter cannot have a taste.

Atheists love to make fun of religious rituals. They are an easy target, but then so too are all conventions, rituals, and ceremonials of royalty, clubs, and societies. Most human rules and regulations are petty and infuriating. It is easy to make fun of a gentleman showing courtesy to a lady, or indeed eating with a knife and fork instead of his fingers. If it is claimed that ceremonies like male circumcision (totally different from female circumcision, because no sense or organ is permanently removed or incapacitated) impose inestimable psychological and physical damage on defenseless children, I would argue that our societies do far more lasting damage by allowing people to get married without preparation and by imposing parental neuroses on innocent children, not to mention corporal punishment and child abuse. And if we balk at seeing animal slaughter, then we ought to ban all killing of all animals for human food and be done with. But until we do, and until we have irrefutable scientific evidence of pain experienced rather than guesswork, which we do not, it cannot be used as an argument against religion alone.

For the past hundred years or so, the most serious battle between atheists and believers has been the issue of creation. Atheists have argued that science in general and evolution more specifically can explain the creation of the universe. Recently the well-known atheist philosopher Anthony Flew recanted. In his book *There Is a God*, he concludes that the world is far too complex and an awe-inspiringly impressive to have come about by accident or any of the evolutionary theories that all continue to raise as many questions as they claim to answer. There are still problems with "the missing links," that transition period from one stage to the next. The odds are such that randomness fails the probability test when compared to intelligent design. I am not that impressed. Because even if one agrees it looks as if there was intelligent design, we still know nothing logically or scientifically about what it was that designed the world. In other words, we are still left with the question "What is God?"

On the other hand, what it does show is that atheism, far from having a coherent alternative, still does not.

The debate is healthy. Religious fundamentalists tend to be both arrogant and intellectually sloppy. So a good challenge is necessary. But the challengers need to be pricked too. False arguments are not going to do it. I do not believe there is any watertight proof of the existence of God. This doesn't mean God does not exist. Empirical physical or scientific proofs are for the physical world, not the spiritual. Even if in the past, great minds thought they had proofs, in all humility I assure you they did not. But God can survive absence of proof just as much as love defies logic, yet thank goodness most of us continue to fall head over heels at last once in our lives.

I had a very useful and valuable debate with the English atheist philosopher Anthony Grayling at Yakar in London in 2002. We ended most amicably with an appreciation of both points of view, and that's how it should be, even though neither of us changed his opinion. Victory is often an accident of debating skills. Valid arguments survive.

HERETICS

There's been a lot of talk about heresy recently. Not just in Jewish circles. I'm not going to defend the others. Neither do I think their problems should distract us from our own. I am concerned with what's happening in Judaism. Political correctness used to be a feature of the loony left. Now religiously correct thinking is a feature of our Orthodox world. It is argued that the extreme keeps Judaism alive. But what it is keeping alive is often a travesty of the genuine article. The fact is that everywhere, in every Jewish community, there is tension between the increasing demands of the Charedi world that impinge on others.

In the 1950s in Israel, it was the secular left-wing Zionists who had the upper hand. Nowadays the scales have been reversed. In Bet Shemesh an extreme enclave is expanding its reach and imposing its dress codes through physical assaults. In Jerusalem the demand to segregate buses and relegate women to the back has been satisfied at the expense of those who do not object to sitting next to the opposite sex. Airline flights are held up nowadays by Charedi men refusing to take their seats if there's a female within striking distance.

All this does not worry me so much as the response that any criticism is heresy. There is no attempt at accommodation. The issues are no longer dealt with through the Halachic process or academic debate but through besmirching any opposition by declaring it heretical, by ad hominem assaults on those who disagree. Sounds very much like another religion I know.

So what is heresy in Judaism? The Mishna lists those who have "no portion in the World to Come": anyone who denies spiritual continuity (defined as the next world or resurrection), divine revelation of the Torah, a person who mutters magic incantations, and finally an *apikoros*. The Mishna also mentions a list of very bad people. So what is an *apikoros*? Of course it sounds very much like the Greek "epicurean," which could either mean someone who enjoys the material world or a follower of the philosophy of Epicurus. According to the Gemara, an *apikoros* should amount to no more than someone who is disrespectful to the rabbis or interprets the words of the Torah in a corrupt way. A bad boy perhaps but hardly what we think of as heresy.

The rabbis are saying, "Anyone who rejects our agenda is out of line." But their agenda was pretty specific. Don't fall for snake-oil salesmen, accept that there may be more than the physical world alone, accept Torah and God as the guidelines for living, don't dismiss out of hand, and keep an open mind. It was only someone who made an ideological issue out of publicly repudiating Torah who was excluded from the community. There was still room for the honest doubter. Agnostics were in. Atheists were out.

Medieval theology complicated the issue. Heresy became linked to truth, and truth was a philosophical proposition. Many medieval rabbis, like their Christian and Muslim colleagues, took heresy very seriously, treated it as a rejection of God, a capital crime. But we have moved away in our philosophical thinking from certainties. As the trend moved away from abstraction toward existentialism, the nature of heresy changed from a thought process to one of loyalty.

But loyalty raised other issues of legitimacy. One of them is over whether accepted tradition trumps the letter of the law. Certainly some customs gain universal acceptance, but many do not. Just compare any two Chasidic dynasties to see how many differences in custom there are. Or consider the various Sephardi and Ashkenazi texts of prayer, traditions and local customs. *Masora*, "accepted custom" has now become the touchstone of legitimacy rather than the definition of theological propositions. It is important of course, but it cannot be a tool for silencing opinions or blocking change; otherwise Halacha would have stopped dead two thousand years ago when we might have argued against the wheel on the grounds that it was an innovation.

Another modern question is whether there can be other truths outside Judaism. Of course there can, even if some Orthodox rabbis declare there cannot. But in no Talmudic text will you find the idea that only Judaism has the truth, the whole truth, and nothing but the truth. To accept truth elsewhere does not invalidate your own truth.

The Bible uses the word *emet*, "truth," to mean either correct or empirically proven. It does not use it as a theological tool. That is very Greek. The Gemara says that "there is wisdom among the nations." I suppose we have to believe that they only meant then but not now. Rabbi Yehuda HasNassi said that the non-Jews were more accurate than we were in astrological calculations (Pesachim 94b). Must be a misprint. What about the Thirteen Principles of Faith of Maimonides? Does it say there that Judaism has the monopoly of truth? No, sir!

Maimonides, again, said that God cannot be totally comprehended by any human being. So no one gets the complete truth. But then his books were burnt. I'd like to see the rabbi who would agree to be operated on by someone who only studied Torah.

Indeed using the word "truth" is fraught with difficulties. The "truth" for a Cohen is that he should *duchan*, bless the community, but it is not the "truth" for a common and garden Israel. The "truth" for us Jews is that we should keep Shabbat, but if my life is in danger, the "truth" is that I should break Shabbat.

"God is truth," we say whenever we say the Shema, indeed, true for us. So, according to Maimonides, is Allah. Can they both be true? Yes, of course, but you have to use the word creatively. If you think about it, "truth" is multifaceted just as humans are. Which is why Maimonides himself comes up with the idea of "different kinds of truths."

The great Malbim, Rabbi Meir Leibush, in nineteenth-century Poland wrote in his introduction to the book of Ezekiel,

> With regard to the commentary on the vision in the first chapter, by our great teacher (Rambam) in his "Guide"…it is void, the foundations upon which he built his commentary, namely wisdom, natural science and earlier philosophies are now superseded. They have been demolished and invalidated by the research of recent generations who have rebuilt the structure of our universe upon reliable foundations.

If we throw the word "heresy" around carelessly or destructively, there are a lot of great rabbis of the past who would be in serious trouble. We have regressed intellectually. Ladies and gentlemen, I rest my case.

PART 2

HISTORY

HOW JEWISH IS JEWISH HISTORY

Once we asked, "Who is a Jew?" Now the big question is "What is Jewish history?" Both questions are largely academic and the products of a particular mind-set that desires to know exactly how to label or characterize human affairs and where other human beings fit in. It is a product of Western philosophical culture, modern nationalism, and indeed scientific categorization.

I don't for the life of me understand why it has taken me so long to read Moshe Rosman's excellent *How Jewish Is Jewish History?* published by the Littman Library, first in 2007 and then in paperback in 2009. I must have been sleepwalking, for it is a most important and essential book for anyone interested in Jewish affairs. It is an overview of how academic theories of modernism are changing and have changed perceptions. It is a vital analysis of how many different approaches to Jewish history there are. It is an illuminating record of the many attempts to describe it.

Even the ancillary issue of when does "modern Jewish history" begin is the subject of constant debate and modification. Was it the French Revolution or the American Revolution or Napoleon, the Haskalah, or the Enlightenment? Perhaps it was the age of mercantilism, the exile from Iberia, the rise of nationalism, the collapse of autonomous Jewish life in Poland, the mass migration to Israel under Yehuda HaHassid? They all have their proponents and academic support.

It all confirms what we inside have always known. You can define neither Jews nor Judaism in a way that will satisfy all the various elements that make, for want of a better term, "the broad church of Judaism and Jews." What is the difference between a "people" and a "nation"? Is Judaism an "ethnic culture," a "religious culture," or neither? Jean-Paul Sartre thought it was anyone whom others think is Jewish. Homi Bhabha thinks it is any group that suffers as a result of imperialist domination.

Modern theory is right to try to avoid "the simple solution," "the grand scheme," or the "neat title," whether it is "The End of History" or "The Clash of Civilizations." They might sell books, but they get just as much wrong as right. We do know that modernism has freed us to think more as individuals than as members of established ideologies. The Internet in all its varieties has, for better and worse, enabled more of us to "pursue our own ideas and goals." Political, religious, and social groups try to control and dominate, but the genius of mankind is its ability to resist category and to allow us to be ourselves as we define it. We might call it existentialism or phenomenology, but the fact is that just as much as some humans need to lose themselves in the comforting but suffocating embrace of societies, communities, and ghettos, many others resist these constrictions.

There are plusses and minuses in both, and it would be wrong to say only one is right and all the others wrong. But that, sadly, is precisely what all kinds of fundamentalisms do. Rosman's book highlights the achievements, advances, and limitations of academia. Old models are challenged, superseded, and they in turn will face revisionism. It is a world in which great minds toil and produce theories, defend them with aggression and determination, devote passion and animosity to demolishing competition, and invariably end up being as doctrinaire, unreasonable, and closed minded as the worst anti-academic fanatics.

If you saw that brilliant Israeli film *The Footnote*, you will know exactly how it works on the academic shop floor. It is hard to find a more competitive and throat-cutting atmosphere outside of a Marxist coven. It makes rabbinic conflict look positively benign, and it explains why so much antagonism toward Israel comes from universities.

Rosman raises all the fascinating issues. Can Jewish history only be about Jews? What about their relationship for better and worse with their host societies? Is an English Jew more English or more Jewish than a French Jew? Is an American Jew more comfortable with other Americans or with other Jews? Is a Charedi Jew more at home with a Salafist Muslim or a secular Jew? Is a liberal Jewish female more at home with other feminists?

Israelis, Russians, Ethiopians, Jews from Arab lands, and Jews from Christian lands…are they influenced more by Judaism or by their cultures of adoption? If Jews are defined as having a common culture, is it one of religion or of card playing? How can all their different histories, cultures, and attitudes be reconciled if Jewish history is concerned with culture? But one might study their institutions and systems under a rubric of Jewish structures. And what about kabbalah? Is it mainstream Judaism or fringe? If it is a category of Jewish culture, in that case Madonna could be more Jewish than a rabbinical Talmudist! But that is the beauty of postmodernism. It opens up new worlds, new ideas that I find liberating. A Jew is indeed anyone who says or feels that he or she is one. The only problem is when you want other Jews to agree with you!

Postmodernism recognizes the variations and validates them, but in so doing creates such an indeterminate category as to be gutless, passionless, and all but meaningless. I don't belong entirely to any of the categories that postmodernism offers as defining Jews, although I belong in part to some. But in one rea, the religious, I live a clearly Jewishly defined way of life that is more animated by the Jewish tradition than any other. I do indeed walk in Athens and Jerusalem, but there's no doubt in my mind which and what matters most, even if my version has little in common with 90 percent of other Jews. In other words, I am who I am. And Moshe Rosman helps me feel very good about it.

BLOOD LIBELS

The twentieth of Sivan is the anniversary of the blood libel at Blois in France in 1171. The Jewish community of about forty people (at a time when the total Jewish population of France was no more than a few thousand) was massacred. Half were burnt to death singing the Aleynu prayer as they perished. The great Rabbeinu Tam instituted a fast day to commemorate the tragedy that for many years was adhered to strictly by the Jews of Ashkenaz.

Earlier, in 1144 at Norwich in England, Jews were first accused of killing Christian children because it was claimed they needed their blood for the four cups of wine at the Passover Seder. In Gloucester in 1168, in Bury St. Edmunds in 1181, Bristol in 1183, and most notoriously in Lincoln in 1255, Jews died as the result of this insane and barbaric charge. A thirteenth-century monk called Rhindfleish claimed that Jews stole communion wafers from churches to beat until the blood of Jesus flowed and hundreds of Jews were killed to avenge this "crime."

One might think it unexceptional given that this was an era of burning heretics, drowning witches, and torturing people to confess almost anything, but the blood libel persisted into the twentieth century. In Kiev in 1913 the unfortunate Menachem Mendel Beilis was charged with murdering a Christian child for Jewish blood-ritual purposes. Although at the trial he was acquitted, the Jewish religion was not! It will come as no surprise that the blood libel is making a big comeback in the Muslim world and is repeated and exaggerated on state-sponsored television throughout that culturally benighted part of our planet. Even in Nepal where Israelis went to rescue earthquake victims, it has been alleged that they really came to kidnap local children for blood.

A few years ago, a scandal erupted because it was reported that the Italian Israeli academic Professor Ariel Toaff was accused of claiming that medieval Jews were guilty of the blood libel. The furor was so great he was pressured to withdraw his book. On closer reading, it becomes clear that all he said was that possibly Jews did use dried human blood in medieval cures and charms and at most might have retaliated for acts of violence against them. Even so, this was based only on confessions under torture. But the idea that we ever drank cups of blood, something forbidden by our laws, is so malevolently false that only distorted minds (or those mistakenly influenced by the Christian belief that drinking communion wine actually turned into the blood of Christ) could conceive it.

Six-year-old Edgar Mortara was kidnapped by the Catholic Church in Italy from his parents in Bologna in 1858, on the grounds that his Catholic nanny had secretly baptized him. He was never returned to his parents. He became a favorite of Pope Pius IX, who ordered and perpetuated the crime. Mortara eventually died in a Belgian monastery. It was argued that he needed to be saved from dastardly Jewish blood drinkers.

Throughout this period of exile, despite the continuous lies and brutalities and the kidnapping, rape, and murder of our men, women, and children by supposedly good Christians, although negative opinions are expressed, nowhere in any major rabbinic authority or source will you find any support for a Halachic position that says you do not have to treat non-Jews correctly and morally and according to the law of the land. Throughout the periods of bloody chaos under both Christianity and Islam (accepting the differences), whether it was Rabbeinu Tam in the twelfth century, Rav Menahem Meiri in the fourteenth, Rav Lowe of Prague in the sixteenth, Rav Yehezkel Landau in the eighteenth, or Rav Yisrael Lipshitz in the nineteenth, they all wrote and spoke out against any evidence of mistreatment, deception, or amorality in dealing with non-Jews and our obligations to adhere to "the law of the land." Logically, this ought to apply to international law too.

Sadly, there are rabbis today who go the other way. Here is the latest example of scandalous rabbinic distortion of our law from the *Jerusalem Post*:

> All civilians living in Gaza are collectively guilty for Kassam attacks on Sderot, former Sephardi chief rabbi Mordechai Eliyahu has written in a letter to Prime Minister Ehud Olmert. Eliyahu ruled that there was absolutely no moral prohibition against the indiscriminate killing of civilians during a potential massive military offensive on Gaza aimed at stopping the rocket launchings. The letter, published in Olam Katan [Small World], a weekly pamphlet to be distributed in synagogues nationwide this Friday, cited the biblical story of the Shechem massacre (Genesis 34) and Maimonides' commentary (Laws of Kings 9, 14) on the story as proof texts for his legal decision. According to Jewish war ethics, wrote Eliyahu, an entire city holds collective responsibility for the immoral behavior of individuals. In Gaza, the entire populace is responsible because they do nothing to stop the firing of Kassam rockets.

Eliyahu is simply wrong. Collective punishment is not halachically acceptable. Maimonides's controversial position justifying the actions of Simeon and Levi in the biblical massacre of the men of Shechem has been overwhelmingly repudiated. If Rabbi Eliyahu is going to take a highly contentious precedent and apply it to modern conditions, then frankly it is in the same category as the Neturei Karta jokers who argue that all the suffering of the Jewish people in Israel and beyond is because they have dared to preempt the Messiah.

I had little respect for the Israeli Chief Rabbinate before this outburst. Even if I give him the benefit of the doubt that he was responding in pain to his suffering constituents in Sderot and the scandalous double standards of others, such abuse of law and lore demeans the person, the system, and is a blot on our tradition. We are descending to the very levels we complain about! No wonder we have stopped fasting over blood libels.

While we have a right and an obligation to self-preservation, and while charity starts at home, we cannot isolate ourselves, and we must meet our obligations to society in general. We who have suffered so much from the lies and distortions of religious leaders must not follow their evil examples.

ALTALENA

Oh, for a Palestinian Gandhi. Gandhi initiated a campaign of nonviolent protest that eventually forced the British Empire out of India. I accept that he failed in many areas too. No friend of the Jews, he was strongly opposed to the Jewish state. But his achievement through nonviolent means was a universal symbol of what human dignity can achieve in the face of oppression and power. There is no doubt in my mind that, had a Palestinian leader been man enough to adopt a Gandhi approach, the suffering of the Palestinians would today be over. Even if it is true that there were occasional men who advocated passive resistance and were regrettably exiled by Israeli authorities, no major figure under Arafat or Mazen (let alone Hamas) has adopted this approach. I recognize, of course, that passive resistance is as alien to the dominant Muslim mentality as it was to Judah Maccabee over two thousand years ago. But if you cannot change, you cannot win.

I was in Israel in 1967 when everyone hoped that after the comprehensive victory the Arab world would accept the reality of Israel's existence and there would be a trade of land for peace. Moshe Dayan said that he was willing to trade everything for a treaty. I also remember how the Palestinian West Bankers welcomed the Israelis. They hated the Jordanian occupation. Then the Arab summit at Khartoum dashed hopes. They refused recognition, peace and negotiations.

I detest the almost inevitable realities of occupation. I agree with the late Professor Yeshayahu Leibowitz that domination breeds inhumanity, not of everyone, but some. I stand ideologically closer to Amira Hass, the Rabbis for Human Rights, and the Peace Camp than I do to Gush Emunim, Kiryat Arba, and those Jews who oppose any sort of compromise. But there is a fundamental evil in suicide bombing cafes, schools, and children that totally alienates me from the perpetrators and those who encourage them. I understand retaliation, though I do not usually approve of it. And I accept that, sadly, in conflict innocents die. I do not approve of targeting, certainly not when children are killed at the same time. But collateral damage, unintentional death, is very different to getting on a bus filled with children and blowing them up. For that there are no words of human condemnation that even begin to be relevant.

I am not equating, but I do say that both sides have their extremists and are engaged in a war of ideologies, words, and ulterior motives. Both sides have their supporters, their funders, and their spokesmen. Both sides have those who wish to sabotage any deal. Both sides have their lunatics, and both sides have an obligation to control their fanatics. But Israel has an example of leadership taking difficult decisions for the greater good of the people. There is a historical precedent for eliminating internal threats.

In the final years of the British mandate in Palestine, there were several competing Jewish militias, just as there are different Palestinian groups today. The main army, the Haganah, was led by Ben-Gurion representing the official Jewish community, the "Yishuv" as it was called, with its predominant left-wing socialist secular ideologies. There were splits in that camp too. The Palmach left-wing fighting units wanted to remain independent but Ben-Gurion would not hear of it. Their official policy toward the British had been one of negotiation not violence.

The Irgun Zvai Leumi, Etzel, led by Menachem Begin, was of right wing in ideology, more sympathetic to the religious community and prepared to use violence to evict the British. They together with even more radical right-wing breakaway groups were responsible both for blowing up the King David Hotel and the massacre of Palestinians in the village of Deir Yassin in April 1948. Of course there were plenty of massacres the other way too.

After the British left Palestine and the State of Israel was declared, five Arab armies attacked. On June 1, the Haganah and Irgun agreed to merge into the Israel Defense Forces, headed by Haganah commanders. The accord called on Irgun members to hand over arms and terminate separate activity, including arms purchases abroad. Ben-Gurion said at the time, "The state can not exist until we have one army and control of that army."

While the negotiations were going on an old American navy landing vessel bought by the Irgun's American supporters and renamed the *Altalena* was en route for Israel. The ship, whose purchase had predated the June 1 agreement, was packed with 850 volunteers, 5,000 rifles, 3,000 bombs, 3 million cartridges, and hundreds of tons of explosives, all essential to bolster the newly born state against the enemies who had invaded it on all fronts.

Ben-Gurion wanted every soldier and bullet he could get and ordered the ship to dock. Begin said the arms should go to Irgun troops. Ben-Gurion insisted and sent Haganah men to intercept the boat as Irgun men headed to the beach to unload. Ben-Gurion realized the challenge he faced. As he said in his memoirs "I decided this must be the moment of truth. Either the government's authority would prevail and we could then proceed to consolidate our military force or the whole concept of nationhood would fall apart."

Begin refused to concede. He boarded the ship, as did other Irgun fighters and Ben-Gurion ordered the Altalena shelled. The Altalena burst into flames. Begin was hurled overboard by his men and carried ashore. The ship sank, along with most of its arms and more than a dozen Irgun members. Others were arrested, and the Irgun's independent activities were finally put to an end.

In his 1953 memoir, *The Revolt*, Begin says he had known hunger and sorrow in his life but had wept only twice. Once was out of joy, when the state was declared, and the second time, in grief, the night the Altalena was destroyed. This was a seminal point in Israeli and Jewish history. But it effectively laid the foundation for a single, unitary state. Unless the Palestinians can follow this example, they are doomed.

In 1996, the Palestinian Authority showed itself capable of confrontation, making widespread arrests of extremists in the wake of several suicide bombings. Thousands of militants were arrested. But most were eventually let go.

The Palestinians must do it again and in a definitive manner. The Altalena is a symbol of that task because it involved genuine confrontation.

The point for the Palestinians is that until their radical militias are put out of action, those groups will always be in the position of spoilers; so too will many right-wing extremists in Israel. Israel today needs to recall the lesson of the Altalena as well.

SEPHARDIM

I spend a fair amount of time with Persian Jews here in New York. I really enjoy their warmth and joie de vivre. But the quickest way to offend them is to suggest that they are Sephardi! Actually, you'd get a similar reaction if you suggest that a Muslim Iranian is an Arab!

The Persian Jewish community existed long before Spanish Jewry, which is the etymological origin of the term "Sephard." The Jews of Persia have been in the same place at least since the first of the two Babylonian exiles around 590 BCE. Some suggest an earlier date. In any case, they have been living in that constantly changing part of the world longer than any other Jewish community. Don't tell that in Gat!

When the Muslim conquerors burst out of the Middle East and reached through Spain almost into France, Jews from the old Persian Empire followed them and seeded the new communities in Spain. The rabbinic leaders of early Spain all came from that mother community. After the great expulsion of Spanish Jewry in 1492 and the consequent wave of Iberian Jews returning east, the term "Sephardi" ("Spanish") came to refer not just to Jews of Spanish origin, but rather loosely to apply to those living mainly under Islam who follow the ancient liturgy and rabbinical influence of Mesopotamia and eastward. Even those Jews of Persian origin who went to Spain were often still called Sephardim when they returned.

On the other hand, those Jews who had settled in northern Europe, the Rhineland, and then Poland and destinations farther east, the area known as "Ashkenaz," came to be known as Ashkenazim. To complicate matters even more, when in the eighteenth century, eastern European Chasidic Jews adopted the ecstatic Lurianic version of mysticism, they called their style of prayer *Nusach Sefard* (an Eastern Liturgy)! A separate category was Italian Jews who had originated mainly in Israel, moved to Rome, and thought themselves neither Ashkenazi nor Sephardi. And those Iberian Jews who migrated to Ashkenazi lands were called "Spanish and Portuguese."

Nowadays in Israel the term "Mizrachi" (oriental) refers to Jews from Oriental (Sephardi) countries. But this name is confusing too. My late father used to be the president of the Mizrachi Movement in Great Britain when it meant "religious Zionist" (he resigned when it went into politics in Israel). Words and names change in their usages and connotations over time. But we do seem to need names and categories, and we get so easily offended by them. Charedi Jews are upset if called ultra-Orthodox. Orthodox Jews who appreciate aspects of Western culture detest being called Modern Orthodox, and many other Orthodox don't like to be called Orthodox altogether because it has different connotations (like Russian Orthodox).

Among the faithful, there are all the different Chasidic sects who battle to preserve their special identities and shut out anyone who does not conform to their specific rituals and dress. The Charedi world itself is full of Yiddish distinctions, a Sheyner Yid (a fine Jew), a Chasidishe Yid, a Heimisher Yid ("one of us"), a kosher Yid, and a "Ben Torah" (conforms to Charedi standards).

All this is without venturing toward Egalitarian, Conservative, Masorti, Masorati (yes, they are different), Reconstructionist, Reform, Liberal, secular, cultural, intellectual, and whatever. I often run into trouble when I use the term "Reform" referring to Reform Jews. In the United States, Reform Judaism is a large denomination that was once the most important sector of American Jewry. It is fast losing that position. It is a radical movement that in choosing to define Jews in a "patrilineal" way has in fact split the Jews into Jews that Orthodox can marry and Jews that Orthodox Jews cannot marry. But in Great Britain, Reform Judaism is closer to Conservative Judaism in the United States. It has not gone down the divisive path of patrilineal descent.

So whenever I refer to "Reform Jews," I have to make sure the English know I am not referring to them.

But I really detest these labels. They are divisive and destructive. Nowhere does Moses differentiate between good Jews, religious Jews, or common and garden Jews, though I have to admit he was keen on the tribal divisions. Even so he talked about the sons of Israel. We are all in it together. Some are more into it and some less. And one of the things I really love about the Sephardi world is that they had no divisive reform movements there. Jews were either observant or partially or not at all. And that explains why their rabbis tended to be more tolerant and lenient. They were not fighting a competing movement and did not feel so much under assault. They could relax more. Instead internal rivalry focuses on city of origin and whether you do or do not like the rabbi.

So why do Iranians not like to be called Sephardim? It has to do with discrimination. Jews from Poland, Lithuania, Ukraine, Hungary, and Germany all looked down on each other and thought they were better than the others. When different groups of secular Jews started arriving in Israel in the nineteenth and twentieth centuries (religious groups had always been coming to Israel whenever the political climate allowed it), each group made the next one suffer. A bit like schoolchildren, the newcomers are picked on, so when they get to the top they make the next generation suffer the way they did.

The Russian socialists came first. By that I mean among the secular pioneers, for pious Jews had been coming all the time when they could. The Russians discriminated against the Germans, who in turn took it out on the massive immigration from Arab lands in 1950, who eventually turned on the post-Glasnost Russians, who felt better taking it out on the Ethiopians.

It wasn't until Menachem Begin won the election in 1977 that Sephardi pride began to turn the tables on Ashkenazi arrogance. There still does exist a layer of prejudice and discrimination against Sephardim in some small, petty-minded, and usually corrupt sectors of Israeli society (including the religious, sad to say), which is precisely why Iranians do not want to be called Sephardi. As if anyone else makes such fine distinctions. But here's the rub. Many Iranians discriminate against other Iranians. Is a Mashadi better than a Kashani, and is a Teherani just an out and out assimilationist?

I am often asked about marrying across these internal Jewish ethnic varieties. And I always say that if you have Torah in common, the rest is secondary. But anyway, it is certainly good for the genes!

CONVIVENCIA

There is a volume of essays I highly recommend by the late historian Yosef Hayim Yerushalmi who died in 2009, far too early. It is published by Brandeis University, and the title, *The Faith of Fallen Jews*, comes from Yerushalmi's fascination with what life was really like for the Marranos, the conversos, the secret Jews, some of whom were forcibly converted when they were given the choice of death or abandoning their faith. After the great massacres of 1391, thousands of Jews converted willingly in the tragically deluded notion that they would be accepted by Christians if only they "saw the light." Indeed this was the official position of the church. But in practice it did not work out.

The success of such converts in rising through the ranks of Christian society was seen as a threat. So "old Christians" fought back by differentiating between racially pure Christians and the originally Jewish parvenus. They introduced the racist concept of "pure blood," *limpiezia de sangre*, to purge Jewish blood, even converted blood, from that of the racially pure of the faith. And even if the concept in theory applied to Muslims, the Moriscos, and others, in practice it was applied almost exclusively to those of Jewish descent.

Yerushalmi argues that we are mistaken in thinking that racist anti-Semitism was the innovation of the nineteenth century. The nineteenth century might have taken the idea of racial contamination of the Jews out of the religious into the realms of the national, but it was a religious disease before it became secular.

He similarly debunks the mythos of the "Convivencia," the fashionable idea that once Jew, Christian, and Muslim all got along famously and equally in the golden age of Spain. There was hardly a golden age but merely brief respites in an otherwise painful state of accommodation and convenience in which Jews were used when it suited their masters. Even then the interaction was essentially with a small layer of aristocratic and learned Christians and Muslims that never reached down to the masses. Indeed one might say that that characterizes much of present-day interfaith activity. Not that I discount it for that. I merely point out its limitations. Both in Christianity and Islam, tolerance meant simply the condescending acceptance of an "other," but never genuine equality. When later such equality was required by law, it was resented in the salons and homes of the established classes.

Yerushalmi points out an important feature of Jewish political life throughout the years of exile. It is that Jews established vertical relationships with the few power players capable of extending them protection. Kings protected them when it suited them. Different religious leaders shielded them on occasion. But political relationships were essentially with the ruling classes and rarely horizontal with the majority, the lower and merchant classes. The result was that whenever there was a political crisis, plague, commercial competition, or the agitation of fanatical preachers, the Christian mob, the Muslim street, turned on the Jews with violence and cruelty. Even if there were always individual relationships and those who helped Jews and tried to protect them, the vast majority of every class did not.

The interesting question is whether it would or could have made a difference had such a policy been altered. Perhaps the profound religious sense that Jews were the enemy of the true faith, regardless of which one (including Marxism), was too strong and deeply rooted to have been influenced. Yerushalmi emphasizes time and again how important it is, in making crucial judgments, to have a historical perspective. He quotes the magisterial Baer as saying that the Jews of Iberia had no historical self-understanding. That was why they were so unprepared for the catastrophe that befell them, both those who converted and those who remained steadfast. "Despite his vast and intimate experience in the political world of his day, even Isaac Abarbanel, the last great leader of Spanish Jewry, did not perceive the impending disaster with sufficient clarity to prepare his brethren."

In an essay based on a talk to the Leo Baeck Institute, Yerushalmi argues that German Jews suffered the same fate. Even if they did have a tradition of Wissenschaft and a secular perspective, they failed to appreciate the lessons of history. They took their place in German society without realizing the depth of common or popular hatred. The same can be said of the failure of the eastern European anti-Zionist leadership to see which way the winds were blowing in the 1930s. Somehow we often got blinded by the periods of peace in our host societies and assumed they would always remain safe, that we would survive regardless.

The same is true in Israel today. There is a reluctance to examine the lessons of history and to forge horizontal political alliances instead of vertical ones. If this is true of Israeli secular society, it is even more so of Charedi society. The leaders, devoid of any academic historical training or understanding of history outside of the Talmud, are clearly unaware how their refusal to accommodate other viewpoints or reach out to create alliances on, say, the question of serving in some form of community service, if not the army, or refusing to allow significant numbers to study other subjects so as to enable them to get jobs and earn a living, is a symptom of the refusal to see things through different, including historical, perspectives. Theirs is just one angle; admittedly it is a legitimate one, but few things in life are black and white.

Some argue that this single mindedness is the result of Israeli political culture, all or nothing, the more noise you make the more cash you get. But if so, that's all the more why the work of men like Yerushalmi is so important and must not be allowed to disappear off our communal radar.

ROME AND JERUSALEM

History fascinates me, if only because we stubbornly refuse to learn its lessons. It might never exactly repeat itself, but it certainly helps us understand what has happened and why. Professor Martin Goodman of Oxford has written many books on ancient Rome and Judea during the Roman occupation and destruction. In his *Rome and Jerusalem*, much of it a restatement of earlier works such as *The Ruling Class of Judea,* he attempts to answer the question as to why Rome turned on Judea with such violence and aggression. Rome was challenged elsewhere in the empire, and it was usually ruthless when it could be, but the viciousness of its campaigns in Judea was quite exceptional.

Throughout the empire, the Romans, like the Greeks before them, tended either to ignore local cults or respect them. Perhaps this was a way of covering their bases. In Judea, Romans, even the emperors from Rome itself, regularly sent sacrifices to the Temple. So religion does not seem to have been the issue. Of course the Jewish conspiracy theorists will put it all down to anti-Semitism.

There was constant commercial and social tension and rivalry between Jews and Greeks throughout the empire, and clashes occurred frequently. But, again, this does not fully explain the Judean experience. Through a detailed analysis of sources, Goodman comes up with two principal answers.

First there was Vespasian, one of a generation of generals who vied for succession after the end of the Julian line of men descended directly or indirectly from Julius Caesar. All his rivals had won significant military victories. He had not. So a crushing, brutal campaign in Judea, continued after he returned to Rome by his son Titus, was essential to his claims to leadership of the empire. He had to be seen as outstandingly tough, and the Judean campaign happened to coincide with this moment in history.

Second, in all other areas the Romans relied on the local wealthy and upper classes to run the provinces, and often rewarded them with high office, even becoming senators. But in the case of Judea, the Jewish upper, aristocratic, priestly classes were divided, and no group seemed capable of dominating to the point where it could rule. They undermined their positions because they allowed such a wealth gap to open up between them and the masses that they were the cause of dissent, which only made matters worse and Judea ungovernable. The Romans also made the mistake of assuming that the high priest was a commanding figure who could function as an effective ruler when there were too many competing and more effective power structures. In addition, as hierarchical and antipopulist, the Romans were reluctant to recognize the power of the more democratic and generally acceptable Assembly of Rabbis. There was the other problem of the individualist, rebellious, antiauthoritarian Jewish nature.

Our main historical sources for this period remain Jewish renegade Josephus, notoriously unreliable and self-justifying; the Talmud, written later and a vehicle of the rabbinic tradition; and the Gospels, written in Greek, an alien language, by people who claimed to be Jewish but probably were not and with an obvious anti-Jewish agenda. Naturally I am biased in favor of the Talmud, which presents three explanations of the catastrophe, two of which support the Goodman thesis. One is that Jewish leadership indeed failed, as illustrated by the famous story of Kamtza and Bar Kamtza. Here's my adaptation of the Talmud in Gittin 55b:

> A man in Jerusalem was friendly with Kamtza, but the enemy of Bar Kamtza. He told his assistant to invite Kamtza to a feast, but instead

> he invited Bar Kamtza. When he saw him sitting there he said, "You are my enemy; leave." Bar Kamtza said, "Let me pay for what I eat and drink, but do not embarrass me in public." He refused. So Bar Kamtza offered to pay for half the banquet. Still the man refused. Then he offered to pay for the whole of the banquet, but still he was forcibly ejected. Bar Kamtza said to himself, "The rabbis were there and did not protest. They must have agreed with him [they all deserve what's coming]. I will go and 'chew the cud' with the Romans." He went and told them that the Jews had rebelled against them.

This failure of human sensitivity, the reluctance of the rabbis to tangle with a wealthy man, the absence of moral leadership, the bitterness, and the betrayal, led ultimately to the destruction of Jerusalem. The legend condemns the arrogance and insensitivity of the rich, the inability of the rabbis to take a moral stand, and the divisiveness and personal interests that overrode national considerations. Nothing better illustrates the disastrous incompetence of the ruling Jewish classes.

The Talmud also sees the collapse of moral society as a religious failure. According to Shabbat 119b, most Jews had abandoned their religion, education had ceased, charity was the exception rather than the rule, and people were too arrogant. Throughout the Talmud there are endless examples of the ostentation of the wealthy. But equally, the Talmud blames wider external social and economic tensions, and this is from Megillah 6a: "If you hear that Jerusalem is settled and Caesarea destroyed, or Caesarea settled and Jerusalem destroyed, you may believe it. But if you hear they are both destroyed or both settled, do not believe it!" Never mind that by the time the Talmud was compiled they had both been destroyed!

In other words, the factors we can point to nowadays as exercising a negative influence on Jewish life, and specifically on life in Israel—namely a failure of moral leadership, wealth playing a corrosive role, corruption internally, external hatred and ideological conflict, and religious hypocrisy—were all present then. Add to this external political exigencies and power politics, and you had disaster then and potential disaster now. The only reassuring factor is that, somehow or other, we survive, thanks to our talents and drive.

ASSYRIANS

As battles rage around the area we now call Kurdistan, it is interesting to recall that it was actually the core of the old Assyrian Empire, the one that carried off the ten lost tribes. Indeed there is quite a lot of literature to suggest the Kurds are descended from Israelites. Benjamin of Tudela (who died in Castile in 1173) visited them and thought that had not the Byzantians forcibly converted one half and the Muslims the other, they would still be Jewish. He detected, he said, several customs they all adhered to that could only have come from us. Now there's a thought. Perhaps this explains why Israel today has a better relationship with the Kurds than with any other ethnic group in the Middle East.

Assyria looms large in the Bible. After it conquered the Arameans of Damascus who had ravaged the Northern Kingdom for years, the Assyrians turned their attention to the Kingdom of Israel. First they bullied King Jehu into submission and finally conquered it in 722 BCE. According to the Bible, they exiled all the population and replaced them with other conquered victims uprooted from other parts of their empire whom they settled around Samaria, the capital of the conquered Northern Kingdom. This explains why those people came to be known as Samaritans.

The newcomers were plagued by wild animals and thought it was because they did not know or acknowledge the local gods. So the Assyrians commanded Judea in the south to send priests to teach and convert them. They became known as *geyrei arayot* "converts (out of fear of) lions." In other words, not genuine converts out of conviction. The struggle between Samaritans and Jews would go on for quite a while. Needless to say, Samaritans dispute this narrative. But it does indicate what a religiously tolerant sort of people the Assyrians were. They wanted your money, bodies, gold, and obedience, but really didn't mind too much which god you worshipped.

Then the Assyrians turned their attention to the southern Kingdom of Judea and besieged King Hezekiah "like a bird in a cage" according to Sennacherib's stele. The Bible tells us that the Assyrians were forced to withdraw. The Assyrian record only says that Hezekiah was forced to pay a massive tribute to avoid destruction. Either way, Sennacherib, the one Byron describes as coming down "like the wolf on the fold," retreated home and set about building a new capital called Nineveh. The ruins are to be found outside Mosul today if the fundamentalist lunatics have not completely destroyed them. Others, putting two and two together, suggest he returned home in a rush because of rebellion in his own family. Sennacherib was eventually assassinated by his son.

The Assyrians themselves finally fell afoul of the Babylonians, and they in turn capitulated to the Persians, whose king, Cyrus, let some Jews return. But the Jews on their return ran into trouble with the Samaritans, who said that this was their land now and the Israelites could jolly well go back to Persia and complain to the UN (or something like that). We keep on running into such problems, don't we? But we persevered! And hung in there. Until, of course, the Romans decided otherwise.

There's an important lesson we learn from the Assyrians that we repeat every Yom Kippur when we read the book of Jonah. He was told to go to Nineveh, the capital of Assyria, to get them to repent their evil ways. He didn't want to go because he knew that if they did repent, they would be used as a tool to destroy his country, Israel. So he fled to Tarshish, a well-known port that was in the hands of the Kittim, the enemies of the Assyrians, the Sea People from Crete and islands around. But God had other ideas. We know the story of the fish that swallowed him and then coughed him up. When Jonah gave up running away, he eventually got to Nineveh. There he started preaching, and amazingly the king listened. They listened to him there, although he was ignored at home. Hence the well-known phrase "There's no prophet in his own country."

Assyria repented. And then proceeded to destroy the Northern Kingdom. The lesson is clear. God does not support Israel if they misbehave. He will use some other power to destroy her. So He must have thought reasonably highly of the Assyrians. At that stage at any rate, they were not just brutal, greedy conquerors, but in fact had a higher standard of morality than the Northern Kingdom. Indeed the Sennacherib Stele proclaims that he was the protector of the widow and the poor, the downtrodden and the oppressed—all things the prophets of Israel campaigned in favor of at home.

Archaeological evidence is increasingly fleshing out biblical narratives that rational, skeptical Western society tends to take with a pinch of salt. A recent exhibition at the Metropolitan museum Museum included the earliest archaeological artifact that refers to the "House of David." It is an engraved stone, a fragment from an arch celebrating Hazael of Damascus's destruction of the House of David found at Tel Dan. As you might expect, the Palestinian archaeologists, anxious to deny there were ever any Jews there, claim it's not the House of David, but the House of Dod (perhaps Dod's your uncle). Given there's no other evidence, record, or hint of such a house, it is just childish if not malicious to suggest it's not what it obviously is. But hey, politics insinuates itself into archaeology too. And the Israeli archaeologists made so sure we would not miss the reference they chalked the words white against the black background for all to see. Politics cuts both ways.

There was a balustrade on display from Samaria in northern Israel. Ahab's son Ahazia fell through one of the balustrades of the palace and died soon after. Ahab's dynasty was done away with by Jehu. And here he appears on display in stone on the Black Obelisk of Shalmaneser III from Nimrud, the Assyrian capital before Nineveh, bowing down low to Shalmaneser. It even looks as though some of those in attendance were wearing four tassels that might have been "tzitzit"!

The Assyrian Empire's tentacles extended to Spain through the Sea Peoples. They were what we now call the Phoenicians or the Philistines. Some suggest the Canaanites are their descendants too. The competition between them and Assyria was fierce. But it was often one of mutually beneficial trade. One sees clearly the connection between the Phoenician alphabet and the early Hebrew script. That was before the Jews of Babylon adopted the square letters we still use today. But it was that earlier one that Moses would have used.

Seeing archaeological artifacts is moving. Biblical events come alive. They remind us of the immense achievements of our ancestors, and their failures too. It is both a source of pride and a warning, that like Ozymandias, great kings end up in the dust and are remembered only by their epitaphs. But ideas live on.

KARAITES

I have several times in the past come across Jews, invariably thoughtful and charming, who have told me that they are so fed up with the excesses of rabbinic Judaism that they have decided to become Karaites. Only this week a delightful young Israeli woman living in New York told me in synagogue that she was so fed up with extra days of festivals and other rabbinic-added strictness that she too was a Karaite and so only kept festivals for one day instead of the custom in the Diaspora to keep two.

Which set me wondering why my little Persian community in New York, most of whom do not bother with second days, did not themselves adopt the Karaite variation? All the more since many of the early founders of the Karaite schism came from Persia. But the fact is that, if you look more carefully into it, becoming a Karaite is not really to be recommended. Though it might solve one set of problems, it would create a heck of a lot of other ones.

The Karaites take their name from the Hebrew Aramaic word for "text," which indicates that they only accept the text of the Torah. They reject post-Torah rabbinic interpretations, additions, and customs. Many of them reject those theological ideas such as resurrection and life after death that are not explicit in the Torah. What makes them popular with Reform communities that accept the patrilineal definition of Jewish identity is that they accepted it too. But unlike Reform, they are most unenthusiastic about conversion.

Some scholars trace them back to the Sadducees, who themselves held such opinions, others to the Dead Sea sects. They were dormant or marginal after the destruction of the Temple, but later and under the dynamic leadership of Anan Ben David (715–795), who some say really founded them, they flourished to such an extent that at one moment in the ninth century they nearly became the dominant sect in Judaism in Persia and Babylonia. The historian Salo Baron thought they accounted for 40 percent of the Iraqi Jewish population.

It was thanks mainly to the great Saadiah Gaon (d. 942), who campaigned energetically and relentlessly against them, that they receded and declined to the very small sect that they are today. Currently some thirty thousand live in Israel and about four thousand in the United States. Despite their differences, Sephardi rabbis such as Rav David-Chaim Chelouche and the late Rav Ovadia Yosef have always maintained that they count as Jews and do not need conversions to "return to the fold." The Ashkenazi rabbinate, surprise, surprise, is not so open to the idea.

So what does Karaite practice consist of? The Karaite calendar differs from the accepted Jewish calendar. It follows the literal reading of the Torah text for festivals lasting only one day. But I don't understand why they celebrate Simchat Torah, which is not mentioned in the Torah as such. They do not include Chanukah, as a postbiblical festival, but do keep Purim.

But before you go out and sign up, let me tell you the downside. Not accepting rabbinic innovation does have its drawbacks. Karaites do not allow lights and fire in their homes on Shabbat, although I am told reformist ideas on this issue now divide them into the "lighters" and "the darkers." They allow no sex on Shabbat. That's a real downer, as are far stricter rules on family purity that really put women in a state of purdah once a month. And the laws of marriage are so strict that any blood relative, however distant, is forbidden. You really are hurting your chances of getting married! That more than anything else probably explains why there are so few today. Since they are not allowed to marry out, the pool of possible partners is ridiculously small.

They don't interpret the Torah texts about tefillin and mezuzot as requiring literal objects. They see the textual references as merely as symbolic. But they are very keen on tzitzit, especially the blue thread. They do not take the four kinds of plants we wave on Sukkot, because they understand the Torah references to mean that they were to be used only in building a sukkah. And because their laws for how to slaughter animals are different and stricter than Orthodox shechitah, this means that a good Karaite will not eat normal kosher meat. If you are interested in learning more, there are several Karaite websites on the Internet. The fact that they disagree with each other must prove they really are regular Jews!

On balance, I conclude, it makes more sense from a social point of view to stay technically within the dominant expression of Jewish religious life. After all, we are small enough as it is compared to the major religions of the world and riven enough by denominational conflict as it is without confining oneself to an even narrower religious network. But then we have never played the numbers games. Still, to claim adherence to the apparently more lenient way of life of an even smaller splinter group based simply on convenience, and usually ignorance, just does not make sense from the point of view of integrity or logic.

If Karaites see themselves as part of the Jewish people, then the variations in their beliefs and practices are no different than those of most Conservative and Reform Jews today. But if someone simply wants a justification for only keeping one day of Rosh Hashanah and the other festivals, there are, believe me, easier ways to go about it.

HENRY VIII

There has been a lot of interest recently in the Tudor dynasty of the English monarchy. Television series, films, and books have provided us with a fascinating combination of drama, titillation, and history. It is an excellent example of the benefits and dangers of watching television. You get some information selected mainly for its viewing interest. But lots of other interesting episodes are ignored. One of them is the Jewish dimension.

The issue was partially religious and partially political. Marriages between royal families were matters of alliances and balance of power. Catherine of Aragon was the daughter of Ferdinand and Isabella of Spain, the nasty fanatics who expelled the Jews from Spain. At the age of three, Catherine was betrothed to Prince Arthur, the elder son of Henry VII of England. Henry had become king after a long, divisive civil war and needed to consolidate his position in a world dominated, at the time, by Spain. In 1501, shortly before her sixteenth birthday, Catherine married Arthur. But after less than six months, he died. Henry needed to keep the alliance alive. So Catherine was then betrothed to Arthur's younger brother, Prince Henry. When he became king in 1509, at the age of eighteen, he married Catherine.

Their marriage produced just one living daughter, Mary Tudor. Henry was desperate for a male heir, and he was a notorious philanderer. He had fallen in love with Anne Boleyn, daughter of minor aristocrats and a star at court. She had persuaded him she could produce a male heir, but she would not allow him to have his way with her until they were married. He wanted Anne in his bed officially. But according to the Catholic religion of the Holy Roman Empire, the religion of all Europe, divorce was not allowed. The only option was an annulment. But as the pope had sanctioned the marriage in the first place, he had to be the one to annul it.

Henry tried all sorts of ways of getting the pope to agree, but the pope was under political pressure from other quarters, notably Spain. Otherwise popes, like rabbis, usually found ways of giving rich people what they wanted, for a price. After several years of fruitless negotiations, Henry declared religious independence. He set up the Protestant Church of England with him as the supreme religious head and got his way, at the expense of not a few clergymen, most notably Sir Thomas More, who remained loyal to Rome and lost their lives. It wasn't only Jews who got put to death for religion in those days. Henry was happy for a while, until he grew tired of his second wife and she failed to produce a male heir. He couldn't face more theological battles, so he became famous for his trumped-up charges, and off went the heads of those of his wives who didn't die beforehand or survive him in the end. As Mel Brooks has King Louis saying in his *History of the World: Part I*, "It's good to be a king!"

Where is the Jewish angle here, particularly since they were expelled from England in 1290, and there weren't any there officially at the time (apart from a few itinerant Marranos, who were outwardly Christians anyway)?

According to Leviticus 18, a man may not marry his brother's wife, and if he does, they will be childless. That, thought Henry, was why he had no sons. No matter that the logic of the law was against marrying them both in their lifetime.

But the pope had sanctioned his marriage based on the levirate marriage described in Deuteronomy 25. In the event of a man dying childless, his brother would marry the widow and have children to carry on the dead brother's name. Henry realized that where texts contradict each other, then interpretation and tradition come into play. If the pope was not willing to play

Henry's game and annul the marriage, he'd have to show that the pope didn't know his aleph from his beth.

The obvious people to turn to were the church scholars, but they themselves were split. So who else do you turn to but the Jews? Of course nowadays we know the Jews can't agree on anything, and certainly not on matters of Jewish law. But Henry hadn't spent any time in yeshiva and knew no better. So he sent his men to Italy, where a Venetian rabbi, Isaac Halfon, wrote an opinion saying that since the end of the Talmudic period, the biblical law of *yibum*, requiring a brother to marry the widow of a childless brother, had fallen into abeyance and only the divorce, *chalitza*, was used. Therefore the marriage contracted with Arthur's widow was against Jewish law, regardless of whether it had been consummated or not.

Furthermore, the same rabbi who had banned polygamy, Rabbeinu Gershom (960–1028), and the later Rabbeinu Tam (1100–1171), both undisputed authorities of European Jewry, had banned the levirate marriage on principle. More good news came from a contemporary responsum to the same effect by Yaakov Raphael Ben Yechiel Chaim Paglione of Modena supported by other Italian rabbis. Henry wanted the sympathetic rabbis to come to his court to reassure him and his bishops of his case. But Jews, despite Oliver Cromwell's support, would not be allowed back into England officially (and not without heavy opposition) until the reign of Charles II. They couldn't or wouldn't come. Instead Henry had to get a Jewish convert to Christianity, one Marco Raphael, to come over on a generous expense account to persuade the local opponents that Jewishly speaking, Henry was in his rights. The King even imported a set of the Talmud to help him find the sources.

Sadly for Henry, all this pursuit proved to be a dead end because the Sephardi rabbinate still allowed a levirate marriage. The pope knew that Sephardi Jews had other customs. Indeed, Sephardi Jews had not been bound either by Rabbeinu Gershom or Rabbeinu Tam. They could have several wives and divorce much more easily, and they had never banned yibum at all. The pope got his own rabbis to say so. Poor old 'Enery had wasted his time and money and found himself back at square one. And that, my dears, was why he broke with Rome and established the first Protestant kingdom and how the reigning monarch of England to this day is also the supreme head of the Church of England.

Little has changed. Where religion and politics come together, both end up the losers. The pope lost out, and the Spanish lost out. In Judaism we might not have a pope, but we have a very wide selection of rabbis and rebbes who behave as if they were and use their authority to terrify their faithful.

No one is surprised if in the United States the Supreme Court justices can disagree over whether the Constitution allows or disallows abortion or the death penalty. So why are we surprised if odd rabbis come out with something that strikes all reasonable people as rubbish and claim it's in the law? It may or may not have some foundation in legal sources, but that does not mean everyone has to agree. At least nowadays no one need lose his head over it.

MYTHS

In 419 BCE, the Persian king Darius issued a decree concerning the Jewish garrison at Elephantine on the Nile delta (near the cataracts of what is now called Aswan). It was directed toward the governor, Arsames, and instructed him to make sure that the Egyptian priests of Khnum did not attack the Jews or try to stop the Passover celebrations at the Jewish temple there. It is a fascinating historical fact that there was a Jewish (perhaps more accurately Judean) military garrison in Egypt twenty-five hundred years ago and a temple where they sacrificed outside of Jerusalem.

Tension between the Egyptian priests and Jews was exacerbated by the Jewish tradition of slaughtering sheep, something the Egyptian religion forbade; this Egyptian antipathy is explicitly stated in the Torah (Genesis 46 and Exodus 8:22). Sadly, nine years later, Arsames no longer there and no one able to protect the Jews, the priests of Elephantine destroyed the Jewish temple and its population.

Long after the Exodus, tensions between Egyptians and Jews persisted. Alternative versions of the Exodus have existed for a long time, just as alternative narratives about the Middle East proliferate nowadays. Each has its own agenda, some constructive and some destructive. Hecataeus, an Egyptian historian who lived around 320 BCE, talks about bands of exiles coming to Egypt, being driven out, and then taking over an uninhabited Judea. They were led by a man called Moses. He founded a new religion that Hecataeus described as unsocial and intolerant!

Manetho was an Egyptian priest who lived in Heliopolis in the middle of the second century BCE. He is mentioned by Josephus. Manetho gave two versions of the Exodus. The first was about shepherds who invaded Egypt and took it over. This conforms to the archaeological evidence we have of the Hyksos invasion of Egypt roughly thirty-five hundred years ago. But then, according to Manetho, they were driven out and settled in Judea, where they founded Jerusalem and built the Temple.

Manetho gives another version, which seems to be a basis of the virulent anti-Jewish sentiment of the Alexandrian Greek world. After the invasion of the shepherds, the Egyptian king Amenophis was told that he would see the gods if he purified his land of lepers and the diseased. So he gathered eighty thousand diseased and unclean and set them to work in quarries. But the diseased ones formed a society of their own under a renegade Egyptian priest called Osarseph. Osarseph made new laws and commanded the diseased not to associate with ordinary Egyptians. This new diseased people escaped their masters, set fire to cities, attacked and destroyed temples and holy images, desecrated holy places, and sacrificed animals that hitherto had been forbidden. Finally, the leader changed his name to Moses and led them out of the land.

There were lots of upheavals, external and internal, in Egypt. One of the most famous was when Akhenaten overthrew the old system for the sun god Aten some thirty-five hundred years ago. Indeed, Freud used this association in his *Moses and Monotheism* when he suggested that Moses was a follower of Akhenaten, and when his boss was defeated he looked around for another job and found leading the Israelites a suitable career. Manetho makes it very clear that these followers of Osarseph or Moses were considered an alien, dangerous, degraded, sick people, rigid and xenophobic. The visceral hatred of Jews as "others" and "enemies" had begun. Josephus uses much of this material in his book *Against Apion*, a defense of Judaism against the notorious Alexandrian Jew hater.

This association of Jews with impurity and being alien has come to be the dominant narrative of Jew hatred from Haman, to the Greeks, and then to medieval and not so medieval Christianity and Islam. Jews are rootless nomads who invade other people's territories and live a life diametrically opposed to the host societies' values and religion, while taking advantage of them and undermining them. They are misanthropes who are a threat to ordinary peace-loving peoples. Thus most Europeans nowadays see Jews as the biggest threat to world peace.

If you are interested in how this narrative is developed from its earliest stages to this very day, it is worth reading David Nirenberg's brilliant book *Anti-Judaism: The Western Tradition*. But I warn you, it is depressing reading for any Jew. There is no question that we have often added fuel to the fire and often been the authors of our own fate, making some terrible decisions. But the pathology of an irrational hatred is documented in Nirenberg's book with even more impressive literary and historical sources than Anthony Julius's great contribution in *Trials of the Diaspora*.

Whenever we sit around the Seder table, surrounded by our children, and tell them tales of our past, enact innocent rituals, drink wine and eat and be merry, we may well wonder what we are doing, bringing children into such a hostile world in which the hatred persists and even grows in many places like dry rot. Yet this has been our narrative for thousands of years. Some argue (not I) that it has made us stronger and helped us survive. Yet for all that, I would not willingly impose this on anyone unless I strongly believed that the Jewish way of life is dedicated to making this world a better and more spiritual place, and that it adds so much quality and depth to one's life, to one's range of experiences, and to one's intellectual development.

We have always been faced with "wicked sons" and daughters who have disparaged Judaism from within as well as without. Just as tradition has it that many Israelites preferred slavery in Egypt to freedom, we tend to emphasize our rights through our suffering. But I would rather argue from the position of the positive contribution our tradition has made to mankind. How much more positive to focus on Torah, a product of the Middle East, rather than the Holocaust, the consequence of Europe.

DARK AGES

We call them the Dark Ages in Europe. Roughly from 400 till about 900 CE, this was that era after the collapse of the Western Roman Empire when the Goths, the Ostrogoths, the Vandals, the Vikings, and other barbaric pagan tribes from northern Europe took over the area we call western Europe today, excluding Iberia, cutting it off from Byzantium and the Islamic Mediterranean. It was, according to historians like Norman Cantor, the monasteries that kept religion alive. Most people lived a life that was primitive, brutal, and pagan. The dominant ascetic response of the monks was to withdraw altogether from society, with its corrupt temptations and distractions, into secure communities. The closed Benedictine communities were islands of scholarship and piety in an otherwise primitive and lawless world, although they too were often attacked, plundered, and their monks killed.

Jews, Greeks, and Muslims were the strange outsiders passing through with goods or acting as middlemen. Towns were few and far between in an essentially agrarian society. There were occasionally strong kings who really acted like Mafiosi chiefs. Charles Martell, who stopped the Muslim advance through the Pyrenees in 732, was one; Pepin I another; and of course most people know about Charles the Great, Charlemagne (768–814). Occasionally a strong pope emerged who challenged the baron kings. Otherwise they were simply corrupt Roman gangsters put in power by their friends. Where the king was strong, the church always fought back, and vice versa. The kings used religion and religious power when it suited them and rejected it when they had other ideas and goals.

Most of the monasteries of the early Middle Ages failed to alter society beyond their own "safe" environments. Such religion as there was relied on paganism, magic, and other popular placebos; hence, for example, the introduction of Norse myths and figures into Christian folklore. Later, new monastic orders developed, more inclined to take their piety out into the community; one thinks of the Franciscans and those great seekers-out of heretics, the Dominicans who led the assaults on the Jews. During the Renaissance, the churches flourished and their power was extended. And then slowly corruption and power began to take its toll. The Enlightenment began the process of weakening the church's grip, so that today it has lost its grip and is slowly being swamped by Islam.

It strikes me that Judaism has always gone through these sorts of movements too with obvious variations. After all, there were Jewish monasteries two thousand years ago down by the Dead Sea. They were the withdrawing Jews while the mainstream Pharisee movement of the rabbis tried to change the nature and quality of urban and agrarian society. When Judaism is weak, we rely on the few isolated "hot spots" to keep the tradition alive. Then when these "hot spots," yeshivas, or religious communities flourish, they deal with expanding numbers either by setting up branches or sending out their own missionaries. Either these missionaries come from the hot spots directly or offer more assimilated or popular opiates that owe more to the host societies.

We are going through a similar sort of period in Jewry now. Let's just take Anglo Jewry. From the period of the establishment of the English United Synagogue in Victorian times until the demise of Chief Rabbi Hertz, the lay leaders often assimilated aristocratic Jews with a sense of noblesse oblige and ran the religious affairs of the community using reverends as their tools and figureheads. They had little contact, if any, with religious "hot spots."

Occasionally a powerful chief rabbi like Rabbi Hertz would stand up to his nonreligious lay leadership. During this period, religion in the United

Synagogue was a perfunctory sort of social institution, meeting at synagogue on a Saturday morning, off to the club or quasi-Jewish restaurant for lunch, and then football or huntin', shootin', and fishin' in the afternoon. There was little knowledge, scholarship, or spirituality.

Slowly over the past century, we have seen a transformation in which most Jews have left Orthodoxy either for other denominations or complete assimilation. The faithful Orthodox retreated back into a sort of ascetic purity reminiscent of the monastic. Orthodoxy has reacted to the challenge of anti-religious modernity by pulling itself inward religiously.

Orthodoxy today is the equivalent of monastic ascetics who initially withdrew into their ghettos or academies and ignored the outside to the best of their ability. After the initial withdrawal, evangelical graduates started to go out into the world to try to change it and fashion it in their image. So today in England the United Synagogue is no longer controlled by its established lay leadership or even by its own rabbinical college. Instead it is in the grip of a variety of ultra-Orthodox "monastically trained" graduates who are paid by the United Synagogue even if they have little sympathy for it. I am not here going into whether this is a good or a bad thing. These trends have always played themselves out in Christian, Jewish, and Muslim societies, and historically they have always been cyclical. Decadence was followed by the Reformation, followed by the Counter-Reformation.

In the nineteenth century, Catholicism went through a period of totally rejecting modern inventions and ideas and falling back on papal infallibility. Judaism did the same in reaction to the Enlightenment and Reform Judaism. Two hundred years ago, the great rabbinic leader Chatam Sofer (Moses Schreiber 1762–1839), decided it was time to reject any innovation (that he did not approve of). His position preserved an Orthodox minority, but it did not prevent the drift toward assimilation.

You can respond to a challenge by opening up, and you can respond by closing up. This cycle and tension has always been there, and it gives comfort to those of us who feel we are out of synch with the current mood of ultra-Orthodoxy despite our commitment to Tora and Halachah; times will change, and so will religious fashions.

Monks and rabbis have a lot in common. They start off as idealists, get sucked into power plays and preserving authority, and then find themselves needing to reinvent the wheel, to return to spiritual integrity. And then after a period of time, financial considerations emerge, compromises are made, and the cycle begins again. Perhaps the moral of the story is that if we believe we are right, we should stick to our guns, and sooner or later we'll be back in fashion again. Or perhaps proven wrong.

JEWS OF PINSK

I have just read almost a thousand pages of the two-volume history *The Jews of Pinsk* published by Stanford University Press. It is translated from Azriel Shohet's Hebrew, and I got hold of a copy through one of the editors of the English version, Mark Jay Mirsky. I should mention that his beautifully written prefaces to the two volumes are reason enough to read the book itself. The volumes are packed with facts and tables, not for the fainthearted or those used to getting their information predigested in abbreviated form. This magisterial work underlines both inspirational and disturbing features of Jewish life in the eastern European Diaspora.

Polish Jewry was the child of the expulsions and catastrophes inflicted on the Ashkenazi communities of England and the Rhineland during the Crusades. Dislocated remnants of destroyed communities headed east. Poland was short of people. First Boleslaw the Pious welcomed the refugees in 1264, even though his own clerics opposed him. Then Casimir the Great (who reigned from 1333 to 1370) granted the Jews extensive charters and laid the foundations for a self-governing quasi-autonomous community that slowly over the years became the most dynamic Jewish community in the Christian world.

Pinsk, on the eastern borders of Poland, sat on the convergence of river systems that linked it with the Baltic to the north and the Black Sea to the south. It came to be the town with the largest proportion of Jews in all Europe, and it eventually merged with its satellite town Karlin. During the course of its history, Pinsk came, in sequence, under Polish, Lithuanian, Swedish, Lithuanian, Polish, Russian, German, Russian, and finally Communist Polish regimes. How's that for instability? Jews were constantly having to readjust to different laws, languages, and religious prejudices. No wonder they needed their own vernacular.

The first volume, dealing with the years 1506 to 1880, describes life initially under the Poles and the self-regulating Jewish Communal Organization, the Vaad Arba Aratzot, the Council of the Four Lands, which combined the regions of Greater Poland, Lesser Poland, Ruthenia, and Volhnya. Each community was in effect governed by its wealthy members and its rabbis, a kind of oligarchy both serving and benefitting from power, united by bonds of financial support, marriage, and vested interests. The state of affairs in which the poor were effectively treated as second-class citizens has been well documented, including the Littman Library's 2004 publication *Yom-Tov Lipmann Heller: Portrait of a Seventeenth-Century Rabbi* by Joseph Davis.

During the Cossack invasions and pogroms under Bogdan Chmielnicki and his allies, too often the rabbis and the rich abandoned their communities, leaving the poor unprotected to bear the brunt of the atrocities. It is similar to how, before the Second World War, many great rabbis in eastern Europe told their followers to stay and not emigrate, but then they themselves got out through their contacts and influence, leaving the poor to suffer disproportionately from the Nazis and their allies.

One gets a picture of the instability of life even under the most benevolent of monarchs. The constant agitation of the church (of every denomination: Catholic, Orthodox, and Reformed), the unpredictability of invading forces, shifting alliances, and constant danger from marauding bandits and mercenaries meant that life for most people at the time was indeed as Hobbes described it, "nasty, brutish, and short." For Jews it was doubly so.

Yet for all the ups and downs, one step forward and two back, the Pinsk Jewish population grew and thrived. The eighteenth century brought not only pogroms and dislocation but also the great popular movement of Chasidism, which henceforth would divide every Jewish community in eastern Europe. Pinsk was the epitome of the opposing Mitnagged tradition. Karlin became a great Chasidic center. As the nineteenth century brought change and challenges, the Mitnagged community tended toward intellectual advance and an appreciation of wider study. Chasidism set itself very much against alien culture.

The second volume starts with 1881 and goes to the twentieth century and the effective destruction of Jewish Pinsk. Life in Pinsk was divided beyond religion. The term Haskalah is often wrongly translated as "Enlightenment." Initially it meant no more in the east than introducing some secular education into the traditional curriculum, something that many leading rabbis favored. In central and western Europe, Haskalah did indeed lead to assimilation in many cases. In Pinsk it was initially seen as helping many find employment and strengthen the community. However, when the Jews of Poland were annexed by Russia and the anti-Jewish culture of the Czarist regime began to weigh down on the Jews of the Pale of Settlement, education imposed by the state was indeed associated with a policy of conscious repudiation of Jewish identity and values.

Under the czars, the struggle for Jewish survival became a daily test. Hundreds of thousands emigrated. Among those who stayed, resistance to the regime in various ways led to serious fissures within communities. Radicals, socialists, and bundists saw the future only in terms of liberation from class oppression and religious narrow-mindedness. Secular Zionists dreamed of salvation in establishing a new Jewish ethos based on labor in the Land of Israel. Different groups competed, fought, and provoked each other. This roiling competitive atmosphere produced great literature in Hebrew and Yiddish, a flourishing cultural life, schools, and youth movements.

The religious too were divided, not just between Chasidim and Mitnagdim but between Zionist and anti-Zionist. The very tensions we find today in Jewish life, particularly in Israel, could already be found in Pinsk toward the end of the nineteenth century.

These conflicts of wealth and ideology continued through the disastrous Polish regime after the First World War, where occasionally only American intervention stemmed rising anti-Semitism, made worse by the fact that Jews were prominent on both political sides and were blamed for everything, as always. It all deteriorates as the German Nazis and their eastern European sympathizers brought catastrophe to Jewish life. That anything survived at all was a miracle.

The myth currently cultivated in certain religious circles about the idyllic Jewish life of the ghettos of the east is dishonest, manipulative, and a betrayal of the memory of those who lived through it. Unless you were rich, it was insufferable and a painful life. Your wealth could disappear overnight. The relatively few students of yeshivas, even the great Lithuanian ones, often went barefoot, coatless, and hungry in winter. Even the numbers studying Torah full time were a fraction of those supported by Israel today, let alone the United States. There were indeed great rabbis and leaders, and Pinsk attracted and nurtured some of the greatest. But for the masses it was hell on earth.

There is something of this dichotomy in Israel today, but it is in no way comparable thanks to social welfare and the dignity of independence. Whether secular or religious, financial or political, regardless of all its troubles and tensions, Israel is a flourishing of Jewish life in the widest sense that puts even Pinsk in the shade. Whether the researchers had an agenda or not, the facts speak for themselves. The pretense that Jewish life was better then, is, as Solomon says in Ecclesiastes, "not a very clever thing to say."

It's a sad story of the disappearance of yet another once-great Jewish center. But Professors Mirsky and Rosman deserve gratitude for bringing this important work to the English-speaking world. We can rejoice in the fact that we have survived and thrived.

CANTONISTS

The story of the cantonists is not just one of Russian anti-Semitic cruelty but also one of the most reprehensible examples of how Jews behaved to other Jews. The rich, the powerful, the religious authorities all took unforgivable advantage of their positions to get themselves off the hook at the expense of the poor.

Russia included the majority of the Jews in the world in the nineteenth century. Czar Nicholas I, who came to the throne unexpectedly in 1825, was a crude anti-Semite who wanted to rid Russia of its Jews. He devised a system that would use military service as a way of cutting young Jews off from their families and communities and converting them to Russian Orthodoxy. In 1827 he introduced compulsory military service for all Jews from age twelve to twenty-five to serve for twenty-five years!

All conscripts under the age of seventeen would be assigned to cantons, military schools inside military camps originally set up a century earlier to train young recruits, before being sent to regiments. While there, they would be denied Jewish requirements and subjected to a harsh and intensive conversion regime. Life would be made easier for those who converted, and progressively tougher for those who refused. These poor Jewish children were called cantonists.

Almost a hundred thousand Jewish children suffered under the system before it was abolished in 1855, after Czar Nicholas died. But of that number, the vast majority died or disappeared under the most cruel and harsh of conditions. Conscription continued after that, but equally for all citizens. Many Jews served in the Russian army, including my grandfather. Even into the early twentieth century, many Jewish young men voluntarily deformed themselves or removed their teeth to avoid the agonies of conscription. But nothing could compare to the sadistic regime these thousands of little Jewish cantonist children were put through. Some did survive and returned to Jewish community life. Often they were discriminated against and excluded because they had had no Jewish education and had lost any outward or religious trace of their Jewishness. There were records of special synagogues exclusively for cantonist returnees.

But there is another dimension to this episode that is in some ways equally disturbing. Government set a quota of conscripts for each community, and it was up to the Jewish authorities to fulfill these quotas on pain of fines and imprisonment. Naturally, no Jewish parents wanted their sons to go through this ordeal, which was usually a death sentence. The Jewish officials were in a difficult position and open to inducements. The rich and the influential got their children off through bribery or persuasion. This meant that the poor and the weak suffered inordinately.

When community officials could not meet their quotas, they employed chappers (from the Yiddish "to grab," *chap*), Jews who were paid to bring in conscripts, rather like the eighteenth- and nineteenth-century press gangs used to force men into the Royal Navy. They would act like a cross between bounty hunters and gangsters. There are documented reports of mothers running behind the carts that carried their kidnapped children in cages, begging for their release, sometimes of an only son or the sole provider for a poor widow.

One of the worst aspects of this was that the rabbis, whom you might have thought the poor and the weak could have turned to for support, were themselves only too willing to protect their own at the expense of others. There are records of debates as to whether it was right to send a young man off to the army who was not religious instead of one who was, or the son of a poor Jewish peasant rather than the son of a rabbi. There is plenty of research on all this. An example is a small, easily accessible book by Larry Domnitch called *The Cantonists*.

This sort of discriminating attitude is still with us, although of course not under quite the same circumstances. Too many of us still think that if I can buy or fiddle or bargain myself a privilege at the expense of someone else, then why not? Who cares about moral arguments? When casualties of the Lebanon War came out, it became clear that most of them were from poorer, disadvantaged families, predominantly new immigrants. And of those who were Ashkenazi, a very high proportion were religious Zionist young men who had studied in yeshivas and were ideologically committed. But more and more of the Tel Aviv beau monde, the Shenkin elite, the privileged children of the wealthy, were skipping the draft. Let the poor put their lives in danger, not us!

As for the ultra-Orthodox, there are now thousands and thousands of able-bodied young men, not all particularly interested in study, who are given automatic exemption. When the Chazon Ish, the great rabbinic figure in Israel when the state was founded, persuaded Ben-Gurion to exempt yeshiva students from military service, there were a few hundred involved. Now it is approaching fifty thousand. This cannot be morally justified.

I agree that scholarly types, the academically exceptional, might claim and merit postponement or exemption. But sixty years ago ultra-Orthodoxy was hanging on by a thread. Now it is powerful, rampant, wealthy, and growing. If it insists that only the nonreligious, or those it disapproves of, go into battle, then there is something morally and ethically wrong. Even if I agree that prayer and spirituality matter as well as fighting men, nevertheless one still needs trained soldiers ready to fight.

The trouble is that everything in Israel is a political crap game of wheeler-dealing negotiation that starts from a tough, seemingly immovable bargaining position in order to squeeze as many concessions as possible. Everyone does this, regardless of party. This means ethics or morality doesn't get a look in. I no longer expect the Knesset to be moral, but I do look to religious leaders at least to make the effort.

JEWS OF IRAN

Esther's Children, edited by Houman Sarshar, is a collection of fascinating essays and photographs about Iranian Jewry. The title alludes to the fact that Queen Esther was told by Mordechai not to reveal her people; to keep her identity secret. The author suggests that most Iranians he knew were brought up to hide their true identity in public. The one abiding impression the book left on me is the extent to which Iranian Jewry has suffered, most noticeably since Shia Islam took power. Apart from a brief interlude under the shahs, the Jewish communities of Iran, in all their magnificent variety, were continuously humiliated and victimized.

Jews lived and thrived in the Persian Empire ever since the exile of 586 BCE. Some say even as early as King Solomon. But the story of Purim illustrates how precarious it was. The Babylonian Talmud itself attests to the richness of Jewish life in Babylonia, and the geonim who flourished into the second millennium expanded on it and beyond. There are references to Persian kings like Shapur, whose mother converted to Judaism. Yazdegerd I had a Jewish wife in the fifth century. But it was not all light and bright before Shia Islam either. The Zoroastrians were a changeable lot, particularly when their priests got the upper hand. They forbade anyone, including Jews, from lighting lights at home instead of in Zoroastrian temples.

Under Islam it started promisingly. The Umayyads were the most enlightened of rulers, the Abbasids too, within the constraints of Islam. The famous Harun al-Rashid had Jewish financiers, doctors, and advisors, but he instituted the yellow badge all Jews had to wear. Jews and Christians were categorized as dhimmis, second-class citizens, which from the time of the Pact of Omar imposed social and economic restrictions upon them that left them very much at the mercy of Muslims. If they were lucky, they were tolerated. If not, they were oppressed.

It was under the Safavids (1501–1731), who turned Iran into a Shiite state, that things got appreciably worse. A Muslim who killed or raped a Jew was not punished beyond a small fine. Jews had to step aside for Muslims in the street and could not eat or drink with, or even touch, Muslims. They were not allowed to ride horses or build their walls higher than Muslims. Jews were forced to live in ghettos (the Mahalleh), which were intentionally kept foul, fetid, and constricted. Muslims were forbidden to sell Jews houses elsewhere. Jews were declared unclean, untouchable. They could not leave their homes when it rained because the wet might transfer their impurity. The penalty for infringement was death. Pressure began to build on the Jews to convert, and violence was often used to achieve results. To be fair, the Armenians, Zoroastrians, and other non-Muslims suffered too, but Jews were singled out. If a Jew converted to Islam, then he would inherit all the family's wealth, leaving everyone else in poverty.

Things got even worse under the Qajars (1795–1925). By the nineteenth century, the Jews of Iran were overwhelmingly poor, uneducated, and at the bottom of the social heap. Forced conversions affected city after city, sometimes for short periods, others for much longer. In 1839, the whole of the Jewish community of Mashad was forced to convert. For many years, they, like the Marranos in Spain, had to live double lives. Only many years later could they return and then they acquired the reputation of being super religious to compensate..

During the nineteenth century, the attention of European Jews began to focus on the plight of the Iranian Jewry. French Jewry established the Alliance Israélite Universelle network of schools in Iran to give Jewish children an education. They campaigned to change discriminatory laws. But they also encouraged assimilation. Thanks to international pressure, things began to change slowly. The Iranian Constitutional Revolution of 1906 sped up the process. By 1911, Jews achieved civil rights (only fifty years after Britain, let us not forget). Jewish life began to flourish. Nevertheless, several memoirs have been written that describe the separations, discrimination, and suffering of Jews during those years.

Under the Pahlavis (1925–1979) things continued to be a mixture of good and bad. It was in fact only after the pro-German Shah Reza was forced out during the Second World War by the British and his son Mohammad Reza came to power and was supported by the United States that Iranian Jewry really did well; many grew rich, and they began to feel part of Persian society. The 1979 revolution brought Khomeini to power. All the social Shia limitations were re-imposed on Jews, including the rules of impurity, once again consigning them to inferior status. Several significant and wealthy Iranian Jews were put to death on notoriously specious grounds. And a mass (though not total) migration led to the establishment of important Iranian communities, particularly in the United States.

We have to admire those Jews who kept their faith under such awful conditions. Imagine if you lived in a country where a group of people who are despised, the inferior dregs of society, suddenly begin to rise and do better than you. If you are a simple Muslim peasant toiling under the sun, of course you will resent these nouveaux riches, as indeed did most Americans and British in their day.

The Jews, after all, were only apes and pigs according to the Koran. Then all of a sudden these apes and pigs are able to establish one of the most powerful, intellectually, technically, and economically advanced states in the area, Israel. They win more Nobel Prizes than you do. Not only that, but these apes and pigs can withstand the combined might of the Muslim states who try to drive them out. The humiliation must be intolerable. And if you yourself are of already limited spirit and intellect, it must be doubly humiliating. Apes and pigs doing better than you. No wonder primitive men like

Ahmadinejad and his fundamentalist allies hate the Jews for having turned the tables on them.

This explains current Iranian foulmouthed anger and invective against Israel and their passionate desire to eradicate those whom they perceive as having humiliated them. Now you tell me, when faced with irrational, deep-seated, visceral hatred, how should you respond? Sit down to a nice cup of tea?

THE GOLEM

On my first visit to Prague some fifteen years ago, I was stunned to see a statue of the great sixteenth-century Rabbi Loew, by the twentieth-century Czech sculptor Ladislav Jan Šaloun. It stands at the side of the New Town Hall. He is depicted as an evil, looming, glowering wizard, like the evil queen in *Snow White*, with "the hounds of hell" glaring from behind his cloak and the supine naked body of the church at his feet. There have been attempts to explain away the obvious, but it won't wash.

Nothing could be more ridiculous and evil than a portrayal of a gentle, saintly scholar as this offensive sculpture. It epitomizes to me the continuing evil of anti-Semitism that portrays the Jew as a dangerous magician out to destroy the world—and incidentally, how art can be misused. The old Jewish quarter in Prague was preserved by Nazi propaganda to portray us as primitive, medieval sorcerers. But the sad fact is that we ourselves handed them the means of regarding us this way.

Almost three hundred years after Rabbi Loew's death, Jewish "enlightened" writers created the myth of the golem. There was not a hint at such a fantasy for hundreds of years after his death, let alone in his lifetime. They had an agenda: to depict the Jewish religion as a dated, medieval culture, dependent on ancient myths, superstition, and magic, a distortion of the kabbalah, that they would now sweep away either through reform, assimilation, socialism, or, when that did not work, through secular Zionism.

The myth was that Rabbi Loew, using magical kabbalah, was able to create a Frankenstein out of the earth and, by putting God's name into his mouth, bring it to life. This golem was then sent out to protect the Jews and attack their non-Jewish enemies in Prague who regularly assaulted the ghetto and its inhabitants. The idea that one might be able to create life through some magical or mystical formula is indeed mentioned in Talmudic legend. There, two rabbis produce a calf through incantations and enjoy a meal. It does not require Rambam to remind us that we should not always take Aggadah literally. This legend has, of course, no legal significance, although if it did it might be a useful way of avoiding animal slaughter and current methods of meat rearing; "cloning" we would call it nowadays, and it's scientific!

By publicizing and even glamorizing golems, dybbuks, evil spirits of the night, and mad kabbalists who could curse and perform miracles, secular Yiddish writers (soon followed by non-Jewish ones) were able to make the association that played into the hands of our enemies and still does to this very day. Now it's true that parts of the Jewish people have always been superstitious and primitive. And it is true that in medieval times and well beyond, Judaism was influenced by prevailing external attitudes. But that does not mean that stories of golems were typical or the norm. It's like depicting American culture through the prism of an era in which Americans murdered the witches of Salem. But it also serves another purpose apart from its distortion of Jewish life.

We are a culture that perpetuates the myth of Superman, Batman, Ironman, Captain Marvel, and all those comic book heroes, now Hollywood blockbusters, that tell us that some extremely powerful spirit can come to our rescue and remove evil and restore order. This is every child's dream of overcoming adults, or every adult's dream of overcoming whatever or whoever it is that either stands in his way, threatens him, or simply lives better than he does. It is dangerous because it is an excuse for inaction and fantasy. It is a justification for refusing to come to terms with a challenge because some sort of miraculous intervention will solve all our problems. It is like expecting the Messiah to come and sort out our personal problems.

This has always been a very powerful strain in Judaism, as in all religions. They have all tried at some stage to suggest that they have all the answers to everything. They have told us that God intervenes to defeat evil and to support good. And when this has manifestly not happened on earth, they have told us that all will be put right in the next world. As against this, the very same religions have added a rider that we must take responsibility for our actions and live with the consequences.

This internal conflict has always played out throughout our history. Do we seek our freedom from the Egyptians or stay slaves? Do we accept Greek authority or fight it? Do we challenge Rome or capitulate? Do we actively try to create a state of our own or wait for the Messiah? Do we withdraw settlements or leave it to God? Do we seek a peace settlement with improbable partners or wait and hope for divine intervention? Do we insist on the ridiculous proposition that every Jew, regardless of his mental capacity, should sit and study Talmud for the whole of his life, or should some at least train for a job to care for their families? Or do we expect soldiers of Israel's defense forces to be our golems today and do our dirty work for us?

The incapacity of too many rabbis to tolerate some sort of practical compromise in relation to the State of Israel is one of the most myopic examples of paralysis that recalls the inability to take steps to prevent millions from escaping the Nazi catastrophe. The state subsidizes their academies, supports their families with welfare, and in return asks for some practical social if not military contribution to its safety. Yet when there is a reasonable request to compromise, the crude responses are the objectionable scenes of religiously garbed and bearded men who ought to know better, accusing other Jews of being Nazis, victimizing those Charedim who do join, calling them rats and traitors, expelling them from communities, abusing them in public, calling rabbis who support the draft sinners and evil men. All this does is proclaim in public for everyone around to the world to see and say, "You see, the Jews are as crazy as the mullahs."

Instead of finding ways of relating to the issue, instead of trying to offer vocational education alongside Torah education for those who will not be the scholars, they are cutting the ground from under their own feet, humiliating Torah, and relying on Superman to save them and their subsidies. They no doubt are, as I write, calling on kabbalists to issue curses and exorcisms and golems to do what common sense and good will could achieve. Perhaps we need a new golem to bash their heads together.

PART 3

RELIGION

GODLESS

What if you just do not believe in God? Does this mean there is no room for you in the Jewish religion? I don't mean the Jewish people of course, because we have always been a collection of different tribes and ideologies, saints and sinners. On the surface, yes, it does. God underpins the Torah. And the Torah is the essential core of Jewish religious life. But the question is what one means by "God." Ask any two people, and you will get different answers. I once tried this at my yeshiva, and it is so. I assure you. The Torah was wise enough not to go into too much detail on abstract ideas.

Maimonides famously thought that you can only describe God in terms of what God is not. The exception was the statement that "God is One." Now if "One" simply means "not many," there is no problem. On the other hand, it is not much clarification either if it is supposed to mean something positive. And if it is supposed to mean "a perfect unity," I am honestly not sure what that really means. What is the difference between a unity and a perfect unity? If for many people God is a feeling—of awe, of presence—then that is significant but very subjective. How do I know if we are feeling the same thing? How does one deal with someone who says he has never had such an experience? Perhaps it is a matter, as Daniel Dennett says, of "the idea of God" rather than God itself. This too leaves the field wide open.

If one thinks that God is an ancient man sitting up in the clouds casting thunderbolts at sinners and bestowing bounteous rewards on the good, or that like Superman, He intervenes whenever bad things look like happening, then I am not sure how many so-called "believers" share such a view. One is bound to wonder why so many innocent and harmless people escape His attention and suffer horrible deaths. Or what if your God had a physical presence or representation? Many medieval rabbis thought so, and many mystics think that way even now. Would that put you out of the official camp that says God has no form or body?

Most of us who do make God the core of our religious lives and the object of our spiritual yearning are constantly struggling. We move in and out of periods of profound conviction and then serious doubt. Each one of us creates his own framework of religious engagement in the light of a person's own mental and emotional characteristics. We are not unique in this. Our sacred literature is full of examples of great spiritual forebears who often felt lost, abandoned, and even alienated. They all needed reassurance. Yet they remain the role models of our spiritual heritage.

The Torah actually does not say, "You must believe in God." The first of the Ten Commandments simply says, "I am the Lord your God." It's an invitation to engage, rather than a theological command to attest to something one may not be able to articulate. For all the divine miracles in the Bible, the people kept on falling back to idolatrous ways and abandoned their God. So why isn't there room nowadays for an honest doubter?

Many Jews have no interest in religion. Their criteria for Jewishness might be literature or Jews who contributed to the wider world. Their heroes will be people like Freud, Marx, Saul Bellow, or the host of acclaimed writers of partly Jewish heritage, with a measure of talent and brains but no claims to Jewish spirituality. Their causes will be civil rights. Their festivals will be musical and cinematic. They might possess a feeling of being defined by anti-Semitism or feel a shared historical destiny. But the life they lead will be no different than that of the liberal academically inclined people they mix with. That, of course, is their right, and if they are also ethical, caring human beings, even better.

There are other positions I can feel a kinship to even if I go a stage further. There is the heightened sensitivity to the divine dimension, to feeling that there is more in this universe than our physical existence. Such sentiments have been articulated by Einstein, or more recently by the late legal philosopher Ronald Dworkin. But neither would accept an idea of God as the great intervener in human affairs. And of course there are different degrees of commitment within "religious" Judaism itself.

The religious person I identify with (insofar as I identify with anyone) is one whose life revolves around a specific religious calendar, who spends time every day in spiritual activity, who tries to relate in practice to Torah values. It is not a profession of faith as much as a commitment to behavior, and this behavior is not just rote but ethical. I take my lead from the Mishna. Rebbi Yeudah HaNasi says in Avot 2:1, "What is the right path for a man to choose? That which is honorable to him and brings him honor in the eyes of others." Or as Chaninah Ben Dosa says in chapter 3:9, "Whoever humans regard as a good person, God considers good too."

I do not consider a Jew to be religious if his behavior toward other human beings is unethical, regardless of his practices or his confessed beliefs. And conversely I do consider someone a good human being if he or she relates positively and kindly to other humans, regardless of religious practice. The two pillars of our religion are the relationship between God and humanity and between humans themselves. If one part of the equation is missing, there is an imbalance. But an imbalance is not grounds for dismissal. It is rather an invitation to engage more deeply.

The presence or absence of religious ritual is a mark of how seriously a person takes his religious life. The value of ritual, of Jewish behavior, is that it helps stimulate and repeat certain types of spiritual encounters and experiences. If someone believes in the importance of being healthy or fit but never acts on it, the belief becomes vague sentimentality. That is why I am in favor of living a religious life, even if one does not believe in God. The rabbis say, "From doing something for the wrong reason one can come to do it for the right one." They didn't set a time limit. Perhaps that person might never be able to jump to the higher level. But they did not reject the honest doubters. Of course I consider a relationship with God as crucial to a full and rounded Jewish identity. But it is not the only model.

We have always been a "broad church." Where Talmudic Judaism drew the line was at the person who ideologically, defiantly denied the possibility of God. That was what defined the person who cut himself off from his religious roots, the certainty of "not" as opposed to the uncertainty of possibility. Like the so-called wicked son we read about at the Seder, though even he kept the Seder ritual. When one encounters men like Noah Chomsky or Woody Allen, one sees where the process of religionless Judaism is leading. And I can respect them as humans even if I do not respect them as Jews. Once, apostasy involved conversion to another religion. Now it is the gentle but certain disappearance from the ranks and from the causes that preserve us.

So here I am, unhappy about religious hypocrisy, worried about those of our family who are leaving us. Why shouldn't I try to include anyone who manifestly lives a Jewish life regardless of intellectual reservation? If an agnostic Jew wants to keep Shabbat, I say, "Good for you, and come and join my *minyan*!"

PRAYER

The way most of us pray today is very different from the way it was originally intended. What goes on in most Jewish "houses of prayer" of whatever community, denomination, sect, or form is more of a social experience, a happening rather than an inspiring spiritual experience.

According to Maimonides (Laws of Prayer 1:11), it remains a Torah obligation to relate to the Almighty every day and in one's own way, one's own language, regardless of what may or may not happen in a synagogue. The Hebrew "to pray" is *lehitpallel*, which literally means "to express oneself." How many people do really express their feelings, their hopes, and fears at prayer services? We tend to think that prayer only refers to repeating traditional texts or being present in a place of prayer. However, there were no places of prayer as such for the first thousand years or so of Jewish existence. People came to watch ceremonies, in the tabernacles and then the temples. The formal community prayers we have today were initially only intended to be a menu of suggested ideas for those who could not find the words to express themselves.

There is a dichotomy between personal, private prayer and public communal prayer. Their functions are entirely different. The Torah ideal remains that individuals should find spontaneous, subjective, and personal ways of connecting with how they understand the divine presence. This is what is called *deveykut*, actually engaging with God. It can rarely be done in a crowded synagogue surrounded by others who often have no interest in such activity and are present for other, perhaps lesser reasons. One cannot pray or meditate while a cantor performs, and most of all it cannot be done "on command."

Sometimes for a moment, such as Kol Nidre, a powerful effect can be achieved. But it rarely survives long. Only in very few situations, such as those yeshivas with a strong tradition of prayer, does one experience extended concentration and excitement during a service. For the average Jew living in no such rarified situation, synagogues in general simply do not offer an experience of the divine. The Great Synagogue in Alexandria where flags were waved to let distant parts of the building know when to say "amen" (TB Sukah 21b) cannot possibly have been a place of personal engagement with heaven.

The services we have nowadays are primarily to give us a sense of community and to actually get people together in ways that most religious obligations do not. Judaism makes demands on us both as individuals and as members of the community of Israel. Personal prayer remained personal. After the destruction of the Second Temple, specific petitions were incorporated into the public services that replaced the Temple ceremonial. There is no evidence that the intention was to replace private prayer whenever one felt inclined or wherever one was.

Later, herded into claustrophobic, foul ghettos under Christianity and Islam, most Jews wanted to escape the overcrowded hovels they often shared with animals. The synagogue was the only large and airy building in the community where one could go to chat and study as well as pray. People needed to come and leave together for safety. That was where they wanted to be and spend as much time as possible. No wonder the services got longer and longer.

The prevailing culture was also one in which any educated persons expressed themselves in poetry. Hence the great payetanim who composed complicated religious poetry (that made the English metaphysical poets look banal) spread under Islam from Israel to Spain to northern Europe and churned out poetry so complicated in formal structures and conventions. Yet they were included, not without objections, into services. Most of them no longer resonate with us.

The great mystic R. Yitzhak Luria was responsible for introducing songs into formal prayer, for walking out into the fields, praying on the hills of Safed. The attempt to experience God moved from man-made structures to nature and back. The existential aspect of prayer, its singing and ecstasy as much as its communal aspect, influenced the great Chasidic reformation. But then like all revolutions, over time it lost its iconoclasm and creativity and sank back into formality. Still to this day in many Chasidic courts, you will hear singing and ecstatic prayer that would be unimaginable in most synagogues in the West.

Over the years I have gone through all sorts of different prayer experiences, and I still find the traditional service meets my "communal" socializing needs. But I rarely really pray there. It is private prayer that satisfies me spiritually, and I can often achieve this best away from the community. Even some great Chasidic rebbes preferred to pray communal prayers alone. Yet I have always encountered other Jews who disagreed with me. Some preferred the big performance, the big event, the sense of being together, to the modest utilitarian alternatives I tried to recommend. It is right that it should be so. We are not all alike. We have different intellects and tastes and needs. There should be alternatives.

We are living in exciting times. More and more people are willing to experiment. Whereas once this inevitably meant casting off the requirements of tradition, now the trend is to find resolutions without throwing the baby out with the bathwater. One of the joys of many Jewish communities where there is a critical mass is that one can on a Shabbat shul-crawl and experience a wide range of alternatives and find one that accords with one's temperament and background.

As for those who are dissatisfied, I believe that more energy should go into trying to find completely new styles of worship than in tinkering with the old. There must, for example, be creative ways in which female spirituality could create totally new atmospheres and experiences without being constricted by established male modes and norms. I approve of choice and, where it is possible, to explore the alternatives in one's neighborhood.

Regardless of the style of service, or the regularity of one's attendance, one really ought to reestablish the practice of personal prayer privately. Meditation and contemplation in a totally secular style, or one borrowed from another religion, have brought relief and inspiration to many in the West. But we have our specifically Jewish exercises and meditations. One need look no further than Avraham Abulafia (or in modern times Aryeh Kaplan) to realize they have been part, albeit a neglected part, of our mystical tradition. We must revive them.

Romantics rely on the externally inspired experience, the stimulation of beautiful buildings, music, canonicals, and ceremonial to induce a sense of devotion, worship, and spirituality. The classicist works on himself to make it happen. I prefer the latter than to expect others to do my religious experiences for me.

AS IF

It is a fundamental principle of Judaism, and the one that differentiates it from other religions, that the Torah was given to Moses on Sinai some 3,300 years ago. But what actually happened on Sinai is not at all clear. The Torah itself gives different descriptions in Exodus 19 and 24. And the rabbis in the Talmud and Midrash give various opinions too. Nevertheless, Torah as we have it is the foundation of Judaism.

One of the most significant divides on religious matters within our community is between the literalists and the symbolists, between those who feel bound to take holy narratives literally, at face value, as opposed to those who put much greater emphasis on the idea, the significance, and the symbolism beneath the surface reading. The latter do not necessarily deny the historical background or that miraculous or amazing events took place, but see the text as a spiritual and behavioral guide to be understood on different levels, rather than a precise, scientific textbook.

The Talmud and Midrash disagree as to exactly how and what was transmitted on Sinai and when it was written down. But there is now a general assumption not only that the Torah comes directly from God in dictation form but that all the written and the oral law were included in that revelation and the text—including punctuation, variations in size of letters, and assorted dots—was delivered in its entirety on the mountaintop. To many Jews, even some Orthodox ones, this seems a trifle fanciful, especially if one thinks that God told Moses on Sinai about future postbiblical festivals like

Purim, Chanukah, two sets of crockery, the rabbinic innovation of the eruv, or indeed how to use a time switch for Shabbat, let alone the custom of wearing two sets of tefillin.

The question, then, is whether one can remain within tradition and still find room and significance for those ideas that rationally one struggles with? What I have to say will not even be considered by the fundamentalist school of Jewish theology. But I am writing for those who do, indeed, try to reconcile rationalism with faith.

There is a solution that preserves both possibilities in the idea first put forward by a German thinker, Hans Vaihinger (1852–1933). Dealing with "reality" and whether what we see and experience is "true," he argued that human beings cannot really know the reality of the world. For example, the way a table looks to the human eye is very different from the way it looks through a powerful magnifying glass. Which is "real"? Despite the uncertainty, in dealing with the world practically, we behave "as if" the reality of the world matches what we see. We treat the table as if it were solid even though we "know" it is made up of moving particles.

George Kelly (1905–1967), an American psychologist, in dealing with patients whose sense of reality differed from most other people, also encouraged people to try different ways of looking at events to see what might happen when they acted "as if" alternative ways might work. In this way they might learn to change their ways of behaving to relate to others. What matters, then, is not if something really IS the way we see it, but how we respond to it and act. A wall may not be "solid" when seen through a microscope, but I do not try walking through it.

I am not convinced we are expected to adopt unquestioningly and superficially those ideas we have sincere intellectual doubts about. I believe the rabbis of Talmud accept this when they say that what they cannot accept is the person who denies or rejects as opposed to those who are still in the process of clarifying how to understand certain ideas. Only a *kofer*, a denier, is excoriated. Not the honest questioner. As for how the rabbis want us to understand what they meant when they said something, the great medieval commentator Rashi himself said that the great rabbis of the Talmud often used language in an exaggerated way to attract the attention of the simple folk (Shabbat 30b "Mutav Techabeh"). They used expressions hyperbolically or even dramatically to make a point or to arrest attention.

One of the most common hyperbolic forms of language used in Midrashic and Talmudic Judaism is the Hebrew word *keilu* which does actually translate to "as if."

We are familiar with the phrase in the Hagadah "In every generation one is obliged to see oneself *as if* one has actually come out of Egypt" (Pesachim 116b). Obviously this means "imagine" and is clearly not literal. But here are some other examples from the hundreds to be found in the Talmud:

> He who eats and drinks on Tisha B'Av [a rabbinic fast] it is *as if* he eats and drinks on [the stricter biblical] Yom Kippur. (Taanit 30b)
>
> Whoever tells Lashon Hara [gossip] it is *as if* he denies the existence God. (Arachin 15b)
>
> Whoever studies Torah one day in the year it is *as if* he has studied all year round. (Chagigah 5b)

The use of "keilu" is important as a homiletical tool. But that does not mean it indicates a Halachic fact or obligation. It is an essential idea. What matters is what one does. One can behave in a way that indicates devotion to God and the Torah or in a way that in practice ignores or denies God and Torah. What the rabbis wanted was for us to treat Jewish law *as if* we personally have heard it from God. *As if* God were speaking to us now. That is why we adhere to Jewish traditions.

The theological ideas of our tradition, as opposed to the behavioral ones, are there to help us avoid thinking of the world we inhabit only as material, but to try to imagine a spiritual world and spiritual values as well. If one wishes to be part of the mainstream of tradition, one needs to treat all the theological imperatives of Judaism with respect and a serious desire to understand what they mean. But ultimately we must try to hear God, a different dimension, speaking to us through them and to understand what the real message is, not just the superficial meaning of the words. Remember the rabbis often chose a way of speaking that had to allow for the simple mind as well as the intellectual giant to take away a message.

To adapt the idea to current politics, one may disagree with the vast majority of Jews either because one is not as right wing or as left wing as one's neighbor. But what matters is how much one is doing to perpetuate the Jewish tradition and keep it alive.

AUTONOMY

Does being a religious person mean you sacrifice your personal autonomy and freedom altogether? There are two seemingly contradictory fundamentals in Judaism (and probably in all ideologies to different degrees). On the one hand, there is the personal obligation to discover, declare, and commit to a personal moral and spiritual imperative. On the other is the obligation to help and be part of a community of people.

Will spiritual values mean more to me than material ones, and will I express this through a relationship with however I choose to understand the idea of God? And am I going to commit myself to a specific community, congregation, or people?

These are the two covenants that the Torah describes as being presented on Mount Sinai: the acceptance of God as the most significant arbiter of one's behavior and the commitment to the Jewish people and the perpetuation of its existence and "constitution."

On the face of it, these two covenants are contradictory. The existential fundamental that has become the most important influence on Western values is the idea that I must take responsibility for my own actions. Life is my choice and I am the most important fact of my life, and this must take priority over everything else. In some expressions of this idea, this extends to the right to commit suicide. The term "autonomy" is often used to describe this principle. It contrasts with the idea of obedience, either to law or to the needs of others or to the dictates of the wise and the learned.

The communal obligation, however, supersedes this principle. It demands our loyalty and sense of obligation to more than just ourselves. Whether it is family, community, or people, there are transcendent obligations that go beyond one's ego. In Freudian terms it is the superego. It is that process of education that enables us to interact with other human beings and to try to accept their alternative narratives and respect their needs.

In Judaism the obligation to accept the experience of God, the interaction with God, is the fundamental. The concept of a superauthority is the basis of and the authority for all Jewish law, even if its development continues when it is handed over to its interpreters. On the other hand, Israel represents the community that we are obliged to defer to and to be loyal to. And this is the most difficult thing to achieve given the variety and often the unlikeability of so many in most communities. And both these ideas are incorporated in our essential declaration *"Shema Yisrael HaShem Eloheynu HaShem Echad"* (Israel, realize that God is our God and God is One).

The two parts of this phrase contrast each other: Israel the community as opposed to the personal hearing or realization or consciousness. And it is right that they should. We live with a built-in conflict between what we want and what we need. What is good for me and what is good for the community. It's not just in the area of religion that this is so. On a personal level, one has to find time for one's parents, one's partner, one's children, one's friends, one's community, and one's job. They all require a delicate balancing act, sometimes excluding the others and sometimes including them. It is so for every moment of our lives. There is no single or perfect answer or formula as to how one balances these conflicting demands on our time and loyalties. Our life is a constant balancing act that we often get as wrong as we get right. And too often it is the person or the situation that makes the biggest noise that gets our attention. We are constantly struggling for balance.

Judaism requires us to engage, not to retreat from the field of combat into an insulated bubble. So we are often commanded to do contradictory things, to work and to rest, to eat and sometimes to fast. As the book of Ecclesiastes says, "There is a time for everything...a time to give birth and a time to die...a time mourn and a time to dance...a time to love and a time to hate...a time for war and a time for peace."

The famous Talmudic debate revolves around the hypothetical situation of two men lost in a desert with only one bottle of water between them. It they share it, both die. Rabbi Akivah concludes that the person in possession of the bottle keeps it because who can say that my blood is redder than yours? Why should I give up my life for yours? But equally the converse is true. If you want to kill me, I should defend myself even at your expense because what right do you have to tell me your life us worth more than mine? These are the broad principles that guide Jewish law, and yet often people have decided to sacrifice their lives for their children's. "We must live by our commandments, not die because of them" (Leviticus 18:5).

This is why all other divine commandments are expendable to save a person's life except three: one may not cause another death, commit adultery, or deny God, even to save one's life. Yet throughout history, just as many Jews have gone to their deaths for refusing to abjure their religion and their God, many others have chosen a way out. And even if this goes against the law, consistently rabbinic authorities have always tolerated the effects of coercion and turned a blind eye when people either converted to save their lives or said something they should not have.

The life of every human is precious, and the obligation of that person to find his or her way to God is indeed a very personal one that cannot be defined or generalized. Each one of us finds his or her own way of dealing with this idea, and rarely do two thinking human beings agree. It is much easier to define and to act on something behavioral than something abstract. Human intellects vary a great deal. But human behavior is essentially the same across the world. No matter where you live or under whichever culture, human eat, sleep, work, reproduce. So a religious system that focuses more on behavior than abstraction will be able to adapt more easily than one based on theology. This is why Judaism has adapted so well to different cultures. Actions are clearer than ideas. It is also one of the reasons why we feel no need to proselytize or to persuade the world that we are right. If correct behavior is what really matters, why care about the different ways of encouraging it? And yet there seems to be a universal tendency to want to do this.

Because I have my doubts and my questions and sometimes my struggles, it is useful to have before me a sort of memo. Such a memo serves to remind me that I must constantly refer to the divine personal experience and equally to the needs of community and others. Sometimes I conform and sometimes I do not. I am me. These decisions I take sometimes to veer in one direction, sometimes in another, define me and make me who I am. And as I have quoted the Talmud, I may also quote Shakespeare's Polonius: "This above all—to thine own self be true." Avoid a one-track mind.

BLESSINGS

Everyone seems to have a story to tell about how blessings from holy men or women miraculously changed the course of people's lives. They rarely tell of the cases where they did not. But what is a blessing? If it were simply a prayer on behalf of someone, it ought to be included in the same term. It wouldn't be called something different. In English the word we use for a blessing is both good and bad, a curse as well as a benediction. So how in Judaism does one differentiate a blessing from a prayer?

Despite, or because of, the advance of science, we have become more insecure. Human beings in all societies expend enormous amounts on blessings, charms, and wonder workers. In Judaism it is common now to go to rabbis for blessings to cure cancer, solve marital problems, and guarantee good investments. This is a reflection of our need for miracle cures for everything from wrinkles to fat, old age, and even stupidity. I believe in spiritual power beyond rational humanity. But this factory-line production of miracles strikes me as medieval. So, how do I reconcile this with our traditional emphasis on *brachas*, blessings?

The word "*bracha*" itself has many different possible derivations. One comes from the roots that can mean "knee," as in bending in worship; this would apply to blessing God. Or it can be associated with the word "soft"; at a circumcision the child is called a *rach*. This second theme implies tenderness, caring. A blessing, therefore, is a way of showing that one cares, about God and one's family. This is the blessing God gives to the world, and that we give to God and, indeed, to our children. Some even say it is connected to the word for a pool of water, *breycha*, that gives us life and sustenance. The common denominator is a source of goodness and care.

But there are two kinds of blessings. There are the formulaic expressions we humans use to bless God before performing religious actions, and then there are the blessings that we give and receive to each other, like "Bless You." In the Creation, God blesses creatures that they should be fruitful and multiply. There was nothing yet to be healed, no promise of wealth or fortune. It simply was the expression of the hope, support, or encouragement that someone or thing should go on to fulfill its potential or that events would play out positively.

When Rebecca is blessed by her family before she leaves to meet Isaac, it is the hope that she and her descendants will succeed. When Isaac blesses both his sons, he is expressing his hope that God will treat them in accordance with their own deeds and qualities. When Jacob blesses Ephraim and Menasha, it is for being who they were. From this comes the idea that every parent should bless his or her child every Friday night. This blessing is an expression of love for someone one knows. It is not a magical spell.

What is the nature, then, of a personal blessing from someone who knows no more than a name on a piece of paper? To think that a clairvoyant or rabbi can know everyone and care about each individual, lovely as it may sound, is rather facile. And if the person had such powers, then surely he wouldn't need a piece of paper, and if his power works, how come it's so selective? The Talmud says one should not treat lightly even the most modest of blessings, regardless of the source. Except we are not talking about humble blessings but talismans, magic, and miracles that usually cost!

If it were simply that a great man expresses to God the hope that someone's prayers will be answered, I could understand that as giving encouragement to the troubled. But there is an assumption of efficacy that strikes me both as superstitious and offensive, and when it is coupled with the demand for money, it is frankly evil, like the two sons of Eli in the Bible.

A quite different idea is that a good or saintly person can somehow call down divine energy because of his great level of spirituality. This was a power that Avraham had, and prophets such as Elijah and Elisha. But these were exceptions, not common as is the case today. The Torah itself has already warned us to beware of miracles and that false prophets would often be able to perform miracles in dishonest ways. As Maimonides says, miracles are the lowest level of faith.

It is one thing for a spiritual leader to radiate love, concern, and support. It is another to set up machinery for raising cash through blessings. Nowadays we are inundated with miracle workers wearing all sorts of different clothes, and each one seems to have a gimmick—read your *mezuzah*, your *ketuba*, your *tefillin*, your skull, your palm, your eyes.

It is a principle of our religion that the Almighty deals with humans according to their deeds. Of course, this is impossible for us to see or measure, for divine criteria are not ours, and there are indeed forces beyond our control, call them fate, luck, or divine intervention. But if one behaves according to the Torah, then one is doing what is expected, and this is what defines success in our religion regardless of whether one is rewarded or not.

Superstition implies something different: that, no matter how you behave, the special person with unique powers can do something for you. This has been the secret behind the ability of many men of God to retain the deep loyalty and affection of even totally nonpracticing sinners!

The Talmud has always been tolerant of superstition. According to Maimonides, this was only because so many people actually believed in it. The role of a *tzaddik*, a saintly person, is to help us humans rise, not to take away our sins or help us win the lottery. A great Lithuanian rabbi was once asked for a *bracha*. "Why?" he replied. "Are you a vegetable?" That has a double meaning, of course. But the fact is that he was no less a Jew for his opinion.

Reassurance is terribly important at every stage in life. But I am offended when Judaism is seen as a placebo, when it is thought that money achieves miracles. My fear is that this aspect of Judaism should come to be seen as an essential ingredient, because then what would there be to differentiate us from the pseudo-kabbalists who also promise heaven for cash?

According to the BBC, in Andra Pradesh in India, a holy man called Yanadi who claimed his leg could cure and perform miracles was abducted and his leg cut off by thieves so that they could possess the source of the magic! That's what happens when people prey on the credulous.

A blessing is an expression of love, concern, or hope. As such it can be reassuring and encouraging. But in the end it is all up to us to do our best and to then accept what the Almighty has in store for us.

TEFILLIN

Every weekday morning after I get up, wash and dress, and, unless it is a fast day, drink a glass of water, I put on my *tefillin*. They are the objects that, for reasons I cannot understand, are called "phylacteries." That word still sounds like a form of contraception to me because when, as a fourteen-year-old, I saw an advert for prophylactics, I was told by an almost equally ignorant teenage friend that it had something to do with birth control. Apparently it is from the Greek for "outpost" or "guard," which implies they are some sort of magical protection.

Come rain or shine, hell and high water, healthy or sick, in a good mood or bad, I put on my *tefillin*, even if I am nowhere near a *minyan* or a synagogue. It is one of the most important rituals of my life. It enables me to start each day in a mood of reflection and spirituality and identification with my Jewish heritage.

As I put them on, I look at the "houses," the "little leather boxes" that contain scrolls of parchment of crucial biblical texts that I dedicate my head and my heart to. I fondle them and turn them over. I notice the details of the leather craftsmanship, the precise, accurate, clean lines of the squares, the relief of the letter *shin* with four branches on one side but the usual three branches on the other, the complicated knots on the pristine leather straps, and the exact number of threads of sewing gut that just peep out from the recessed channels they are threaded through, and I am both amazed and perplexed at the creativity and persistence of traditions.

I often wonder, can it possibly be that Moses and his followers wore things like these thousands of years ago? Of course it is not impossible. Egyptians had been building very complex, technically sophisticated structures for a long time beforehand, and their jewelry and other crafts were impressive even by modern standards. But such things were luxuries confined to the minute stratum of wealthy aristocrats, not for the masses.

The Torah is vague. "And you shall bind them [these words which I command you today] as a sign on your hands and they shall be decorations between your eyes" (Deuteronomy 6), sounds to me as though it was meant symbolically, that the constitution of the Torah should be there with us all the time to guide and affect every action. In the same way "write them on your doorposts" sounds paradoxical in an era of tents. It sounds more like an injunction to dedicate a habitation to divine values. But still, the fact is we have an oral law, a tradition that helps explain what was meant by the written law or how the oral law came to understand the idea. So for example when the Torah says, "Take the fruit of a fine tree" on Sukkot, it is clarified by oral tradition as the *etrog* (rather than a kiwi or a kumquat), which we still use to this day. It does not strike me as necessarily unlikely at all that that was exactly what was meant by people at the time even if we have to take it on trust.

There is an old argument between the medieval scholars Rashi and Rebbeinu Tam over the actual order of the texts in the *tefillin*. Remember this debate comes some two thousand years after many males among the children of Israel had, one assumes, been putting them on daily. So they should have known! Now, hundreds and hundreds of years later, because of this difference of opinion, a few kabbalists started wearing two pairs (some doing so consecutively, and others simultaneously), and that caught on among the Chassidim, who now wear two pairs of *tefillin* every day, one with Rashi's order and one with Rabbeinu Tam's. I do not, because my father did not, and what was good enough for him is good enough for me. Similarly, there is a debate as to which blessing should be said. So to compromise we say two. Didn't they know then which one to say?

It also seems likely that an ancient argument is responsible for the fact that on the head the four texts are in four separate but conjoined sections, while on the arm they are all together in one. As indeed is the unique use of a letter *shin* I mentioned above, with four branches instead of three. Not only that, but the great archaeologist Yigael Yadin discovered ancient *tefillin* that were round. So, on the one hand, it is clear that *tefillin* of some sort have been around for thousands of years. And that's precisely why I would not be surprised if the ones we have today had not gone through changes since Moses's day.

But then does it matter if the little black disks (or the multicolored knitted ones) all Orthodox and not-so-Orthodox people wear on their heads might be a more recent development? Similarly, putting something on or covering our heads all the time or just for ritual occasions is such an integral part of Jewish law and custom and certainly has been documented as such for two thousand years. Does it matter if head covering itself originated as desert protection or a reaction against Roman and then Christian custom? I know nowadays we are expected to believe that Moses wore a fur *shtreimel* and full Polish seventeenth-century baronial gear. Indeed I have seen Charedi illustrations where Talmudic rabbis were wearing *shtreimels*. But that surely is fanciful and a tool of socialization rather than historical accuracy.

I am not a slave to conformity by any means, but I do love our traditions and customs and see the value of investing most of them with authority. *Tefillin* mean so much to me and play such an important role in my life that frankly, even if someone could prove they were invented a hundred years ago in a Romanian beer cellar, I'd still put them on every morning never fail and still feel a little bit closer to heaven.

Why? Because once I tried praying only whenever I felt the mood, and at one moment in my past tried only performing a ritual act when I felt I wanted to. But too often I just missed the opportunity, got distracted, or simply gave in to laziness. Having to do something and do something physical that requires focus is incredibly therapeutic. It is helpful in ensuring that I really do devote some time to meditation and escaping from the seductions of materialism every day. It's a wonderful habit to have, and it's a connection to another world that helps me enjoy this world more. Regardless of how many changes have taken place.

HUMAN NATURE

We seem to be caught at present in a terrible battle against evil extremism. But the sad fact is that human beings have always been and continue to be prone to violence, of ideas and actions. For all that Stephen Pinker might argue in *The Better Angels of Our Nature* that on balance the world is a safer place now for more people than it was in the past, still the amount of evil and suffering we humans inflict on each other is simply inexplicable and often overwhelming.

Catholics believe in "original sin." Humans are born bad, physical beings with no redeeming divine soul. This is why humans do bad things. Only through accepting the dogmas of Christianity can they "save" themselves. In their natural state, the very nature of human beings is one that Hobbes described as "nasty and brutish."

The Torah, on the other hand, sees humans as neutral, with a tendency to do good and a tendency to do bad. This tendency, "*yetzer*," comes into people during their youth: "There is a negative tendency in the heart of man from his youth" (Genesis 8:21).

It is true that one can find references in the Talmud to "original sin," that the mistakes of Adam and Eve had ongoing repercussions. But it is not the accepted or indeed the general response. The problem of why we do such bad or crazy things as humans was tackled in the Talmud in many different ways.

For example, "When Adam was created he reached from the Earth to Heaven. But when he sinned God placed his hand upon him and shrank him"

(TB Hagigah 12a). You could not ask for a more simple and unequivocal expression of humanism. Humans have the potential to span the world, to make it a wonderful place. But because we also have the capacity to make the wrong choices, we end up diminishing ourselves.

If this is true of humanity, it is equally true of the children of Israel. "Why are Israel compared to the stars of the Heaven and the dust of the earth? Because when they rise they can rise to the heavens but when they sink they sink to the dust" (TB Megilah 16a).

From the very start of the tradition, the story of Adam and Eve in the primordial Garden of Eden, human beings always tend to blame someone else. Adam blamed Eve, and Eve blamed the snake! Blaming others is usually a smokescreen for human failure. But the biblical narrative does not accept excuses. It is almost as if the Bible is telling us that if this is the human condition, we have to live with it, to try to ameliorate it but not to expect that it will be different. Not in this world anyway. This is probably why "life after death" seems to offer the only solution in rabbinic literature. Pushing off resolution to another state avoids the issue.

The alternative is to try to come to terms with the present. Consider the debate between Beit Hillel and Beit Shamai (Eruvin 13b) over whether it would have been better for a person not to have been born. They argued for two and a half years before agreeing with the proposition but added the conclusion that we have no alternative other than to evaluate our own actions and try our best to get on with living in the here and now.

Aggressive human beings use whatever means are at hand physically, whether it is a fist or a bomb, to impose their selfish wills on others. They start with personal antipathy, move on to tribal rivalry, and end up with national conflict. We see some of this progression in the Bible from Cain killing his brother to a series of bloody wars against opposing armies. In our world we start with arguing, spitting, throwing stones, beating up, and go on to throwing acid, raping and then using guns.

Ideologies make matters worse. No matter whether they are political, religious, social, or even sporting, the idea that I or my ideology is better than you or yours has led to the greatest catastrophes and orgies of destruction that humanity has caused. Millions of humans are currently seeking an escape from the hell of religious fanaticism, in the Middle East, in Africa, and beyond, even in Europe. Many die in the process. And it shows no sign of letting up. Historians debate the causes of world wars, and in the end one concludes like Plekhanov that "the inevitable always happens through the accidental." Politicians are constrained by personal and political considerations, by constituencies, votes, trade-offs. They rarely take difficult, vote-losing, long-term solutions. They are invariably reactive rather than proactive.

The Talmud consistently blames the Jews themselves for the disasters that overtook them. They betrayed their spiritual traditions, they betrayed their social obligations, they made all the wrong political decisions, and the few good people were simply outnumbered by the selfish and the corrupt. And it sounds exactly the same today. Fanaticism exists with our people just as much as tolerance and sensibility. We like to think we are better, that we set an example. In some ways we might. But the sounds of internal conflict and brutalism toward the other—be it a female, a different religious position, a different people—are so painful one can understand why so many prophets fled to avoid having to deal with the impossible.

Let us consider our own central conflict in the Middle East. Can we not solve it because we are all evil? Most of us desperately want to see an end to conflict, needless deaths, occupation. I cannot see the light. We are like two punch-drunk fighters slugging it out until one drops or the referee separates them. And then after a few years of recovery, we are at it again. None of the so-called solutions I have seen on either the right or the left work in practice. And it is not good enough to say that the Almighty will get us out of this mess. It did not always happen in the past. So what can we do, we ordinary human beings who care about humanity and about our ways of life?

We ordinary people can pray, and that helps soothe. But practically? The politicians will decide, and behind them the fanatics will maneuver. We can only get on with doing our best wherever we are, to increase the amount of goodness around us and to try to shine a little light in a dark world. And so it is with evil. It is there, as God says to Cain, "like a dog always crouching by the door." That is life. We can blame whomsoever we like. Some give up hope and claim it is all a matter of "predestination." But we argue that we still have to live with it, and it's up to us to try to find a solution. So to blame our nature is simply to refuse to deal with reality. To refuse to act is to relinquish responsibility.

CREATIONISM

How was the universe created? Scientists will present their theories based on technical observations that support their different points of view. Creationists, on the other hand, base their ideas of creation on holy texts. Yet these texts themselves may be understood in different ways. Others rely entirely on a sense that there must have been a creator. The world could not have happened accidentally or randomly. However, they can offer no objective observations to support their ideas. They are based on faith.

Without judging either side, it is clear that scientific theories form part of the world of universal scientific education. Faith, on the other hand, is a matter of religious education. To teach either one in the other's curriculum is like teaching the Spanish language in a mathematics class. I am not impressed by attempts to trash science based on the fact that its theories change or that they modify earlier theories. Of course scientific endeavor involves guesses that are either validated in whole or part or are not (and sometimes scientists fake results). But they usually involve a documented theory that can be examined and tested. Religious theories may tell us something about design, but in fact tell us nothing about who the designer is. Both have something to teach us, but they should not be confused or considered equivalent. Stephen Jay Gould once called them "nonoverlapping magisteria." They might actually overlap, but they are certainly very different magisteria.

During the late 1950s, my parents became close friends of Sir Monty (and Lady Miriam) Finniston, then the director of the government Atomic Research

Center at Harwell, not too far from where we lived on the banks of the Thames at Wallingford. Monty was one of the top scientists in Britain at the time and ended up as the head of British Steel. The friendship between a major scientist and a rabbi involved theological discussions. The question of the age of the universe was one of them. My father took the view, as I do today, that science is one kind of process and religion is another and the two are neither mutually exclusive nor necessarily contradictory but ideally complementary.

Inevitably the issue arose of why it was thought necessary still to believe that the world was some fifty-seven thousand years old when all the scientific information led to the conclusion that it was millions of years older. My father's position was that it was not necessary to believe anything about the world physically other than that the Almighty created it and was essential to its continuity. But the process of creation and indeed the time scale were open to interpretation and opinions based as much on close reading of biblical and Talmudic texts as on science.

As a result of their discussions, my father wrote a letter to the Lubavitcher Rebbe asking his opinion. My father was convinced that the rebbe, whom he admired greatly and who had briefly studied engineering at the Sorbonne, would come down forcefully on his side in favor of a scientific approach to dating the universe as older than the traditional fifty-seven hundred years, while certainly believing it was created by a divine power.

I well recall his dismay when the rebbe's reply came back attacking the arrogance and certainty of science and arguing that all the scientific evidence was flawed and if tradition had sanctified a date, then we were bound to go with it. My father reluctantly defended the rebbe's response by arguing that a religious leader coming from the ultra-Orthodox camp probably needed to both reinforce his core constituency in its battle with the secular world and ensure his own position within it. Besides, public statements were very different from private ones, and this letter was one that would be widely circulated, as indeed it was. Even so, he felt, as did I, that the rebbe disappointed us.

Intellectual honesty ought to trump pragmatism, particularly with a religious leader.

A few years ago Monty's widow, Miriam, gave me a faded copy of Monty's response to the rebbe's critique of the scientific method. Toward the end of his reply he says this:

> If you ask me why I do not accept the biblical account of creation it is because there is a body of factual evidence which allows for a rational and logical interpretation granted certain rational assumptions. These assumptions may turn out to be wrong, but since the conclusions deriving from them at present create a self consistent picture, albeit leaving numerous questions unanswered, I am prepared to accept them until proven false. The biblical explanation makes no such appeal in the context of the known facts and on the contrary actually conflicts with observed evidence…I do not believe that if I reject the biblical age of the universe I reject religion per se. Religion to me means the establishment of a relationship between man and God and man and man. Neither of these essential and unique features of religion seem to me to depend upon the blind acceptance of the age of the world based on reading the bible.

Nevertheless, the vast majority of Charedi rabbis persist to this day in claiming the world was created just over fifty-seven hundred years ago on Erev Rosh Hashanah. And one must not question this.

Rav Shternbuch, the highly regarded (and English-born) Charedi authority, recently said, "A person who casts doubts on this accepted tradition—even if he is widely respected person by the Jewish people is to be considered as a non-believer. That is the halacha…simple calculations from the Bible concerning the generations from Adam lead to the clear conclusion that the world is less than 6,000 years old."

The great Maimonides, in his introduction to the last chapter of Sanhedrin, says that one should not take the sayings of the rabbis at face value, either to accept them or to ridicule them. By his own admission, he admired and followed Aristotle's scientific method, and I have no doubt that had he lived in Galileo's era, he would have been on his side rather than against him. But we should remember that some of the Charedi rabbis of his day burnt his books too.

Traditional Jewish, Christian, and Muslim leaders who reject the freedoms and abuses of modern societies do indeed put the blame for its abuses on science. But to condemn science for the abuses of some scientists is the same as condemning religion because some religious people are corrupt. I agree a totally materialist scientific outlook on life is the antithesis of a religious way of life. But it need not necessarily be so. Doubt falls into different categories, the benign and honest versus the destructive and negative. That, after all, is the lesson of the four sons who ask four similar but differently nuanced questions at the Seder table.

There is too a post-Holocaust element that sees Western values and indeed scientific materialism as responsible for everything that went wrong in the last century for us Jews (just as it does for many current Muslims). If science and culture could produce Nazi homunculi, there must be something inherently corrupt in them. And I have some sympathy with this critique, particularly as one sees the corruptions, distortions, and hypocrisies of the media and intellectual fashions.

But to condemn scientists for the way scientists examine the physical world strikes me as self-defeating and narrow. That, after all, is the method that has brought us so many technological, medical, and agricultural advances that have made our life on earth so much better.

ORGAN DONORS

What is the Jewish religious attitude to organ transplants? Some will tell you it is not allowed, but I belong to an organization called HODS (the Halachic Organ Donor Society), an admirable institution that involves rabbis and laypeople in encouraging organ donation and ensures that the religious requirements of how to define the moment of death and provide respect for and proper disposal of body parts are adhered to.

There is a serious shortage of organs for transplantation, and the hope is that as science progresses we will be able to clone or manufacture replacement organs and even use genetic engineering to prevent diseases that may lead to requiring them. Meanwhile there are two issues. Every year across the Western world there are cases of parents who sue hospitals for removing organs from the dead without consent and then trying to hide the evidence. This lack of respect is just typical of all bureaucratic organizations. But it contributes to a reluctance to donate that often results in unnecessary deaths.

This shortage has led to a growing world trade in human organs. The most common are kidneys, taken mainly willingly from the very poor to furnish the needs of the wealthy, or at least the wealthier. In the early 1990s, most of the buyers were from Gulf States who travelled to India to buy kidneys. Now buyers come from India, the Middle East, Britain, Canada, and the United States. Most Western countries forbid commerce in human organs. The World Medical Association also frowns it upon. In 2002 the British Medical Council for the first time banned an individual who had participated in commercial organ transplants. But there is no effective international regulation. Sadly, in recent months a series of scandals involving Israelis, Brazilians, and South Africans "harvesting" organs for commercial sale has highlighted illegal transactions. But I am certainly not going to justify nor even discuss the criminal side of things.

The trade is often supported on the grounds of shortage; demand creating a market. Many very poor people are only too willing to sacrifice a kidney for sums ranging from $1,000 to $10,000 that will either clear debts or set up their families for the future. Opinion among doctors and philosophers is varied. Some approve of a free and open trade with market forces applying. At least if it is in the open, there is a chance of proper medical treatment rather than butchery, reminiscent of the old back-street abortions. Proponents argue that this trade actually helps those less well off because the rich, jumping the queue by buying organs, enable more organs when they do become available to go to the poorer. Some object to the monetary incentives as crass materialism and argue for donors receiving no more than medical expenses and insurance policies. Others advocate only "ethical incentives."

A recent article in the *New York Review of Books* argued that it is the hypocritical Jews, Asians, and Muslims whose culture is biased against donating organs who are mainly responsible for encouraging this trade that takes advantage of the hopelessness of the poor.

Judaism is not opposed to organ donation to help other human lives. Sadly, the terrible toll of homicide bombers in Israel has led to several well-publicized examples of organs from victims helping others live. But it seems to me that there are two moral problems here. There is the right of a person to dispose of his or her own body, and the much more troubling issue of rich versus poor. I believe as a citizen of a liberal democracy that people should be allowed to do whatever they want with their bodies provided they do not harm others. And if they take such selfish action that leads to their deterioration and illness so as to burden the community with having to clean up their mess or take care of them, then they should be taxed or fined for their selfishness. If the State allows them to knowingly destroy their organs by ingesting poisons of all sorts, then I would argue, if a person willingly gives up an organ to help another, this can be regarded by the State as praiseworthy.

Of course as a halachically bound Jew, I believe we have other standards and responsibilities. We should not do anything that degrades our own bodies. But these are options we are free to adopt or reject in open societies. We must take good care of our bodies, officially, though I am amazed that any religious Jew is allowed to smoke anywhere that bills itself as a place of religious worship or study. We are supposed to take care of our diet and fitness, but you wouldn't know it from observing what many religious people do. There is a very huge gap in the religious world between what ought to be done and what is done.

Religions claim and often try very hard to ameliorate the plight of the poor. And this means not just giving money but valuing them as human beings and trying very hard to make them feel valued and respected despite their lack of resources. Unfortunately, the way the rich were and are treated in religious societies propagates distorted values. There is a well known the old Yiddish proverb. *"Baal Hameah Hu Baal HaDeah"* (the person with a hundred is the one whose view counts). This, sadly, goes for too many societies, but I just don't hear enough pious rabbis speaking out against it. Instead they encourage it by giving excessive honor and preference to big donors.

What worries me about the trade in organs is that poor people are taken advantage of because they are so desperate. Halachically one may not take advantage of another's distress. I can well imagine a scenario in which a desperate man might offer his lungs or his heart. There is a huge difference between a sane, rich man deciding to end his life and a desperate poor man offering up his heart so that his children might have food.

This is not a new problem. One of the realities of eastern Europe that is forgotten in the nostalgic yearning for the good old days of the shtetl is that there was an enormous white slave trade in young poor Jewish girls. Bertha Pappenheim (otherwise known as Bertha O in Marcel Breuer's notes) campaigned relentlessly, and although some rabbis supported her, most were indifferent.

The issue is one of sensitivity to the plight of the poor. I do not see how one can legislate for this any more than one can legislate for the rich being able to afford better treatment, life-prolonging luxury treatment, better education, and better aftercare than the poor. But the very notion is ethically disturbing. It was to avoid this that the dreamers who founded the welfare state hoped to institute one health system for all. And in the slow decline of state welfare we are also going to see the erosion of the ethical values that assert that all human life is equal.

The most common exhortation of the Torah is not a law as such; it is to remember the poor and the disadvantaged, for if their cry goes up to heaven, says the Talmud, God will surely hear it. We need to be sensitive to the circumstances that create both the need and the supply. Desperation is never a fair basis for ethical decisions.

SABBATICAL

The Jewish attitude to the Land of Israel is completely missing from the current propaganda and hatred directed against the Jewish people. Our commitment to, love for, legal obligations toward, and desire to return to this land have pervaded our traditions for thousands of years, long before the rise of Islam. Nothing illustrates this more than the biblical law of *shemittah* (the seventh year release) that is still adhered to by many residents of the Land of Israel. The Bible mandated a release of slaves, debts, and tribal lands.

Every seven years, says the Bible, one must leave one's fields and orchards fallow and not cultivate plants, vegetables, and fruit. Whatever grows by itself is treated with sanctity and has to be shared with others. This law applies only to lands that were part of our ancient heritage. No reason is given in the Bible other than that we need to appreciate that everything belongs to God and is on loan to us. One can guess it was an agricultural preservative system like the rotation of crops that originated in the Middle East some six thousand years ago. But one could equally argue it was an opportunity in a predominantly agricultural society for a break to enable national education and spiritual reflection and to refresh and reinforce one's connection with Torah.

It was Nachmanides (1194–1270) living in Catalonia who said in his biblical commentary that all its laws were intended primarily to be adhered to in the Land of Israel. Beyond its borders in exile, we keep them so as not to forget them for the time when we will return (so much for the claim that Jews abandoned their claim to their lands). Everyone agrees the laws of *shemittah* only apply within the inhabited biblical boundaries. Not surprisingly, there is much debate as to whether the laws of *shemittah* still apply, whether they depend on the defunct institution of the Jubilee, are of Torah obligation or now simply rabbinic, to keep the memory alive. So just think. For three thousand years the actual land has been part of our religious psyches.

In the case of many biblical laws that became impractical or anachronistic, the rabbis found ways to accommodate them to new conditions. The *shemittah* also required cancelling all debts. What was a humanitarian act, lending to the poor, in early times became unworkable if the debt could be cancelled every time a sabbatical came along. As commerce spread with the Romans, Jews had to decide. Either ignore the law or forget making a career for yourself in real estate. Now you can guess the choice they made. Hillel realized something had to be done, and so he found a way, according to the Mishna, of getting around the law by transferring the debt to the courts. He invented the *prosbul.* Scholars still argue about the origin of the word. In Aramaic it could mean "take the contract" or even "a deal that benefits rich and poor." Greek experts prefer its link to the Greek for "community contract."

You might wonder why he didn't just cancel the law. It has always been accepted that we do not eradicate a law altogether. Even if unworkable, its principles remain as an expression of a religious ideal. We rather try (at least the few adventurous and strong ones among our leaders) to find a way around it while preserving the concept. Times change, human society advances in cycles, and what was thought to be modern at one moment becomes medieval at another. Thousands of years later, we have now adopted the idea of an intellectual sabbatical. Even crop rotation is coming back into organic fashion. How shortsighted would we look now if we had written the law out altogether?

Another example. The Bible warns us against lending money for interest and wants us to lend money in a charitable way. There can be nothing wrong with that in principle. If anything, the error is rather with a society that only sees lending money as a commercial venture. Yet two thousand years ago this sort of thing was the very basis of international trade and commerce as it is today.

The Talmud discusses various ways of getting around the problem. Later in medieval Europe the *hetter isska*, business permit, developed. This is a contract that substitutes partnership fees for interest. It is used pretty widely nowadays by religious Jews throughout the world and is rather similar to the procedure used by Muslims to deal with the very same problem. By insisting on a way around the law instead of scrapping it, the rabbis at least ensure that the principle remains in place, and for those who care, it stands as a moral and religious issue.

Yet another example of a rabbinic fiddle, as some call it, is selling chametz before Pesach to a non-Jew and then buying it back again afterward. This was originally intended to help Jewish merchants who might be holding serious stocks in their warehouses waiting for the right deal. Similarly, the rabbinic eruv is a much-maligned device designed by rabbis to circumvent the ban on carrying loads on Shabbat. It was created to help people carry personal effects on Shabbat as settlements began to expand beyond city walls. Both were devices for making life livable while preserving the concept and the principle of the law.

To return to the shemittah, settlers always migrated to Israel whenever conditions allowed it, particularly after the expulsion from Spain in 1492. Then the Ottoman Empire welcomed Jews. The pious sultans of those days would be shocked that now in the name of Islam Turkish President Erdogan spews out crude hatred against Jews whenever he gets a chance. Later Jews began to arrive in response to other waves of hatred in the nineteenth century and began to till the land. The religious ones among them could not have survived if they had had to leave their lands fallow and wait two years for another crop. The great Rav Yitzchak Elchanan Spektor adapted a well-tried device for getting around the law: sell it notionally to an Arab and buy it back at the end of the year.

Thus the practical link between religion and the land was preserved. The idea remained, even if the practicalities led to finding ways around it. As the Jewish presence grew and agriculture flourished, the first chief rabbi of Palestine, Rav Kook, made this sale the policy of the rabbinate and it became automatic for many years. As with many such laws, individuals found other ways of circumventing it. One bought produce from Arabs. Then one imported it from Cyprus, and more recently Israeli enterprise and innovation in hydroponics has helped meet the need.

Once only the few religious kibbutzim and moshavim kept the *shemittah* and relied on the fictional sale. Nowadays the Charedi world does not accept the rabbinate loophole. More and more individuals in Israel see the *shemittah* as a way of asserting their new piety and/or their ancient bond with the Promised Land. As one would expect, asking for financial support has now become a fundraising tool to help more people keep the rigors of these ancient laws. And why not, if modern methods and charity make it achievable?

Shemittah has another function. As our connection to the land is being disavowed, delegitimized, it is a powerful reinforcement to us, at least, that this is a land we care for and have loved for thousands of years. This, I insist, does not mean it cannot be shared as it often was.

Dr. Margaret Brearley, a medieval historian and former advisor to the archbishops of Canterbury, has shown in her research the difference between Jewish and Christian poems about the Holy Land at the time of the Crusades. To the crusaders it was an abstraction, a theological mission into alien territory. Jerusalem was a town in Europe beyond the sea. To the Jews it was the dust, the boulders, and the ruins that made the land not an abstraction but a reality, a place that existed in this world, not some other.

After two thousand years of such dreaming, it is hardly surprising that we Jews did not want a quiet plot in Africa or the Russian steppes. Instead we wanted to return to our ancient land. For that is what our religion is based on, regardless of how well or otherwise we have adapted to exile.

DA'AT TORAH

You cannot understand Orthodox Judaism today without coming to grips with the concept of Da'at Torah. Da'at Torah literally means a "Torah opinion," and it was originally used to refer to a legal opinion that fell within the framework of Jewish law. Much, much later it came to mean the only authentic religious position in Judaism. Even later still it mutated into that position officially endorsed by "the council of great rabbis" without of course specifying who those rabbis might be. Since nowadays there is so much disagreement about who actually is a great rabbi, it now means "whatever position *my* 'great rabbi' endorses." So we have been treated to a series of examples where one "great rabbi" says, "Vote for this party," and another "great rabbi" says, "Vote for that party." For those in the middle or those following a third "great rabbi," this is rather confusing.

Da'at Torah is an ideology that emerged toward the end of the nineteenth century in response to the challenge of assimilation and Reform and secular Zionism. It is as near as you can get to the Catholic dogma of papal infallibility (itself a nineteenth-century reaction to challenge). Over the past century, it has been constantly modified and tweaked to the point where it has become the defining distinction between Ultra or Charedi Judaism and every other brand of Orthodoxy.

Da'at Torah is an interesting expression of an idea that is more political than religious. Of course there has always been a tradition of following religious authority. You can find its origin in the Bible, in Deuteronomy 17:8–10:

"If there is something you do not understand in Jewish law, a disagreement between people or a conflict within your gates...you shall take it to the priests or the judges whoever is the authority at that time, and you shall do as they tell you in accordance with Jewish law." Throughout the Talmudic period, there were mechanisms of authority, processes of decision making. These have continued to this day through the medium of *teshuvot*, responsa, published learned legal opinions. Such mechanisms have always allowed for differing opinions, as there have always been on matters of politics, civilization, and personal choices.

Post-Talmudic Judaism has developed into different traditions based on locations, influenced by host nations and intellectual trends, sometimes mystical and sometimes rational. Nevertheless, the constitutional integrity and continuity of the Halachic process has been what has kept the common core and link between these different religious communities and sects, as one sees most vividly in Israel today.

Yosef Karo, the author of the handbook of Jewish law, the *Shulchan Aruch*, said in his introduction that the purpose of his book was to enable the average Jew to know what to do and only have to resort to a rabbi when he did not have the information. The dogma that one had to go to a rabbi or a kabbalist to answer all and every matter of one's personal life is a recent development that owes as much to the Chasidic concept of the rebbe as the tzaddik (the saintly man with a hotline to heaven) as it has to do with traditional or Talmudic sources.

Of course some rabbis, some people, are on a higher spiritual level, some more knowledgeable, and some more talented in understanding human nature. But that is not the same as saying one is obliged to go to a rabbi for every issue, be it ritual, political, or personal, and that one is bound to adhere to his advice.

This dependence on rabbinic authority was tested during the run-up to the Holocaust, when many eastern European great rabbis told their followers to stay put rather than flee into the jaws of American materialists or Zionist heretics. Yet many rabbis who told others to stay got out themselves and were worshipped nevertheless. Which only goes to show that devotion has nothing to do with logic or history, but is an act of faith. No evidence can ever dissuade someone who chooses to believe. That is both the strength and the weakness of faith.

In a world where money and power are dependent on votes, leaders of religious communities, like political parties, know they must keep the faithful loyal so that they can produce a voting bloc at election time. This is why politicians in Israel and the United States go out of their way to court "great rabbis": they want their votes. So the concept of inerrancy becomes a mechanism of control and political power. That is why the rabbis I respect most are precisely those who refuse to use such power, morally, fiscally, or politically.

Once such a phenomenon characterized Chasidic courts and kabbalist miracle workers. But now even the Lithuanian Yeshivish community mimics the Chasidim because they have realized the cost-benefit factor. It is a sad moment for Judaism as a spiritual tradition, as opposed to a social one.

But this ideology is beginning to fray. The Council of Sages is no longer effective. More and more followers have abandoned such features of Da'at Torah as refusing secular education, or serving in the Israeli army, and banning the Internet and smartphones. Much of what Da'at Torah objects to may be justified. Secular culture is increasingly destructive, corrosive, and morally ambiguous. But the answer is not to imitate Catholicism, for as we know, it hasn't succeeded. The answer is to follow the great tradition of "both can be (right) the words of God" (TB Eruvin 13b). There can be differing conclusions within the parameters of Jewish law.

The great and the good have the expertise and scholarship. I believe they should be respected and deferred to. However nowadays "great rabbis" have such carapaces of assistants, secretaries, bodyguards, gatekeepers, and fixers that it is impossible to know what actual message gets through to them and what they actually said in response. That is why I find it hard to rely on reported responses. It's like Chinese whispers both ways. Books have been banned by men who have not read a word of them.

Thanks to the Internet and computer technology with massive databases, we can all get access to the facts with a basic yeshiva education. It's how one uses those facts and which ones one selects that should define a great rabbi, rather than simply falling back on received conclusions. In an ideal world, it is the ability to filter the information and the type of decisions that are made that should define Da'at Torah.

The idea of Da'at Torah has developed into a positive theological political ideology. Ironically it is almost identical to Ayatollah Khomeini's way of thinking.

BE HAPPY

When we consider religion, we rarely think of fun or joy. Usually it is control, discipline, and awe. There is an early tradition of combining joy with restraint. In Hebrew it is the idea of *Gilu BiRe'ada*, "serve the Lord with awe and rejoice with trembling" (Psalms 2:11). The Talmud asks,

> What is meant by "rejoice with trembling?"...Mar the son of Ravina made a marriage for his son. He saw that the rabbis were getting too merry, so he brought a precious cup worth four hundred zuz and broke it before them, and they became serious. R. Ashi made a marriage for his son. He saw that the rabbis were getting too merry, so he brought a cup of white crystal and broke it in front of them and they became serious. The rabbis said to R. Hamnuna Zuti, at the wedding of Mar the son of Ravina, "Please sing us something." He replied, "Alas for us that we will die. Alas for us that we will die!" They said, "What can we respond?" He said to them, "There is Torah and there is Mitzvah to help us!" (Brachot 30b)

Living a life that is guided by rituals has a purpose. I do not suggest the reason for doing them is necessarily for material benefit or pleasure. But there are certainly positive consequences. So much depression and aimlessness comes from not having a structured life and a framework. The daily rituals are reasons for getting up and for getting involved in the practicalities of daily life. The rituals that revolve around eating food are ways of stopping and thinking before stuffing our mouths. Ideally they lead to appreciating one's good fortune. Behaving in appropriate ways, being aware of right and wrong, of the ups and downs, the bad as well as the good, helps us cope with the challenges we face. Even when faced with serious crises, we are enabled to deal with situations of illness or of impending death because we can see a larger picture.

Our secular society is preoccupied with pleasure. If one only lives for pleasure, then one is ultimately bound to feel let down because all physical pleasures can so easily lead to going too far and then feeling let down. Eating too much makes one sick. And so people constantly try to find antidotes. It is like those Renaissance paintings of distinguished men with a skull in the background to remind them of mortality. Or the *Et in Arcadia Ego* of Poussin's neoclassical paintings; death lurks in the Garden of Eden, too. The paradox is that one wants to enjoy life, but we need to realize how transient it is.

Yet our religion keeps on emphasizing the need for joy. So what is joy? And what is happiness, so often connected to the idea that it can only be found in pleasure? The fact is that there is a lot of disagreement among academics of all kinds as to what happiness is and how it might be achieved. Some find evidence that humans are predisposed to characteristics and those who are happy by nature will be so regardless of whether they are rich, well educated, married, or healthy. Others are disposed to be sad, unhappy, and miserable. We will not solve this issue here. But I do believe there is no such thing as a state of happiness one enters into and everything goes swimmingly thenceforth. Rather I think certain actions make us happy or satisfied.

The Hebrew word "*simcha*," does not just mean being happy in the sense that, as the Beatles said, happiness is a warm gun, or a hot bun, or a new car. When I hear people say they just want to enjoy themselves and I ask why, I am told because it makes them feel happy. But that kind of happy is purely physical well-being. How is this different from a pig wallowing in the mud or a cow contentedly chewing the cud in a field? Important as it is, it fades as quickly as a good meal or a farewell kiss.

Simcha is not just physical. It is physical linked to spiritual, a higher goal. It is a sense that one's life has a purpose, direction, and meaning, that one is doing something valuable. That is why the Mishna talks about the rich man as being "happy with his lot in life." Being happy with what one does can also be painful, like visiting a hospital or helping a frail elderly person.

There is another related Hebrew word, *ashrei*. It too translates as "happy," but to the best of my knowledge it is only used in the metaphysical sense, being happy because one is living a good life, a considered life, a life with meaning. Isaiah 56 is more specific: "Happy is the person who keeps Shabbat." Or in the words of the psalm we say three times a day, "Happy is the person who lives in God's house," or "Happy is the person who trusts in God." Being happy here, similar to being grateful, might not always be fun or even make one feel happy at all in the usual sense.

The purpose of serious holy days is to spend time in introspection, self-evaluation. It is not to feel guilty or bad, but to give one a sense of priorities. This does indeed help one cope with the vicissitudes of life. And having a ritual that imposes this can be very helpful. They are not supposed to be sad days, but rather serious and reflective ones. If one spends time assessing one's values and priorities and comes out feeling that one is on the right track, it can give a sense of great joy and happiness, a feeling of physical well-being and of intellectual and moral self-justification.

To return to the earlier quote from the Talmud, *gila*, "to rejoice," also requires constraint, the trembling, the seriousness that does not prevent happiness and joy but rather qualifies and restrains it through presenting a balance. Each religion has its own trials, its own special days, and its own subcultures and hidden agendas. What differentiates the religions is not necessarily in the goals, but rather in the ways prescribed to pursue and achieve them. In this respect Judaism's emphasis on daily ritual for everyone, not just an elite, is to me the crucial reason for valuing its distinctiveness. It is not ascetic religion.

It demands that we sample, taste, and enjoy life within the constraints it imposes. Happiness is a means to an end, not the end in itself. It is the means to self-fulfillment that can only be achieved within the context of appreciating the need to consider and care for others, to appreciate life and its benefits, and to be prepared to deal with the bad as well as the good.

I really enjoy most of our very specific rituals. I enjoy the sense of historical continuity. I even enjoy the poetry of the services. Above all, I relish the challenge of examining myself, accepting my failures and faults, and considering whether the targets I set last year were met and what new ones I need to set for the coming year. And doing it in the Jewish way will give me enormous joy and happiness on levels we don't usually associate with those words. And that is the added value of being Jewish. I feel incredibly privileged, happy indeed, that I am an heir to the great Jewish religious tradition. That makes me happy even when I am sad.

AFTERLIFE

The Bible does not explicitly say there is life after death. Which seems strange given the tremendous significance all the surrounding Middle Eastern cultures attached to the idea. Just think of the Greeks and Hades, the Egyptians and their pyramids, and the Babylonian ziggurats, all testaments to the significance of what they thought happened to the body after death. Not to mention Hindu concepts of the transmigration of souls and reincarnation, as well as the Buddhist graduation to another level of understanding and "life." Perhaps the Bible chose quite intentionally to focus on how to live life in the present rather than spend any time on the intangibles of something beyond the physical world. Maybe it simply assumed such a universal belief could be taken for granted. And of course there is the possibility that it simply did not think the idea had any merit.

The counterargument to the deduction from silence is that there are references to the fathers, Abraham, Isaac, and Jacob, dying and being "gathered to their people" (for example, Genesis 35:29). Talk of "spirit" in its various forms implies something beyond the physical, and odd phrases such as "until Shilo comes" (Genesis 49) are usually understood in a transcendental way.

The oral tradition, however, placed, and continues to place, tremendous emphasis on the importance of the next world and read into all kinds of texts, hints however improbable. Both the Talmud and Maimonides conflate the idea of resurrection and afterlife. The Mishna in Sanhedrin talks about those who have no part of the afterlife and then proceeds to discuss those who reject the idea of resurrection. What has one to do with other unless they conflated both ideas?

Maimonides was accused of not believing in resurrection because he did not mention it at all in his major Halachic work, *Yad HaChazaka*. Instead, in *Hilchot Teshuva*, chapter 8, he talks about the significance of the world to come and about those who cultivate their souls, enabling them to continue on a spiritual level after death, while others simply obliterate their souls through neglect and die like animals. Thus he fell afoul of those who thought souls indestructible, and the kabbalists who claimed Jewish souls had an eternal life of their own.

Maimonides was no stranger to controversy, but even he buckled under pressure and wrote a specific little pamphlet reiterating his belief in resurrection, though even he could not really explain rationally how it worked. And he made up for it by listing resurrection in his simple, handy guide to Jewish thought, the Thirteen Principles of Faith, but surprisingly makes no mention there of life after death.

For many Talmudic thinkers, the only way one could explain reward and punishment, disasters affecting the innocent, or why good people suffer and bad people prosper, was through the idea that accounts are settled in the afterlife. But still, the whole idea is so difficult to explain, because as the Talmud itself says, "No human has ever seen it, only God" (Sanhedrin 99a, etc.).

Talmud in Kiddushin tells the story of how a group of rabbis saw a boy follow his father's instructions to climb up a tower to send a mother bird away from the nest before taking the fledglings. He fell and died despite the promise of the Torah that those two commands, obeying one's father and sending away the mother, would guarantee long life. Some rabbis responded by saying long life meant eternal life. Others wondered about his motive, and yet another suggestion was that the ladder might have been faulty. The apostasy of Elisha Abuya was put down to his having no patience with the idea of life after death, and this explained his defection to Greek philosophy for its more rational approach.

Nevertheless, Rebbi Yosef the son of Rebbi Yehoshua Ben Levi took ill, had a sort of near-death experience, and reported that he had been to the afterlife and returned and discovered that those on top on earth were on the lowest rungs up there and vice versa (Talmud Pesachim 50a). Did he really believe he had been to Heaven and come back? More likely he was trying to make a point.

Aristotle said that one's immortality was in one's children, and other Greek thinkers talked about the legacy of the good works one leaves behind. Of course, comforting as it might be, this does not help with the question of whether there is an afterlife, and that seems to be a mystical rather than a logical matter.

Doubts about life after death go way back to the Bible. Ecclesiastes 3:21 asks, "And who knows if the soul of man rises and the soul of animals sinks to the dust?" And yet for all that, overwhelmingly rabbinic opinion holds firmly to the idea. Some might argue that it's a way of coping with the long, sad history of Jewish suffering. Others might say it's a way of coping with the inequalities and stress of life. Either way, the rabbinic position is that one has to do one's best on earth in the here and now if one wants to be part of the next world. It is not an escape but rather a culmination. And for those who have difficulty accepting the idea, it remains a mystery among the many we have yet to solve.

MOURNING

Recently I had three houses of mourning to attend in as many days. There was a sad symmetry to the three *shivas*. In one case it was for a ninety-year-old man. The second was for a middle-aged woman who died of cancer. The third was for a young man whose life was tragically cut short, to the incredible pain of his parents and siblings.

For the benefit of the uninitiated, the institution of *shiva*, which literally means "seven," requires a mourner to spend the seven days after the burial at home surrounded by relatives and visited by a constant stream of friends, well-wishers, do-gooders, and clergy.

Some argue that this is therapeutic. The constant presence of people helps create an artificial atmosphere that forces one to engage rather than retreat into one's own world. It helps carry one through from the unreality and tragedy of loss to the adjustment required to reenter mundane society and pick up where one left off. Others suggest that it imposes a process of mourning that we need to go through as a way of learning to cope with loss.

I do not personally adhere to Jewish custom and law because of any utilitarian or practical benefits. I am delighted to know that divine wisdom might on occasion coincide with ours, if only because it isn't fun being the butt of skeptical agnostics who spend an inordinate amount of time and energy attacking the iniquities of religion instead of giving it some credit for helping the human condition. However, even if no benefits could be seen, I'd still follow the rules.

But I must confess I find the *shiva* incredibly difficult to handle. First as a rabbi, clergyman, or simply a comforter, it is so difficult to know how to respond to those who have just lost someone dear and important to them. Their life has suddenly changed dramatically and sometimes cataclysmically. Instinctively I want to show my feelings by hugging or touching. One wants to connect, to find some tangible way of expressing one's concern or friendship, whether it is a male or a female. Of course the Orthodox world does not encourage such free physical expression of feelings, especially with people one is forbidden to have sexual relations with. Touching is regarded as a "fence around the law." I remember how in my youth many people used to make fun of such religious sensitivity. But nowadays civil law in the West has caught up. With so many cases of sexual molestation, harassment, and perversion, very often on the part of clergymen of many religions, it is impossible for a teacher to touch a pupil or a doctor to see a patient alone in his surgery.

So when touching is not possible, what are you left with? Words. Words. Words! The trouble is that very few people have the skills to use words felicitously. Even those of us who live by the word often find it very difficult when faced by tragedy and human pain. Just think of the usual clichés: "Our hearts go out to..." "We extend our sincerest condolences..." "They have passed on to a far better place." I once heard a rabbi in Glasgow declare, "The community's loss is the cemetery's gain!"

And then you have all those well-meaning explanations of untimely death. "Everyone is given an allotted task in life, and some of us accomplish it earlier and others later." This was to explain to me why my father died at the age of forty-eight, and then years later why I lost a son aged two months. In neither case did the Shiva achieve anything except to make me want them to stop digging their own graves. I suppose someone who is in a coma for years and then dies, this departure might be seen as fulfilling a necessary function. Oh yes, I will be told they are giving something to the family, if only indirectly, even in their comatose or premature state. Yes, I know these people meant well. This is one of the less satisfactory aspects of a *shiva*, having to sit and listen to these endless inanities and ridiculous nonsenses.

When my father died, there was a veritable procession of people who assured me they were my father's best friends and fervent supporters, but I know how much he suffered because he was not supported in his great work and how few of the people who claimed to be his friends really were. Did they think I didn't know? If anything, for me the *shiva* hindered the process of grieving, made me very angry and resentful, and left me longing all the more for solitude.

One of the beauties of Judaism is that there is a tradition of berating God. Yes, we are expected to give thanks for the bad as well as the good because in one way or another everything comes from the same source and is for the best. Both King David and Job were stoic in their sufferings and never raised a word against the divine decree, but on the other hand, the Chasidic masters were not at all inhibited in their complaints against the way God treated His creatures.

The fact is that a true believer takes what comes and bears it without any acrimony directed to God. What happens to us on earth is part of the natural way of things. Some bodies are more prone to diseases than others. Some situations are more risky, and some people's genetic makeup makes them more likely than others to end up in a mess.

Belief in God does not change the natural order, neither does it answer why things happen that we humans call "bad." When someone dies and we ask why, we do not want the rational, medical explanation. We want to be comforted, and as with a crying child, a hug is often better than a word. Logically, the dead person must be better off, whether you believe in an afterlife or not.

We are mourning for *our* loss, for *our* pain. And that is why comforting is so important. Once upon a time, every word counted. Nowadays words are cheap. So we babble to cover up our awkwardness, and our words get us into trouble. Job's comforters sat in silence, and in that silence there was no reproach. It was when they started talking they got into trouble.

The law is that we should remain silent until the mourner starts speaking. But I've often seen silent comforters sit awkwardly waiting for the word that never came. This is one of the sicknesses of our times, that we need to speak, speak, speak. Whenever a rabbi turns up, some duffer says, "Rabbi, we expect you to say a few words." They are rarely few, and even more rarely are they helpful. To be fair, sometimes words can help, and a sensitive rabbi can comfort.

To me the most important lesson of the shiva, and indeed of life, is that we should be forced to focus on the living rather than on those who have gone. But if one is ever asked "why" the only honest answer is "I do not know."

HOLINESS

When I read Leviticus (Vayikra chapter 19) and see all those magnificent laws about being nice to one's neighbor, helping those in need and those less fortunate than oneself, not taking advantage of other people's frailty, not telling tales or gossiping, I am always amazed that a code written down so very long ago should contain such phenomenal moral, humane ideas. Yet here we are thousands of years later, and I doubt very much whether an infinitesimal proportion of the human race actually follows these rules. They are so uplifting and yet seem to run counter to basic, natural human instincts.

No one, I think, would say these rules are out of date or barbaric. And yet most people seem to think that all the rest of the Torah is to some degree or other. It is one of the challenges of Judaism in modernity to try to reconcile the paradox that Torah contains so much we can admire and identify with and yet so much that seems to us to be so irrelevant to our times. So we can read chapters about leprosy of bodies and clothes and buildings, priests, sacrifices, temple purity and impurity that leave us feeling alienated and that seem devoid of constructive messages.

Mary Douglas, the great anthropologist and author of, among others, *Leviticus as Literature* (published in paperback by Oxford University Press), explains the structure of Leviticus in a way that makes incredible sense even to the most critical and secular of minds. She points out the emphasis on different spaces, private, public, and holy. There are different states, of health, sickness, and spirituality. Different foods, different ways of treating different parts of a sacrificed animal. Different ways of sexual behavior. It is possible to read important messages into the rituals and laws that are not so obvious to us moderns if we try to look a little deeper and widen the context.

Yet so many of us are turned off Judaism both by unsatisfactory experiences and above all by a very limited education. It has been left to other religions to take our basic ideas and spirituality and to popularize them in ways that we have clearly failed to do. And we can explain this both in terms of the experience of exile and oppression and in terms of the intensity and complexity of our special brand of religious behavior.

Yet it is clear that the Torah intended us to set an example and to behave in a way that would indeed elevate us and mark us out as an example to others. It must be admitted that we have not succeeded. Some argue that in passing on a popular form of our religion to Christianity and Islam, we have indeed changed the world. But in terms of being a good example, I am not sure we have. All the evidence shows that in areas of ethical behavior, family life, and business life we mirror the values and mores of the host society.

There are indeed occasional exceptions. Many wonderful women spend their time and money visiting the sick and tending to the poor and the dying and dead. There is a tremendous amount of charity, goodness, and kindness in many sections of our community, and yet it coexists with corruption of some sort or another at virtually every level.

So what has gone wrong? Perhaps this is simply the way humans are, and we need the disciplines of whatever religion to keep us in line. In every religion you can find corruption coexisting with good deeds. In every religion there are political divides and internal tensions and divisions that can even sometimes become murderous.

Is there hope? We are like horses that without bridles will just go off where the whimsy takes them. According to the Torah, God tried just giving a few guidelines to Adam at the beginning, but that didn't work. So it seems we need more reins. Sure, Torah is just one example of how to achieve a considered and controlled life. It is the starting point of our particular tradition.

We Jews are such a peculiar people. As Balaam says in the Torah, we are "a nation that dwells alone." Will we ever change? Can we ever change? Are we just fated to have our corrupt ministers and drug smugglers, our crooks and our prostitutes, as well as our scholars and saints just like everyone else?

We are cursed and blessed. We are blessed to have an amazing tradition, and we are cursed in that we are constantly destroying it and ourselves. Indeed you cannot read the Bible without sensing this message of heights and depths. Our isolation can be an excuse for turning our backs on the world or for rising to a new challenge. I see both within our community.

Among the many jewels in Leviticus 19, there is the command to "rebuke your neighbor" (when he is doing wrong) so that "you do not bear his guilt" (19:17). The Talmud says you have an obligation to rebuke, otherwise you share in his evil. But then it qualifies this. If you see you will have no effect on a bad person, then there is no point in trying. Don't encourage him through provocation to be even worse. But the phrase itself is very ambiguous. The second part in Hebrew goes "*VeLo Tissa Alav Cheyt*," which literally means, "And let not him carry the sin." The obvious question is, who is "he"? Is he the sinner or the person who is telling him off? Logically, it means that the person who is pointing out the error of another should not stand by while the bad guy continues to do bad things. Just as previously the Torah commands one not to stand by while another is being killed or suffering, the same concern for another requires us to take responsibility for trying to get him or her to do the right thing. This is consistent with the Torah's values of having a sense of community and belonging to a people.

The dreaded ArtScroll translation (which is often as far from literal as you can get) takes this second part to mean "and do not bear a sin because of him." It refers to the person who is trying to correct another actually sharing in the crime. As interpretation this is fine and indeed moving, that we share in the guilt of the crimes of others. But it is not what the text says. We are not guilty for the sins of others. That is the approach of other religions, not ours. The crime is his, not ours.

There is a beautiful Chasidic take on this line, not meant to be literal, which goes like this: "Tell off your neighbor." But if you can't "VeLo," then "Tissa [share] Alav Chet," share his burden, his pain, the situation he is in. You can tell someone off when he feels you are sharing the burden, you are committed and on his side. But if you are not, then the purpose of the rebuke is suspect.

In Leviticus 19 we are commanded to be holy, *kadosh*. But the word in Hebrew is double edged, often called a Janus word because like the Roman god it looks both ways. A temple is *kadosh* and a person can be *kadosh*. A temple prostitute is *kadesha*. The object, the person, is neither good nor bad. He or she can be used well or badly, positively or negatively. It is up to us to choose, to choose life and to choose to be holy. It doesn't mean we should or could be perfect. It just means that we should always try to be better, more sensitive and more aware.

PART 4

CULTURE

SEXUAL EXPLOITATION

According to the Bible, Noah's flood destroyed humanity because they were violent. How much have we changed? Many of us seclude ourselves in our protected worlds and often have little idea of what is really going on beyond our walls. We who live in Western "civilized" societies and are reasonably well off know about the millions of refugees or poor, exploited human beings around the world, but it rarely touches us personally. More worrying is the delusion we have that our societies are safe places. They may be safer, but they are not safe. It's not just a matter of terrorism, gunfire, fires, and auto accidents. Hundreds of children, men, and women disappear off the streets each year and are never heard from again. Are they victims of sexual abuse, murder, or simply people who want a child? Abuse of women (and men) remains a blot on the record of the males of our species, and it is far too prevalent even in the "free world."

I want to focus specifically here on the violence, the rape. The Torah, in Deuteronomy 22.26 compares rape to murder. But there is a degree of violent aggressiveness in males worldwide. But even here in a free society, there seems to be a streak of male violence that glorifies this wanton abuse. Columbia University student Emma Sulkowicz has been protesting at the inaction of university authorities by carrying a mattress around campus until her reported rapist is removed. Fifty assault survivors spoke out recently in a campus demonstration supporting Sulkowicz. More and more female college students are coming out to fight against both the abuse and the reluctance of college authorities to act.

Governor Jerry Brown of California has now passed a bill requiring all colleges that receive state money to enforce a standard of "affirmative consent" or "yes means yes," meaning only a positive "yes" at every stage can lead on to the next. Such a law was first instituted at Antioch College twenty years ago. Until recently no one else adopted it. Harvard still hasn't. Hardly a month goes by without some new story of women being abused or raped on university campuses. President Obama has begun a campaign to highlight the problem of college rape in the United States. Here are the statistics, according to One in Four (www.oneinfourusa.org/statistics.php):

- One in four college women reports surviving rape or attempted rape at some point in their lifetime.
- Each year, 5 percent of women on college campuses experience rape or attempted rape.
- Among women currently attending US colleges and universities, 673,000 have experienced rape at some point in their lifetime.
- In one year, 300,000 college women, over 5 percent of women enrolled in colleges and universities, experience rape. This does not include other forms of sexual assault.
- Every year, 5 percent of women in the US military academies report surviving rape, as do 2.4 percent of the men.
- *Time* magazine on September 22, 2014, reported that 13,079 women in the United States experience domestic violence every day in the United States.
- The *New York Times* on September 30, 2014, reported female firefighters suffering job discrimination, harassment, and sexual abuse every day.
- One in three women has been physically abused.

The boxer Mike Tyson was a classic example of male physical crime against women. His rape landed him in jail, and for a while the public took notice. But interest subsided. The issue has been brought to the public by the recent revelations of the number of American football stars, "heroes," who have been guilty of abusing women. A video of Ray Rice's attack on his fiancée has gone "viral," in current terminology, and has forced the NFL to start taking action after years of pretending there was no problem. Another footballer, Adrian Peterson, was indicted for beating his child. Jonathan Dwyer was arrested for aggravated assault against a woman and a child. These massively rich Neanderthals have for years been getting away with physical abuse. So too have college sportsmen and ordinary common and garden males of the species.

The defense has always been that women invited the men's attention, even threw themselves at them, that they dressed provocatively or drank too much and invited it. It's true that modern fashions tend toward the provocative, and it is true the amount of male and female drinking on college campuses and city bars is excessive. Recently examples of college girls dying from immoderate amounts of alcohol have been publicized.

But nothing justifies the crude brutality of males forcing their unwanted attentions and testosterone-inflamed bodies on women. Many parents are bound to wonder whether sending their daughters away to college is such a good idea. The traditional antipathy of ultra-Orthodoxy to allowing girls to go off to college away from home might even have some justification. The trouble is that it's not just away from home that violence is a problem. Within homes, all kinds of physical abuse are reported at phenomenal levels. It is estimated that 46 percent of cases are not even reported. And that is just physical abuse, not mental.

We who value the intensity of our religious tradition are proud of the quality of our religious life. We look with a degree of condescension on the decline in the moral standards of the world around us. We are bound to wonder whether we are doing enough to protect our families from the sexual predations of society within and beyond the home.

It may be true that nowadays women have much more power and greater access to legal means to defend themselves. Nevertheless, recent revelations that police forces across the United States neither took complaints of rape seriously nor processed evidence in their possession show how primitive are the attitudes toward this in a so-called modern world. The problem exists at every level of society and, sadly, in every religious community as well.

The religious world considers itself an antidote to the corruption of the secular world. But it too has a poor record of dealing with abuse within its own communities. Often the clergy themselves are the guilty perpetrators. Sadly, this past year we have witnessed highly regarded rabbis being found guilty of theft, bribery, and sexual corruption. It is a blot on our world. The case of the rabbi of Washington's Modern Orthodox community who was found guilty of spying on women going to the Mikvah, is yet another sad example of how men of religion, all religions, use their positions and power to take advantage and abuse others, men and women. There has been too much of this within the Orthodox community of all degrees.

We recognize that if we leave our children's morality to society's default position, we are failing them. The whole purpose of religion is to raise the level of morality and spirituality. But this does not happen accidentally or by itself. Religion should not be concerned only with our souls. It also requires of us that we take responsibility for our own community and its leadership where it is failing in its obligations, as well as the world beyond. What goes on around us ultimately affects us. Just as a rising tide lifts all boats, so a sinking one leaves them high and dry. Noah's flood is a reminder that violence by humans against humans can destroy a world.

HYPERSENSITIVITY

I was in the Metropolitan Museum of Art the other day, standing in front of a painting by an artist I much admire, Giovanni Battista Caracciolo (not as good as Caravaggio, but a close second). The painting, entitled *Tobias and the Angel*, is based on a weird story in the apocryphal book of Tobit.

Briefly, Tobit is a member of the tribe of Naftali exiled by the Assyrians to Nineveh. Horrible things happen to him. He gets blinded. His son goes off to try to collect a debt, and the angel Raphael sends him on a journey to Media to help a widow called Sarah who is possessed by the demon Asmodeus. Tobias is attacked by a fish as he crosses the Tigris. The angel tells him to use its innards to scare off the demon. He rescues Sarah and, back home, uses the miraculous innards to cure his father's blindness. Tobias and Sarah marry, and they all live happily ever after. Not really the sort of book you'd expect to find in the Tanach, and it isn't. But it certainly has Jewish flavor.

In the gallery the caption reads, "Based on the biblical book." My hackles began to rise because it might be in the Catholic and Orthodox Bibles, which include the Apocrypha, but it is not in ours, or in most Protestant Bibles either. Couldn't they get it straight? Then I got worked up about their calling it the Old Testament, for us primitive old fogeys, as opposed to the shiny New Testament for the good guys. And then I thought, "Am I crazy to get worked up about such a trivial issue?"

A few months ago, a friend in London involved me in a complaint he sent to the director of the National Gallery in London about a painting called *The*

Rich Man Being Led to Hell by David Teniers the Younger, in which the rich man is clearly painted as a Jew, complete with kipa and beard, not to mention exaggerated features. The director replied amenably, and tried to put it in the context of the painter and his time. But I did think a few lines added to the blurb might have put the portrait in the context of say, *The Jew of Malta*, *The Merchant of Venice*, or indeed *Oliver Twist*, not to mention *Der Stürmer*. I suppose one could have argued that a beard by itself does not necessarily indicate a member of the tribe. Neither would a skullcap for that matter, though the combination, with the added refinement of a hooked nose, seems pretty obvious to me.

Now if I am so hypersensitive, why am I so surprised when other people are? I have always been very quick to take offense at any perceived slur against my religion and my people, even if I am myself among the first to criticize them when they are wrong. Doesn't Proverbs say, "Better the wounds of a friend than the sweet talk of an enemy"? Perhaps it was growing up in England where in my youth Jews and Judaism were indeed regarded as not quite acceptable. We were still called Christ Killers, Jew Boys, and Yids and were accused of being devious, rich, unpatriotic foreigners who should "go home." Except, of course, many Brits didn't want us to go "home" either!

Yet whenever people made fun of religion in general, pompous vicars or duplicitous priests, I enjoyed the fun. Jewish humor is predominantly self-critical and makes fun of God, Moses, rabbis, and the lot of us. But as society has changed, we have been forced to become much more sensitive toward those who suffered from racial discrimination, sexual discrimination, indeed any kind of discrimination. The doyen of American writers, Joyce Carol Oates, has been mangled online and in the press because she tweeted, "Where 99.3% of women report having been sexually harassed & where rape is an epidemic, in Egypt, it is natural to inquire: what's the predominant religion?"

Some of the criticism has been that Ms. Oates might have mentioned other factors such as social, economic, and historical. It was not fair to blame religion only. But why are some religious groups more prone to sexual assault and violence against women than others? Might it not be, in part, because of religious attitudes? We can all see that within religions there are extremes and fanatics and bad guys as well as good guys. If people set themselves up as spiritual leaders, we have every right to expect them to behave as such and take responsibility. Toleration of corruption or distortion must be excoriated. That, after all, is our tradition. The prophets, musar, and Torah all require self-analysis, self-criticism, and self-discipline.

Ironically Ms. Oates has undone herself. She is now in in the forefront of this retreat and capitulation to politically correct hypocrisy. She has objected to PEN, the organization of writers, for freedom of expression for giving an award to the Charlie Hebdo cartoonists. Clearly she has been got at for her earlier criticism of Islam's treatment of women. Culture is obviously bendable, depending on political correctness and pressure.

So despite my hypersensitivity, I do not get angry over reasoned criticism of Judaism (or of myself). I don't expect thinking Muslims to object to a reasoned critique of Islam. Is this insensitive? No, I don't think so. Religious leaders or authorities should expect criticism over mistakes or poor judgments. The Ethics of the Fathers declares, *"Nagid Shmey Avad Shmey"* (A name made is a name destroyed). If you set yourself up above the crowd, you must expect scrutiny and criticism.

If American politicians who lost office through their own sexual misdeeds, choose to run for office again, they must expect the scrutiny and explain why they should be trusted with high office. They cannot be treated with kid gloves. It is not insensitive to challenge them about their past behavior. I recall John Profumo, who in 1963 lost office against a background of sexual impropriety. But then he lived a life of good deeds, modesty, and charity. We all have choices. If we take the high ground, we must expect to have to defend it.

Of course there is still racism, anti-Semitism, and anti a whole lot of others. The Supreme Court opened up a debate over preferential treatment for minorities. New York is arguing over police profiling. All sides are getting their oars in openly and blatantly. That is the beauty of robust, open, contrary debate.

In Britain and Europe, where state broadcasting systems affect the narrative and in practice dictate the manner of debate by imposing a wet blanket of political correctness and bias, it is much harder to find a fair, open, and honest hearing of a contrary point of view. Just read Melanie Phillips's blog to see what it's like to try to offer an alternative narrative.

The United States also contains different states with different laws and different biases. Some are pro-business and some are pro-union. Some impose state taxes, some do not. If citizens do not like one state's laws, they can move to another. The freedom to insult in the United States often surprises Europeans. But in the end, I believe its brutal openness is healthier. In other words, being sensitive ought not necessarily to mean you cannot say what you believe is right. If I am hypersensitive, I need to get over it.

T. S. ELIOT

Anthony Julius has a reputation as one of the brightest English lawyers of his generation and has a PhD on T. S. Eliot. Recently he was praised for his role in the defense of Deborah Lipstadt against the revolting David Irving. Julius has spent many years studying anti-Semitism in all its varieties. He concludes it has felt like swimming through a sewer.

His book *Trials of the Diaspora* (Oxford University Press) is magisterial. Some of the critical reviews have been predictably nitpicking, and Harold Bloom's positive review in the *New York Times* brought the secular anti-Zionists out in force, so it must be good. No Judaica library should be without it.

The disease has proved uniquely persistent, mutating from religion to religion and from nation to nation. It exists even where no Jews are present. What every outbreak has in common is illogicality mixed with paranoia and politics.

There is nothing new in Julius's chapters on English history. England gave the world the blood libel. The crusaders slaughtered Jews as the easily accessible heretics. Jews were blamed for everything from the Black Death to famine and war, just as later they were blamed for being capitalists and Marxists, internationalists and nationalists, too weak and too strong.

In England Jews were used and abused and then expelled in 1290. Yet hatred of Jews persisted even when there were none around. When, under Cromwell, the question of readmitting Jews was discussed, sections of the Anglican Church raised the specter of Jews destroying churches, killing

Christian children, banning pork. Merchants argued that the Jews would simply swindle everyone else and put them out of business. Similar charges were made in 1753 when Parliament passed a Jew bill and King George actually signed it, giving Jews equal rights. The uproar was so great the bill was repealed! In anti-Semitism, every one of the medieval calumnies has a modern equivalent.

Julius's specialized contribution is how anti-Semitism is deeply embedded in English literature. From Chaucer to Marlowe, from Shakespeare to Dickens, and on to Eliot, the Jew is invariably depicted as the dangerous, malicious symbol of evil and everything good Christians oppose. All of this makes the exceptions all the more amazing. There are those in the field who think Julius exaggerates anti-Semitism in English literature right up to modernity. But Julius makes a powerful case.

In the most relevant part of this book, he examines current anti-Semitism in England in general, and specifically in the context of anti-Zionism, which is now commonly used as a surrogate. A major factor is Islam, which, like Christianity, always had a problem with Jews precisely because they stubbornly persisted with their "old" ways. Perhaps under parts of Islam, Jews suffered less at certain times, but the Jew was always regarded as the outsider, the dhimmi. Jews were allowed to live in Muslim countries provided they paid a tax and put up with humiliating legislation.

One can, of course, understand the modern political antagonism. When two nations fight over the same home, there will be a lot of bitterness and violence on both sides. But it is the completely irrational hatred and demonization of the other, regardless, that betrays the disease. Rwanda illustrates how easily "the other" can be dehumanized. Most disturbing because it is inflammatory and has led to violence against Jews around the world is the medieval anti-Semitism that floods the Muslim world and underlines how easily human minds can be distorted by manipulators.

The church remains problematic. Catholicism has tried to eradicate anti-Semitism. But mainstream Protestantism (as opposed to the Southern

Baptists) has adopted an anti-Israel narrative as the biased language of the recent Methodists report illustrates only too well. To make matters worse, many acculturated Jews and Israelis have always cooperated and conspired with prejudice in order to secure their own positions in society. Julius demolishes secular Jewish anti-Zionism. The issue once again is not whether Jews or Israelis deserve criticism or condemnation. It is the assumption that all evil is on one side only and that only Palestinians deserve a homeland, not Jews.

Some ultra-Orthodox Jews have long opposed secular Zionism. Nevertheless, most of them still wish to live in the Holy Land and perpetuate their ancient link with it. But secular and left-wing anti-Zionism goes back to the struggles within communism. Much of Russian Jewry opposed the very idea of a Jewish state (ironically so too did the majority of Anglo-American Jews). They fed the left-wing and labor movements of Russia, America, and Europe, and their grandchildren are the secular Jews who today feel embarrassed by the Jewish religion and Jewish particularism. For a while some could identify with a secular socialist Zionist agenda. But as Israel proved to be as fallible as any other democracy, abandoned its socialism, and allied with the great capitalist United States, many of them turned on Israel to cleanse themselves of their embarrassing Jewish identity and reject the idea of a specifically Jewish homeland. Now that the communist "god has failed," all that is left is anti-Americanism and antiglobalization. Israel is an easy target. This also explains the strange alliance between secular left-wing Englishmen (and other left-wingers) and those who despise women, gays, and liberals, and wish to overthrow the Western democratic process.

Julius makes the point that no other country suffers from a campaign of delegitimization, irrational hatred, and double standards as much as Israel does, and he believes it is precisely because of its Jewish character. It is the loss of objectivity, the language of hate and prejudice that explains the exaggerated odium directed at Jews and Israel, and of course Islam's own internal problems.

It is often said that it is Israel that causes modern anti-Semitism. Julius debunks this theory. The antagonism would still be there, regardless of geo-political circumstances. Hatred will always find a way of seeping out of the sewer; if it cannot find one channel, it will always look for another.

Recently an English judge, Bathurst Norman, instructed a jury that a gang of political terrorists who broke into and smashed up the offices of a company that dealt with Israel should be let off. He compared Israel to Nazis and said that the protest was a legitimate democratic expression of sympathy for the plight of the Gazans and against Israeli oppression. Now let us see if he or any English judge exonerates any other case of gratuitously smashing up private property on political grounds or compares any other state to the Nazis. If not, we will know for certain that Anthony Julius is understating the problem of anti-Semitism in Britain today, rather than exaggerating it.

This important but depressing book needs to be read by anyone who cares for the health and sanity of modern society. When violence is directed at Jews, it never ends there.

BOSTON, CAMERAS, AND CIVIL LIBERTIES

America is a crazy land of contradictions, and yet if ever there was an argument in favor of dysfunction, the United States is it. Its politics are hampered by the incapacity of the Republicans and the Democrats to agree on anything from reforming taxes, to immigration, entitlements, the environment, global warming, oil pipelines, or foreign policy to make any meaningful changes. Meanwhile big money, businesses and unions buys votes, representatives, senators, and presidents.

So for example Senators could not agree on requiring its citizens to be checked before being allowed to buy guns. Or to put it another way, this is a democracy where the National Rifle Association can buy enough senators to carry out its wishes. And which normal healthy state could possibly object to limiting the size and arsenals of guns readily available to the ordinary man and woman in the street? No state except for the United States of America. And this regardless of how many mentally unstable mass murderers have already killed so many innocents, how many tragedies have occurred, or that the death from gun-inflicted wounds is so massively higher than anywhere else on earth. As they say, "You cannot be serious."

OK, so the Right is crazy. What about the Left? Two brothers set off bombs at the Boston Marathon that killed three and inflicted on innocent bystanders some of the most horrific injuries it has been my unfortunate lot to see on television (and outside Israel). They were identified before they could execute a far wider planned campaign of violence only because security cameras caught them on video. In Boston, the ACLU (American Civil Liberties Union) had successfully blocked the city from placing cameras in the city center's public places and had prevented others from being activated because, they argued, it was in breach of civil liberties. Fortunately, private stores had their cameras turned on, and it was thanks to those of Lord & Taylor that the terrorists were identified, and so quickly. Yet still the ACLU continues to campaign against cameras in public places. They too are either misguided or naïve ideologues.

How can we deal with evil, amoral enemies with our hands tied behind our backs? Surely safety overrides libertarian considerations. Indeed, according to Hobbes (whom the Founding Fathers admired), this is the very basis of society. We give up freedoms. We accept taxes and limitations precisely as the price for protection and safety. OK, so they don't agree with Hobbes, but I do! Besides, if you are doing nothing illegal in a public place, what have you got to fear? No one has suggested putting cameras in the homes and bedrooms of American citizens (without a court order). If you are not doing anything wrong, why shouldn't you be caught on security cameras? You might rightly be worried about abuse of data; abuse happens all the time wherever data is collected. We try to stop it, but hackers are everywhere, even without public videos. But in the end we need whatever might protect us. And that, I believe, should be a priority.

The ACLU's mentality is of the same breed as the refusal of so many sections of US society to accept that this kind of violence is indeed a product of Islam. What Islam was intended to be, or was once, is not what huge swaths of it are now. Similarly in Judaism, what was intended and how many practice it or don't is a far cry from its ideal past. Are we to pretend all is healthy and rosy in our garden and not admit what is distorted? Should we say that the religious anti-Zionists who demonstrate with our enemies are not really Jews? I might like to, but it won't help. I thank the Lord they don't explode bombs. But political correctness prevents dealing with issues and only prolongs the agony.

Western states are irrational and all but ungovernable. They encompass so many radically different ideologies, ethnic and religious groups, so many contrasting ways of life. Yet for all that, somehow they find ways, through trial and error, of coping. They are more popular places to live in than those countries that are controlled and commanded by religion or political "isms" that stand in the way of progress and resolution and only delay transformation. You can gauge the success of a country by whether people are clamoring to get in or not!

Yet I believe good governance requires a spiritual, ethical dimension. If I had to put my finger on why the United States has been relatively successful, it is precisely because its founding ethical utilitarianism was combined with a spiritual persuasion, even if it was antinomian and separated officially from state.

To return to civil liberties, nothing better illustrates the difference between a Jewish religious standpoint and the values of the ACLU. Once I believed the ACLU had a vital role to play, like the unions. But now, like the unions, it has betrayed its mandate, and it stands in the way of progress rather than for it. Its prevailing spirit is to enthrone individuality over all else. And while I agree with the importance of individuality, it cannot be the overriding principle in a communitarian world. Look, the United States is indeed dysfunctional. But tell me a country that is not in its own peculiar ways. It is just a matter of which poison you prefer.

Our religious culture assumes we do need checks and balances, a restraining principle. This is provided not just by our moral system, but also by the idea that we are always being watched. As the Mishna in Avot says, "Think of three things and you'll never go wrong; an eye is looking, an ear is hearing and everything is being recorded." Now they were thinking not of the FBI but of God, and of course the obvious difference between them is corruption.

In our tradition, having someone look over your shoulder is a good thing. In my musar Yeshiva (musar is the ethical religious movement started by Rav Israel Salanter (1810–1883) and introduced into Lithuanian yeshivas to raise the moral and spiritual level of yeshiva students), we were all allocated a senior student to keep an eye on us during the day and to tell us in the evening what we had done that was inappropriate or whether there was anything, any characteristic, that could be bettered. We called that moral training. It is no bad thing to imagine that everything is being recorded.

As the Talmudic giant Rebbi Yossi once said, "All my life I have never said anything and then had to turn round to see if anyone was listening." How many of us can say that! Indeed, how many regret half the comments and photos they allowed to go up on Facebook and now feel embarrassed or ashamed! It would be no bad thing to have a friendly heavenly voice telling us when to watch out. In our tradition we have security cameras. God is watching. We live with it! But for others the mechanical kind is better than nothing.

THINKING FAST AND SLOW

I heartily recommend Daniel Kahneman's book, *Thinking, Fast and Slow.* I was won over at the very start when he describes his conversations with his late friend and collaborator Amos Tversky in the Rimon restaurant in downtown Jerusalem, just off Ben Yehuda. Ah, the memories flooded back of the many times I sat there in the 1960s for a quick lunch. But unfortunately it was one year short of their era; otherwise I might have become a wiser man.

The Israeli Nobel Prize winner for economics has written a popular analysis of how we fool ourselves into believing that we think rationally and our actions are logical, most of the time. It would fascinate me anyway because of its insights into human behavior. But, as always, I look for a religious angle and a rationalization for my own religious behavior. Many of the examples are old chestnuts. But I want to focus on two of them that relate to the function of religion.

The main theme of Kahneman's book, supported by many case histories and examples, is that we tend to think on two levels: a fast track, useful for quick and easy decisions, and a slow track for dealing with more complicated and demanding problems. The first includes quasi-automatic behavior like driving a car or solving very simple mental arithmetical calculations and intuitive judgments of people. The other is the much more demanding solving of complex problems and challenges we need to work harder and longer at solving. Too often we use the wrong type of thinking for the relevant problem.

There are two examples he uses that have a bearing on religious behavior. The first is a much-quoted study by the psychologist Walter Mischel and his students in the 1960s. They exposed preschool children to a dilemma. They were given a choice between a small reward, one treat they could have right away, and a larger reward of two treats if they waited fifteen minutes under stressful conditions. They were alone in a room facing a table with a single treat and a bell that the child could ring if he or she wanted the one treat ahead of schedule. No toys or books or other distractions. The experimenter then left the room to return only if the bell was rung, or after fifteen minutes to come with the other treat. Meanwhile, the children and their antics during the waiting period were observed through a one-way mirror and recorded.

About a third of the children managed to wait fifteen minutes for the bigger reward. Ten or fifteen years later, a gap had opened up between the "resisters" and the "indulgers"; the resisters registered a higher degree of executive control in cognitive tasks, especially the ability to redirect their attention effectively, and they were less likely to take drugs. The children who resisted had substantially higher scores on college entrance exams and better "emotional intelligence." Researchers from the University of Oregon took the experiments further and demonstrated a close connection between children's ability to control attention and to control their emotions. I am not interested here in the technical issues or whether one can argue that other factors count just as much—genes, environment, child-rearing. I am only interested in the way this makes so much sense to me, given my utilitarian attitude to ritual in religion.

I have always argued that the purpose of the many behavioral mitzvot, commandments, that regulate us from the moment we wake to the moment we sleep are utilitarian. They are designed to get us to think before we act, to ponder, to appreciate our good health, good fortune, and to try to be positive. It is this that differentiates instinctive behavior from considered behavior. Even if one then acts merely out of habit, the habitual rituals reinforce one set of actions over another, which on balance are preferable for society. Giving charity out of habit is qualitatively more beneficial than not giving at all, although obviously it is better to give with thought, intent, and goodwill.

But more important is the issue of delayed gratification. Whether it is tantric sex or just pausing to say thank you before enjoying something, the benefits are huge. One of the aims of Jewish ritual is precisely this, not as Freud suggests, to deny pleasure, but quite the contrary, to increase it through delay, consideration, and heightened awareness.

The second issue is that of "priming," influencing by suggestion how people act. It is possible to affect the way people behave by giving them sets of words that suggest something. If the idea of "eat" is on your mind, you will be quicker than usual to recognize a word such as "soup" when it is spoken in a whisper or presented visually with a blurred font. In an experiment conducted at New York University, collaborators between eighteen and twenty-two were asked to assemble four-word sentences from five jumbled words. One group was given words that could suggest old age: "forgetful," "bald," "gray," "wrinkle," "Florida." When they had completed their task, they were sent down the hall to do a further experiment. It was the walk that mattered, because as the researcher, John Bargh, had predicted, those who fashioned a sentence out of the "elderly" words walked slower than those who made up sentences of completely different words. They were primed to think of infirmity and moving slowly. Another example, in Arizona in 2000, showed that voter support for a proposition to increase school funding was approved of far more when the polling station was in a school, with its images of classrooms, teachers, books, and pupils.

This explains a lot about the text and purpose of our communal prayers, as opposed to our private and personal ones. It is the value of the set and repeated text of formal prayer throughout the day that primes us with certain concepts and ideas that are at total variance with the language of the workplace. Even if one only concentrates on some of the words, one is being reminded, subliminally or consciously, of alternative—call them spiritual—values and concepts. So even if the intended aim of prayer, to communicate with or be conscious of a divine, spiritual dimension, is not activated, at least the subject matter will have some impact.

I still have not explained why exactly the same rituals can have different effects on different humans. Why do some from identical backgrounds become more charitable or more aggressively evangelical or prefer prayer to study or vice versa? But it does say to me that the intentions of the founders of our religious system were way ahead of their time in putting the emphasis less on theological abstractions and concepts and much more on human behavior. Freud accused Moses of imposing rituals to inhibit and repress. I would argue rather they were intended to help liberate ourselves from that natural human tendency that Kahneman's book is concerned with: to think fast, act out of impulse, and take the easiest options, rather than to think slower, harder, and more rationally to achieve greater self-control and considered action.

HALLOWEEN

Why do I feel so negatively toward Halloween? Surely it's just an opportunity for harmless fun, getting dressed up in weird costumes, festooning homes with horror characters and scenes of witches, dungeons, skeletons, blood, and fear. And what could be bad with kids running from house to house asking for sweets, candies, and gum?

Rituals in most religions are, after all, quite arbitrary. More often than not are based on earlier pagan customs—lights in winter, masks and disguises in spring—and so many of our Jewish customs are borrowed from earlier fears of evil spirits, like driving them away by breaking plates and glasses or covering mirrors and lighting candles. However, it's not the ritual itself but rather what lies behind it that really matters. What is the deeper, real message, as opposed to the superficial one? To be fair, all our major biblical festivals were once pagan celebrations, orgies, or human sacrifices that we sanitized. But what was this sanitization? It was not just to break with the past. It was to require of us to think before acting and to take responsibility for our actions. A religious ritual brings us closer to religious values (or should), whereas a magic ritual brings us closer to magic and unpredictability.

In simple terms, the pagan world believed we were at the mercy of the gods of nature who determined everything that went on in the world. Humans had to placate them. Sacrificing children, rites of blood and magic were ways of winning their approval. It was a world that believed that the greatest gifts we could give were of our bodies, our bodily fluids, and our children. Paganism wanted to perpetuate the fear of the natural world rather than try to overcome fear, because that made you dependent on their magic to survive. Superstition was based on randomness: a black cat, a broken mirror, and you never knew what antidote the shaman would require.

Monotheism emerged as a counterforce to say that although God did represent and control the world, what He wanted was good behavior, good deeds, and respect for humanity. He wanted us to refine our bodies rather than simply use them. In God's religion you knew in advance everything that was expected, even if you might not have always felt able to do it all.

Monotheism introduced the "marshmallow principle" of deferring pleasure, the concepts of self-control and self-improvement. Of course we know how hard this is. How often the Israelites found it much easier, not to say more fun, to go off to pagan orgies. Everything was allowed, not forbidden. Not all pagans were the same, of course. Some tried to rationalize their gods, just as today people justify their actions, lusts, and weaknesses.

Spirits were quite useful in explaining things people didn't understand. If clothes wore out, it was because spirits were tugging at them. If you fell ill, it was because a bad spirit flew through the air to get hold of you. Or else someone else had cursed you or put an evil eye on you. Some rabbis in the Talmud seem to have believed in evil spirits, sheydim. The Talmud even contains advice as to how to see them. You should spread sand at night and look for the footprints in the morning, or kill a black cat that has just given birth and spread the ashes of its placenta over your eyes. Perhaps they accepted the credulity of simple people, and they did not want to take their props away from them. It also gave them power and a useful tool for helping the weak and the sick.

Overwhelmingly the greatest of rabbis argued that there was no such thing as luck, *mazal*, in Israel. It was a characteristic of the non-Jewish world, not ours. It was our actions that determined what we made of our lives, what happened to us as individuals and as a people. However, they conceded that if a people or society was doomed, innocents would suffer the consequences too. And external forces, both natural and human, could be unleashed to terrible effect. Our world was one of human choice, not helplessness in the presence of magic or ghosts. The downside, of course, was and is that humans make the wrong choices sometimes.

Why does superstition persist among us now after all this time? Perhaps it's because Jews suffered so much for so long that they needed emotional, magical, superstitious support and turned to any crazy idea that might help them get through the day and the night. Even now we seem helpless and confused in the face of so much antipathy.

What I have against Halloween is that it reinforces the fear of magic and evil spirits, even if most people have lost the significance of the occasion or refuse to make it. The witches, wizards, and devils are all symbolic of the uncontrollable pagan world. They are linked to the world of tarot cards, astrologers, and pseudo-kabbalists with their spells, their tricks, and their magic to help you cope by giving you dishonest but plausible answers.

As our society has become more scientific, more rational, and yet more stressful and demanding to live in, we seek these placebos and fake answers. We become even more superstitious and dependent. We go to horror films. We love zombies and vampires. We want to see more blood, more violence, more terror, more corpses, and more humans suffer, even as we need to know it will all turn out fine in the end because some superhero or strongman will eventually save everyone and good will triumph.

There's another issue here. We are becoming anaesthetized to blood and horror, just as there's a danger that the violent computer games that are so popular also affect our sensitivity to suffering and pain. The jury is still out, of course, but my gut tells me that glorifying blood and gore cannot be a healthy thing.

It's true that all this Halloween nonsense can be harmless, and perhaps I am taking it too seriously. But I strongly believe that if as parents we encourage such customs that do not convey the positive values that really matter, we had better make sure we give enough counterexamples of the thinking, caring, and spiritual world if we want our children to learn a positive lesson.

JAMES JOYCE AND THE JEWS

Gordon Bowker's recent biography of James Joyce reminds me why I have such a soft spot for Joyce in contrast, say, to George Bernard Shaw, another Irish writer but one who was openly anti-Semitic.

Much has been written about Jews in Western literature. But what is it that determines whether writers are pro-Jewish or anti-? Shakespeare's *The Merchant of Venice* and Marlowe's *The Jew of Malta* were both written at a time when Jews were perceived as dangerous, evil aliens. If either ever had met a Jew, it would have been a refugee from Iberia who was trying very hard to disguise his Jewishness because Jews were still officially banned from England.

Why, one asks, did Shakespeare manage to look for something positive in Shylock and even give him some strong arguments in his defense, whereas Marlowe's Jew is just a nasty, evil, unattractive caricature? How is it that George Eliot could write *Daniel Deronda*, in which a Jewish character is portrayed as a noble idealist, while most of her contemporaries, such as Trollope and even Dickens, saw them merely as financial manipulators and unsavory upstarts?

To be fair, Dickens did have a character called Riach. Some have tried to argue that he gets his name from the Carpathian pronunciation of *ruach*, spirit and he represents the "good Jew." Martin Amis is far removed from his anti-Semitic father might stand in for the "good gentile" in contrast to American-born T. S. Eliot who describes Jews in the crudest and most negative of terms. James Joyce too, saw the good in Jews. He gave Leopold Bloom a starring and sympathetic role in *Ulysses*. And he personally helped many escape from Europe when the Nazi disease began to spread.

It is not just in literature that Jews were defamed or caricatured. In 1655 Oliver Cromwell convened the Whitehall Conference to rescind the 1290 expulsion of Jews from England. But to his surprise he found that both the church and commercial interests were strongly opposed. He had to let the matter drop (and turned a blind eye to the small number of refugees). In New York, Peter Stuyvesant refused to allow Jewish refugees from Brazil to settle until the Dutch West India Company overruled him. In 1753 both houses of Parliament, and King George II all agreed to give the Jews equal rights; but the outcry was so great, again from church and business (both fearing competition), that the bill was repealed after it was initially passed. Horace Walpole, commenting on the fiasco, said that it was "an affair which showed how much the age, enlightened as it is called, was still enslaved to the grossest and most vulgar prejudices." This ambivalence toward Jews, more than to any other minority I can think of, runs deep and strong throughout Europe, and indeed many other Christian and Muslim societies. Outsiders are rarely popular, and we are the archetypal outsiders. Our survival stands as a challenge to the dominant aspirations of those religions that hoped to supersede us.

This brings me back to James Joyce, because he was one of the few writers who actually saw the morally corrosive, destructive influence of church and society, and made the difficult decision to flee Ireland to get away from the pettiness as soon as he could. The Italy he escaped to was just as bad, but at least it was different, and he had cut the umbilical cord. I suggest that this was precisely why he could identify with the Jews of his day. They were the underdogs. The Irish struggled for independence from the British occupiers, and during the great migration of Jews from Eastern Europe, a significant number ended up in Ireland, where they flourished. Irish society was always divided between the rural primitives and the urban elites, the ruling classes and the workers. The Jews were regarded with fascination but not revulsion. Yet there are plenty of other writers from minority or oppressed groups who are unremittingly and illogically anti-Semitic.

Irish politics has changed since Joyce's day. The struggle with the old enemy, Britain, has been won. After staying neutral in the Second World War, even being partly pro-Nazi, Ireland joined the EU and has adopted much of its mentality. So that now again the Jews are seen as the aggressors and manipulators. Attitudes toward Jews have run a gamut of emotions from fear of the different to sympathy for the underdog to anger at their strength. One senses this transition in Irish public opinion today as much as one sees it manifest in the attitude of the Church of England, which is increasingly antagonistic to Israel. This, together with the old Marxist hatreds, has transmogrified into political correctness that picks specifically on Israel and, inevitably, Jews.

Underdogs love to turn on others when they emerge from their inferiority, and so the tables have turned. Now in Ireland, as in London, the mere whiff of an Israeli sportsman or actor is enough to bring out crowds of howling furies (none, as far as I am aware, seem to be so offended by Assad or the caliphate). One is no longer surprised at the overt hatred of acclaimed writers and academics, for they all have their biases and blind spots. But the worse it gets the more we should treasure those few great writers who did not succumb to anti-Semitism in one of its forms or another.

The fact is that I have adored Joyce for other, purely literary reasons. Ever since I first read the Victorian poet Gerard Manley Hopkins, I realized how excited I was by the ability to create a language of one's own, to play with words and manipulate them for literary effect. No one does it better than Joyce. True, that makes him difficult to read, and the more banal modern literature becomes, the less inclined people are to want to struggle with a book. And Joyce's *Finnegan's Wake* is even harder to read than *Ulysses.*

And here comes my version of "Joyce and the Jewish Question." Maybe the reason I love Joyce is because with him, as with our religion, it is not for the fainthearted or those who want an easy life. Joyce struggled and suffered. Only if you struggle with it, with life in general, do you get to appreciate its majesty.

DANIEL DERONDA

"Every Jew should rear his family as if he hoped a Deliverer might spring from it."

Amazingly this is a quote from a great non-Jewish Victorian authoress, George Eliot. It is from her last novel, *Daniel Deronda*, and the words are those of Daniel's father as reported by Daniel's apostate mother who represents the self-hating Jew eager to abandon her religion to succeed in an alien world. Yet at the very end she is still capable of remembering the nobility of one of those who remained committed to Judaism.

You may have seen the recent TV adaptation recently shown in Britain. I don't think it did justice to the book in many ways, but that is not my point here. George Eliot did a lot of research, took Hebrew lessons, and read widely on Jewish history and religion before writing the book. Her notebooks indicate the extent to which she was familiar with Midrashic and Halachic sources.

Daniel Deronda is adopted by a kindly, honorable English gentleman. He grows up in a privileged world believing himself to be the illegitimate son of his "uncle." After rescuing a suicidal Jewish girl from the Thames, he slowly gets drawn into the Jewish world and finally returns to his roots. The story ends with his setting off east to try and establish a home for the Jews in the Land of Israel.

Eliot describes the differences between the noble and the ignoble in English society, its prejudices and the way circumstances affect people in different ways. The exploration of Judaism contrasts the less well-educated Jews, some good, some disreputable, with the idealistic and the scholarly. In both societies there are good and bad, realists and idealists, those who rise above misfortune and those who succumb.

Prejudices and ignorance about Judaism are exposed. The book is a plea to look at Jews as human beings, not as stereotypes. Bear in mind that this was written as anti-Semitism was regarded as quite normal among European literary circles. Remarkably Eliot, through the mystical Mordecai, argues powerfully for a Jewish homeland. Deronda spurns the love of an English rose who seems devoid of any spiritual dimension. Instead he chooses a dark-eyed Jewish beauty who has suffered loss and trauma and even attempted suicide. He discovers that his mother was a Jewess who desperately and vainly tried to hide her Jewish identity in the hope of assimilating into the upper classes. He gives up a comfortable existence as an English gentleman for the uncertainties of life as a practicing Jew.

Here's another quote from the book. This is Deronda describing Mordecai to Mrs Meyrick:

> I call a man fanatical when his enthusiasm is narrow and hoodwinked so that he has no sense of proportions and becomes unjust and unsympathetic to men who are out of his tack. Mordecai's an enthusiast I should like to keep that word for the highest order of minds—those who care supremely for grand and general benefits to mankind. He is full of allowance for the condition of other Jews.

I can't think of a better way of describing how an Orthodox Jew should appear to the rest of the world. Neither can I think of a better description of the narrow-mindedness we ought to avoid. Enthusiasts of the world unite!

SPARE THE ROD

"Spare the rod and spoil the child," goes the old English saying. It is based on the line in the book of Proverbs 13:24 "He who holds back (from using) his stick, hates his child." The stick is a poetic way of talking about the need for and benefit of discipline. But like so many other biblical texts, it was taken too literally. The principle may well be true. If you care about your child, you should discipline him or her. Not to do so is an act of selfish indulgence and cowardice. But to use corporal punishment? I am strongly opposed to it.

If we stick to traditional Halachic attitudes, the sixteenth-century Shulchan Aruch in the section dealing with teaching Torah says, "A teacher must not hit his pupils cruelly and aggressively with staffs and rods but with little straps" (Yoreh Deah 245). It is true the Talmud warms against overdoing the physical assault on your elder son for fear of driving him away and into bad company. And although a flick round the ear is even recommended by Maimonides for the rebellious wife, the most the Talmud allows is a display of husbandly temper if it helps keep everyone in line.

I was a very, very naughty boy. Some people think I still am. My father, who was also my headmaster, used the cane on me more times than I care to recall. He always prefaced the beating with the mantra "This is going to hurt me more than it will hurt you," and the fact was that after a few hours of stinging pain I was soon back to my old tricks. In my father's last weeks of life, he apologized to me for hitting me. I remember reassuring him that

I thought I really deserved it. He had, as I grew older, compensated for his early strictness by establishing a different and deeper kind of relationship, which sadly came to an end far too quickly with his death at the age of forty-eight. And it was this positive relationship that had a far greater impact on my life than the negative beatings. But those were the times. That was accepted in a British society that thought the best schools should allow elder pupils to bully and beat younger ones, that it would toughen them up and equip them to run the empire. No wonder it collapsed. Incidents from *Tom Brown's School Days* were considered the norm.

When I became headmaster of Carmel some ten years after my father died (the classic case of a poacher turned gamekeeper), I found the very canes that had been used on me behind the desk in the headmaster's study and I destroyed them. Did caning make me a violent person? I sincerely hope not, and I recoil from physical violence to this day. I am excessively squeamish. Yet I have lost my temper with my children on, I am glad to say, very rare occasions. But lashing out physically is a sign of a lost temper. And as the Talmud says, "An angry man has no God." God requires of us self-control.

Britain has for a very long time been a society with a strong undercurrent of violence beneath the outwardly controlled and polite exteriors. The darker sides of Victorian England were almost certainly due to the violence perpetrated on the upper classes by corporal punishment and bullying in their top schools. The working classes suffered from excessive degrees of violence from their masters and as a result exerted it in turn on their children and wives. Sexual excesses are very often the result of childhood repression and frustrations, and most of the people I know who exercise no sexual self-control are seriously underdeveloped human beings.

Nowadays in many parts of the so-called civilized world, corporal punishment is forbidden in schools, but there is still some resistance to forbidding it at home. In Britain the government decided to throw out a bill making any physical act against a child illegal. The proponents of the bill argued that

Britain has the worst record of child deaths in Europe and that child abuse tends to start with a slap and end up with multiple assaults. The traditionalists on both sides argued that to criminalize a parental slap would lead to nonsensical prosecutions, and as we have seen recently, it is easy to prosecute the innocent on matters of child abuse. We have also seen how incompetent social services invariably are in dealing with the real cases. The issue of a slap is now the subject of a popular television series that originated in Australia and has been adapted in the United States.

It is a bad sign if a parent loses his or her temper. It is a sign of failure and weakness. Societies that allow violence at any level too easily become unhealthy societies. If parental discipline is not considered and controlled, it can become disastrous. The answer though does not always lie in legislation so much as in personal values. I loved my father more than I can describe, but although I cringe at the thought that he might have been prosecuted had this law been passed, hitting children is still something we must avoid.

Good family upbringing is essential for a healthy society. So much of what is wrong in America is indeed due to the breakdown of family life and the rarity of parents and children interacting positively, eating together and spending quality and intellectually stimulating time together. Children of intellectually interactive parents will acquire a much wider vocabulary than those of parents who do not communicate as much.

But what happens if we have bad or careless or absentee parents? One of the episodes in the Bible deals with the rebel Korach in the book of Numbers who tried to usurp the mantles of both Moses and Aaron. The Midrash says that Korach's wife encouraged him to rebel and challenge the logic and consistency of Moses's leadership, whereas another plotter, On Ben Pelet's wife, encouraged him to withdraw from the fight and covered up for him when he was too scared to pull out. The text first says that all Korach's family perished. But a little farther on, it says the sons of Korach did not die. We need not go into textual discrepancies or contradictions. The traditional approach is to use every textual variation to learn a lesson.

In this case the Midrash learns that it is possible for sons to overcome the handicaps of a poor or troubled background. A person in the end is responsible for his or her own mistakes, but a good, caring upbringing and a parent or parents in the home can make all the difference!

TATTOOS

I hate tattoos with such a passion it's almost illogical. Nowadays you can hardly open your eyes without seeing them: the faded black, dirty red, dark blue, and mud green, on arms, ankles, butts, necks, and, most revoltingly, whole arms or legs or torsos. It's not my idea of art. There's nothing beautiful or aesthetic in them (I guess "pop art" might disprove that opinion), just ritualized self-desecration and self-mutilation. Yet almost every soccer player, Hollywood actor, or model seems to need one or many. Getting a tat together is even considered a way of mothers and daughters bonding.

All over the New York subway, you find adverts offering to remove tattoos. I guess if "Lola Forever" has turned into "Lola the Slut," you'll not want to advertise the fact. Or if Joe no longer loves you, you might not attract new custom if his name stares up at a suitor whenever you undress! Crosses become a problem if you convert to Islam and vice versa. I am reliably informed that California plastic surgeons are swamped with requests to undo circumcisions! I suppose there was a time when circumcisions were less visible than most tattoos. Clearly this is no longer the case in San Francisco!

Why do I hate tattoos so? Well, frankly, it started as a class thing back in postwar Britain. Then the only people who had tattoos were lower ranks in the armed services and, in particular, sailors who had the reputation of either having a man or a woman in every port! Think of Popeye and his anchor. Tattoo parlors were seedy, tobacco-shrouded cells you would pass in the red-light district of Soho (I was only passing through MiLud) or the back streets of cold, wet, and seedy British holiday resorts, surrounded by cheap stores selling rock, candy floss, and Kiss Me Quick T-shirts.

Rockers and brutish motorbike riders who travelled in gangs and associated with the criminal classes flaunted tattoos. The murderers in Sam Peckinpah films always had tattoos. And there were stories about needles spreading diseases, and drugs and abortions. So in my youth, respectable youngsters would no more have entertained the idea of getting a tattoo than they would have considered castration!

Then there was my Jewish upbringing. The Torah describes how Jewish men removed their jewelry after the golden-calf episode, so I knew that good Jewish boys wouldn't wear jewelry. And only Hebrew slaves who couldn't face freedom had their ears pierced, so I certainly wasn't going to have an earring and be identified as a slave. Similarly, tattoos were against the law, as stated in Leviticus 20:28, "You shall not make any cuttings in your flesh for the dead, nor print any marks upon you; I am the Lord." So leaving aside the residual class snobbery of my English upbringing, my Jewish side was heavily antithetic to tattoos.

Another reason for a Jewish reaction against tattoos was that the Nazis tattooed numbers on the arms of their victims. Tattooing was a reminder of hell on earth. Who in his or her right mind would want that?

From a situation where no self-respecting man or woman would sport a tattoo, before my eyes, society began to change. The pop culture of the sixties, the films *A Clockwork Orange* and *If*, angry young men like the playwright John Osborne, and working-class actors like Terence Stamp and Tom Courtenay all helped elevate cockney and working-class culture into the icon of the day, so that upper-class snobs started trying to speak like Michael Caine and cockney photographer David Bailey became an honorary aristocrat. Slowly the values and standards and hypocrisies of Victorian England were turned upon their heads. This process took time and slowly gathered pace as British society opened up and sucked in millions of others. Even so I do not recall the Beatles having tattoos.

In one way I welcomed the collapse of the old, class-ridden, racist, hypocritical standards. As a Jew I no longer felt the need to hide, to be a Jew at home and a Brit in public. But a lot of the change was for the worse. Fashion came to dictate morality and superficiality, and dumbing down slowly swept away the good standards with the bad. Yet together with the deterioration (others might prefer to use the word "evolution") of certain respects of Western secular standards, scientific and medical expertise continued to advance. One result of this was the ability to change our appearances through plastic surgery. Now it is possible to totally transform the way people look. Sadly, the Barbie doll look became the ideal that millions of Western females began to aspire to and plastic surgery enabled. In many groups, even in very Orthodox, wealthy communities, you can see lots of these clones. Inner qualities gave way almost exclusively to outer appearance, and outer is dictated entirely by the entertainment and fashion industry. I guess Torah values still leave plenty of room for individuals to pursue their own holy grails!

Nevertheless, you will not find tattoos in Orthodox communities (except among late arrivals who were brought up secularly and then became religious). New Halachic literature does discuss the issue of tattoos and where you can put your *tefillin* on them or not, so there must be quite a lot of new arrivals with tattoos in place. And in fact this was the case in Roman and Persian times. But to intentionally have one when one is aware of the religious prohibition makes a nonsense of say, Madonna's claim to be a kabbalist. The very proof that her kabbalah has absolutely nothing to do with Judaism is her fashion for tattooing spurious kabbalistic hocus-pocus onto her body.

Now that Entertainment and Fashion have become, for millions, the gods of the twenty-first century, if they decide tattoos are good, then everyone has to think that tattoos are good. But I find them ugly. Tat as in tattoo! Is this the result of my childhood conditioning? I don't think so. Because objectively, aesthetically, tattoos are limited both in color and form, far more restricted than other forms of art. I always liked bold bright colors. But even the latest and brightest tattoos are faded and dull in comparison to, say, an Yves Klein blue. I'm not going to say it has no value at all, but rather as pop is to classical, it is ephemeral and transient.

I am of course excluding anthropological and ethnic tattoos from my condemnation. They are required by some societies and have important functions in defining the class systems and the rituals of others. They do indeed play an important part in their culture. But in ours? We are no longer cannibals.

Sure, there are some intelligent academics who wear ponytails, earrings, and tattoos. And usually it is a safe bet that they align themselves with views that are the antithesis of mine on Jewish identity and Israel's right to exist. Real value lies in something far deeper than tattooing or piercing one's body. Their current omnipresence is a sign of our times, and not everything in our times is for the best. When Angelina Jolie's or Madonna's or David Beckham's body decoration becomes the touchstone of what society approves of, I know we are in real trouble!

KNAIDEL

In 2014 a young Indian boy living in New York won the National Spelling Bee, the annual spelling championship. The winning spell was "knaidel," that Yiddish description of a mixture of matzo meal, egg, fat, and spices, rolled into a ball we usually put in our chicken soup. Incidentally, I cannot imagine any spelling competition in Europe that would include a Yiddish word. That would offend too many sensitivities. But that was not what caused a kerfuffle in New York. Almost immediately the press was afire with controversy. How can you say there is only one spelling? Would he have been wrong had he suggested "kneydle"? After all, that's how Max Weinreich's authoritative *History of the Yiddish Language* spells it!

The derivation of this Yiddish word is from the German "knoedel," a kind of dumpling. The fact that eastern European Jews spoke Yiddish, a language that derived from German rather than from a Caucasian dialect, knocks into oblivion the infantile theory, first proposed by Arthur Koestler, that Ashkenazi Jews (Zionists) really descended from non-Jewish Khazars. It suits anti-Israelis to pretend there never was a link between Jews today and the Land of Israel. Every clever mind has a blind spot.

But Yiddish is a strange language that was and is pronounced differently across the geographical and sectarian divide. There is an old joke about how it is possible to write Noah (in Hebrew) making seven mistakes when it was spelled with only two letters in the Torah. But take Moses's name. It is spelled and pronounced Moshe, Moishe, Mowshe, Moyshe, and Maishe in different communities.

What I know as a kneydel is sometimes pronounced in the Jewish world as keneydel, kneydl, knoedel, kniydl, and kenedel. Yiddish was spoken in a sort of European dog dialect but usually written in Hebrew characters, and how it was transcribed varied from locale to locale. Who on earth has any authority to say one spelling or pronunciation is right and the other is wrong? OK, so the French have a centralized Académie Française that decides to the letter what is correct and what is not, and that probably explains why France is such a mess and most of us would only live there if we had no alternative except for very short periods of the year, usually summertime.

As for transliteration, it really is quite arbitrary. It is all but impossible to say that only one version can be the correct one. It can only be whatever convention, the publisher, institution, or person chooses to follow. I have in the past month been invited to contribute essays to three different institutional publications, and each one sent me a sheet giving the required translations, transliterations, and styles *it* requires, and they all differ. To be fair, I am hardly consistent. I use "Pesah" when writing for a Sephardi audience but "Pesach" for an Ashkenazi one. Sometimes it is "Rosh Hashannah" and on others "Shana." It might be Sukkah or Suca or Sucah. I often write the word "Charedi" but also Haredi, Hassidism, Hasidism, or Chassidism.

Take the Hebrew word for a wise man. A Sephardi will call him a haham (and by the way, why *ph* instead of *f* in Sefardi, for goodness sakes?). Others, mainly academic, will prefer an *h* with a dot underneath. I prefer *ch*, and others insist on *k* with or without a dot, and yet others *kh*. I have often used an *h* without a dot. Sometimes it simply depends on what side of the bed I wake up on. And how do you spell and write "Chanukah"? Hanukkah, Hannuka, Hanuka, Chanooka, Chanuka, or Chanukah? When do you decide there will be an *h* at the end of a Hebrew word? Only when there's a final *hey*, *hay*, *hei*, or *he*?

Neither can we agree about the word or the spelling for what men put on their heads. Is it a capel (or cuppel or cupel or kapel or kappell), a kippa (or kipa or cipah), let alone yarmulker, yahmulkah, or perhaps a toupee? Can only one be right? Translation is subjective, we know. The Latin word for betrayal is virtually the same as "translate." What then of pronunciation, spelling, and transliteration? Can there only be one correct spelling? Of course not. That would be arrogant, inconsistent, unfair, and dishonest. We are corrupting the minds and values of innocent young spelling champions, imposing our subjective and arbitrary decisions on them as a matter of life or death, or financial reward.

But, you see, that's one of the curses of our era. We want to know exactly how a word is spelled (or spelt), pronounced and written. We want to know exactly what it means, even if by now we have all heard Wittgenstein's aphorism that "the meaning of a word is its use." We want everything prepackaged, predigested, predecided, in black and white, with no room for variety, variation, or inconsistency. In fact, real humans are not like that. And if young Arvind Mahankali (the winner) wants to be a great scientist as he says, he'd better get out of the habit of accepting arbitrary conventions.

And that's my gripe with Judaism nowadays. People are too busy defining! Are you Reform? Conservative? Reconstructionist? New Age? Modern Orthodox? Orthodox? Ultra-Orthodox? Yeshivish? Chasidic (one or two *s*'s?), Charedi (Haredi)? And are you Ashkenazi, Yekke, Pollack, Litvak, Hungarian, Romanian, Ukrainian, or White Russian? Are you Moroccan, Egyptian, Syrian, Iraqi, or Persian? And I can tell you the difference between how a Jew from Glasgow, Manchester, Leeds, or London pronounces his Hebrew and thinks he's better for it is nothing to the differences between a Mashadi, a Kashani, an Esfahandi, and a Teherani!

Do you "keep" glatt, gebrocks, cholov Yisroel (Yisroel, Yisrael, Israel)? Are you shomer negia, shomer shabbes, or shomer fiddle your neighbor? And now in Golders Green we have another one called "shomer interfere with someone else's wife." But for that you need a full beard.

If I refer to a member of the Jewish clergy do I use the word rav, rebbe, rebbi, rabbi, or Rah Bi (yes I do know that's derogatory, Bad for Me, in Hebrew, but that was how the late Rav Moshe Feinstein used to dismiss Conservative and Reform rabbis). And when it comes to liturgical systems in Judaism is it Nusach (Nusah) Ashkenazi, Italqui, Sefardi or Nusach Sfard) ? And does one pray in a shtible or shtiebel or shtibel. Either way, someone will say its either wrong or spelled incorrectly.

Gosh, we take ourselves so seriously. Where's the humor? Where's the variety, and why, for goodness' sake, can't we embrace differences and love them, instead of using them to discriminate, humiliate, and to fight about, let alone to prize young love apart? So don't tell me how to spell, or pronounce or enunciate, and above all, don't tell me that your customs or nuances or idiosyncrasies are essential to being a good Jew or anything else. And if you do not agree, you are an apostate or an ignoramus!

ASSISTED SUICIDE

Religious authorities have submitted opinions on the issue of "patient assisted dying" to the government and to the House of Lords in the United Kingdom. Universally, they are opposed on various grounds. The most common objection is that people might be pressured to end their lives when in other situations they might not want to. Perhaps a younger generation eager to inherit or an older one reluctant to take on responsibility might apply pressure in subtle or unsubtle ways. Perhaps a hospital needs a bed or a care home the room. But then we get the usual simplistic generalizations like "we believe in the sanctity of life" or "our bodies do not belong to us alone." I strongly object to religious leaders in Britain and elsewhere speaking on my behalf, and I object to the arguments and positions they took. They certainly do not speak for me. But nowadays everyone seems to think they can speak on behalf of everyone else.

Euthanasia is an evil idea. Dr. Mengele was only one in a long list of German pseudoscientists who wanted to refine the human race. Their views were associated with the theory of eugenics. Humans with deficient or antisocial genes could and should be eliminated. Of course no religion, no civilized society could possibly support such a program. Judaism and most religions do indeed take the sanctity of life very seriously. We do not distinguish between one human life and another, and we expect in principle each person to accept his or her allotted life span.

But let us differentiate between euthanasia, putting people to death, and suicide. As a citizen of a liberal democracy, I believe society should permit lots of things that I personally or through my commitment to Torah totally reject for myself. For example, we allow humans to bequeath millions of pounds to animals rather than to humans. As a Jew what I allow is within the framework of Halacha and with the limitations that Halacha imposes. As a citizen of the world, I believe women who are not circumscribed by Torah should be allowed to have abortions much more freely, but not late-term abortions. Yes, it is true that civil law does indeed intervene and set limitations. Similarly societies try to regulate experiments with stem cells and genetic engineering, although it is far from clear if they can succeed in slowing down progress or agreeing on how to. If science is to have a voice in all this, so too should religion. But if religious views should be included in the debate, I do not believe they should be determining or imposing on others. Too often religion has and is standing in the way of progress for no valid reason.

So given the caveats, if a person out of strong personal desire wishes to end his life, I believe he should be allowed to. The counterargument is that under extreme pain one may rush into a mistaken decision simply to escape agony.

But most of the cases we have been reading about recently concern people who are suffering from degenerative diseases or serious incapacity and decide, calmly and rationally, they do not want to continue. The late Arthur Koestler and his wife decided together they did not want to go on living and quietly took their own lives. No doubt had they failed they would have been prosecuted and jailed.

Most health systems do whatever they can to assuage pain. Most hospitals allow giving cancer patients morphine to reduce pain even when they know full well that this will hasten death. And indeed there is sufficient Halachic authority to justify this. One cannot do anything to hasten death as an act in itself. But one may help relieve a patient of suffering even if there may be other consequences down the line. The two sisters from Iran, joined at the head and who sadly died on the operating table, illustrate the predominant Halachic position. So long as there was a reasonable chance of success, so long as death was not a foregone conclusion, they had the right to try.

No one is going to introduce legislation compelling or pressuring. But if, with safeguards and involving a range of opinions of those close to the person concerned, Britain were to follow the example of Holland and Switzerland, I as a British citizen would welcome this.

"When a person dies in a tent" (Numbers 19:14) is the phrase used in the Bible to preface a section that deals with ritual purity (not to be confused with cleanliness). Rabbinic interpretation moves the subject away from its original theme and plays with the word "tent" to imply the tent of academic study and say that a person should be prepared to die in the process of struggling to master Torah. In another source it is adapted to being prepared to die for Judaism. But this figurative talk cannot be taken to mean that they literally approved of suicide even in a good cause. Martyrdom was highly controversial, and the issue split Judaism at the time of Greek as well as Christian oppression. Similarly being prepared to die for one's religion was interpreted differently at different times. It always struck me as so humane that even if one contravened a religious principle under duress, rabbinic authorities tended to turn blind eyes and humanely respect that people are frail beings who cannot always cope with what life throws at them.

No, I don't approve religiously of suicide. But as a free citizen of a free country, I approve of maximum freedom so long as I do not harm others. Regardless of the standards I may set myself, I think, by law, people should be free to end their own lives if they want to. I know I do not want to be resuscitated if I am stricken with a serious illness and the quality of my life will be dramatically impaired. But only I should be allowed to make that decision and to make it without pressure or duress from the outside.

ELECTRICITY

When a virus attacked the Microsoft network a few years ago, it wrought disruptive damage to its system and mine. I spent hours trying to get MSN technical assistance. Anyone who has had to deal with these technical centers knows what it's like. You get a whole raft of automated questions before you even get a chance to wait for the next available assistant. The lines are busy, everyone needs help, and then after perhaps after an hour and a half you get an Indian lady whom you couldn't understand or a Montana logger who couldn't understand you, and after a further half hour of trying and failing to put things right, they ask you to wait and you never hear from them again. By Wednesday, after four different fruitless waits, I had given up and was looking around for an alternative means of transmitting my weekly rush of quasi-religious adrenalin to you.

Such happenings, being cut off from the Internet, or worse, an electric power cut, can be sobering. They can make us angry and catatonic. But they can also serve as important lessons on the extent to which we take our modern facilities and inventions for granted to the point of utter dependency. In big cities we become arrogantly smug, looking down at those who live benighted lives remote from civilization. Americans live under much more extreme conditions than the British who are ill-prepared for their heat waves or for their big freezes. Their equipment and their utilities are usually unable to cope with extremes. In the United States whole cities from Phoenix to Miami can function only because of air conditioning. And that is dependent on the electricity required to run it all. But wherever we are, we take electricity (and potable water) for granted and rarely think twice about it until there is a crisis.

Several years ago I experienced such a crisis in New York. At 4:30 p.m. on Thursday, August 14, the city was completely blacked out. Millions were trapped in the subways and trains as the afternoon rush to escape the city was underway. People were stuck in elevators, in cinemas and department stores, without air conditioning or light. Traffic gridlocked in the streets because the traffic lights were not working. Tunnels in and out of Manhattan were blocked, no ventilation, the tollbooths unable to function. As time went on, refrigerators and iceboxes lost their coldness, and vast amounts of food began to rot. The telephones were not working, neither landlines nor mobiles. You couldn't boil water or cook unless you had gas. There was no television, no electronic entertainment, only battery-operated radios if you were lucky enough to have prepared them in advance. If you were in an apartment block, say twenty or thirty floors up, the elevators were not working, and unless you were really fit, you were stuck. Looking out of the window, you could see thousands and thousands of office workers trekking homeward on foot, clogging up the sidewalks and most of the traffic lanes.

For those of us who keep a traditional Shabbat (and for outdoor survivalists) the experience was not as unnerving as it might have been. We are used to managing without electrical appliances and even sitting in the gathering dusk. We are used to not using the phone, cooking, or watching the box. We do it once a week. We are used to walking or climbing stairs. I won't pretend there were not anxieties. The unknown is always a challenge. Uncertainty is always destabilizing when you cannot plan ahead or know when the period of abstinence will end. But having to go through Shabbat and festivals regularly living a different sort of existence, not completely independent of electricity but certainly less dependent, has its benefits. There is some similarity with the experience of fasting, unpleasant though it may be. You at least know that you can survive, you know your capacity, and it certainly makes you more appreciative of what you normally take for granted.

The one common and universal link in all Jewish rituals is that they all get a person to think about daily actions in contrast to the habitual norm and what everyone else in the world is doing, the way a person behaves and the things they do. If one thinks about one's actions instead of simply performing trance-like mimes, one inevitably appreciates the nature of one's life, the pleasures one derives and the positive rather than the negative. Making the best of things and looking on the bright side become essential aspects of one's daily life. Doing without or restraining oneself always heightens the pleasure when one gets a chance to do the very same thing later on in a different context. It is an important assertion of what differentiates (or should) Jewish culture from pop culture.

The power came back on at 6:30 in the morning. Major relief. Everyone talked about the great spirit of mutual support under and above ground, the New York spirit (the spirit of Dunkirk, of being in bunkers or sealed rooms in Israel), rising to the occasion. When a person is deprived, it makes one think and appreciate all the things normally taken for granted when they came back on again. And if accidentally it made us more thinking, grateful humans, then why not go through the same process regularly but with intention rather than by accident?

It needn't take God or religion to impose a thinking lifestyle upon us. However, we do seem to take it more seriously if it is indeed associated with a spiritual dimension, a forceful tradition and feeling for community solidarity and common values. Perhaps that is why so often in the Torah, perfectly rational laws like being a good neighbor and doing the right thing are predicated on obeying God. It is not just a matter of common sense. On the other hand, religious observance or commitment can also be the result of individual choice, of human endeavor. People are different and think and behave differently, so approaches to religion are bound to vary too.

People outside of Orthodox Judaism find the prohibition on using electricity on Shabbat and festivals unfathomable. It even sounds regressive and

Luddite. And it seems even less logical given that you can have all the benefits, provided you arrange it all beforehand or by using time switches. They can in theory understand the advantages of giving oneself a break from the tyranny of the cell phone or the constant thumping of music or the television one day a week. All the more so if instead one concentrates on human interaction, talking, reading, and doing family activities together.

The Torah forbade fire on Shabbat not because it was work but because it was how society ran in those days. Electricity is its modern application. We were reminded that once we were slaves to society. Now we could free ourselves, not by denying in a masochistic way the benefits of human ingenuity, but rather by appreciating it all the more, for having to relate to it in a different way once a week.

We have indeed become slaves to technology. I believe that the deeper we are sucked into a society whose god is electricity, the greater the need to free ourselves from such slavery every now and again. Electricity, regardless of where it comes from, has its benefits, but it also has its costs. Freedom is the right to be different, to assert our humanity. But as with many things, it takes a crisis to wake us up or get us to rethink our lives and see things differently.

SOCCER HOOLIGANISM

I am getting old! English soccer today is not what it was. There is barely a handful of local players in the top clubs. It is predominantly a game of foreign stars, foreign managers, and yahoos with bodies heavily tattooed and barbaric haircuts, all gesticulating at cameras, the crowd, and heaven. In my day if you scored a goal, the scorer modestly acknowledged the applause and perhaps got a slap on the back. Nowadays they are hugged and kissed and disappear beneath a mountain of bodies and limbs before getting up to do a war dance in front of the cameras. They reveal their naked torsos or messages painted on their undershirts. Now there is the addition of neo-fascist salutes and abusive gestures. And of course at long last, something we have known for years and been unable to change, FIFA the governing body of the game, is now finally exposed as a corrupt self-perpetuating oligarchy. Which, given the claims of the guilty that it is all a Zionist plot, leads me to anti-Semitism.

Supporters of the London soccer club Tottenham Hotspur attract the violent attention of fascist thugs occasionally when they play in England but almost always wherever they travel abroad. Soccer is a battleground in Europe and too often an outlet for racism and Judeophobia. It has now spread right across the European Union.

In Britain, football clubs were often in the past proxies for religious wars. In cities like Liverpool, Manchester, and Glasgow, the major clubs were traditionally and until recently either Protestant or Catholic. I once experienced a Glasgow Rangers versus Celtic derby sitting between a Catholic priest and a minister of the Church of Scotland. When the Protestants stood to sing the national anthem, "God Save the Queen," the Catholic half of the stadium booed and cursed. And when the Catholics sang their anthem, "You'll Never Walk Alone," the Protestants erupted in vitriol, hurling abuse at the pope. I was kissed on my right check when Rangers scored and on my left when Celtic did. Mercifully, the game ended in a 1–1 draw.

For some reason, London avoided the religious divide. Most Jews in working-class London tended to support Arsenal, whereas the more genteel middle classes went for Tottenham. Tottenham Chutspa (rhymes with "Hotspur"), as we called them, but mostly known as "the Spurs," was my father's team. He took me to watch them play several times. I remember fondly, in those days of standing terraces rather than seats, the crowds delighted in shouting out running commentaries and abuse, sarcastic comments that mercilessly lambasted unfortunate errors and made fun of any player off his game. "Hey, Jimmy! Yer shorts are too long." Or, "Danny, ar yer playing for the other side?" It was done in a spirit of good humor that made it an art form that was every bit as entertaining as the match itself, and my father used those same skills to humiliate our school team every time he watched us play! It spurred us on to try harder.

As British society began to fracture and change during the sixties, hooliganism became the norm at soccer matches. Thugs went to fight as much as to watch the game. Pitched battles were the norm. Families no longer dared to go. Chants became crude, hate-filled rants. Black players were taunted unceasingly. But then a series of tragedies slowly forced the authorities to think deeply about the way the game was going and how to separate warring gangs of rival toughs.

Television poured huge sums of money into the game. Stars who had earned working-class wages now joined the league of millionaires. Young, barely literate toughs suddenly strutted the social scene, flaunting their wealth in the demimonde world of nightclubs, crooks, and hookers. And of course they fuelled the pathetic cult of celebrity. Television series highlighted the crass and the dirty side of the soccer world. Money attracted investors. For the first time, successful Jewish businessmen entered the fray. Soon both Spurs and Arsenal had Jewish owners, and even Chelsea, once regarded as the most anti-Semitic of clubs, found a vaguely Jewish Russian oligarch to pour millions into it.

Nevertheless, Tottenham Hotspur seemed to have more of a Jewish presence than the rest and, slowly, working-class fascist thugs around the country started to chant anti-Semitic invective against Spurs supporters, calling them Yids, among other epithets. The Spurs fought back. Even the non-Jewish supporters reveled in calling themselves the "Yiddos," and they actually adopted the name as a badge of honor. The taunting backfired.

In Britain, anti-Semitism was always lurking there among the thuggish elements (as well as the elites), but it wasn't the biggest problem. Racism became the toughest hatred to dislodge. One might have expected the arrival of the large black and Muslim population to lead to violence between them and Jews at soccer matches. This didn't happen significantly in the United Kingdom. The immigrants, both black and Muslim, stayed away in significant numbers (the rising cost of entry tickets didn't help). They concentrated on sports the British Empire taught them, such as cricket, where skill alone enabled the former colonials to regularly humiliate their old imperial masters.

Just as Spurs was the Jewish club in London, so in Holland was Ajax. Ajax Amsterdam had, in fact, been founded by Jews and was known as a Jewish club long after most Jews had left. Its supporters took to waving Israeli flags, and of course this inspired reactions. Similarly in Ireland, Protestant soccer clubs adopted a pro-Israel stance in reaction to Catholic anti-Semitism. Any whiff of an Israeli player or team in Ireland produces a hate fest of anti-Semitism such as "Send him to the gas chambers!" Somehow, away from Britain, anti-Semitism felt freer to flaunt itself. And things have been getting increasingly evil.

There was a time when it was British supporters travelling abroad who instigated the violence. But as Britain toughened up on its own game, the notorious football riots of twenty years year past have receded. Violence, racism, and indeed anti-Israelism still erupt at English soccer matches every now and again, but at least the players and the authorities are responding. Still, soccer players in Britain are not the most cultured or educated example of *Homo sapiens* or even of soccer players. That's why England rarely wins anything.

In Europe after the war it was unfashionable to be anti-Semitic and indeed anti-Israel; this has now changed. We are seeing an increase in attacks on any sign of Jewish or Israeli presence. That is why so many Tottenham supporters travelling abroad in Europe are being attacked and injured. This is not new of course. Rival bands of chariot team supporters used to fight pitched battles in Rome. Young people rioted regularly during medieval times over local games. And deaths were much more common. But still the heavy hand of authority eventually got things under control.

Nowadays the disease of bringing politics into sport has spread to disrupting the world of classical music and demonstrating at concerts featuring Israeli performers. The dream that culture could exist detached from politics is certainly dead now. Of course you can't blame the game or the music. But you can blame people. Unless the authorities act quickly and forcefully to stop racial or religious abuse, of any sort, the disease will spread.

PAUL CELAN

There are Jews who think, write, paint, and compose. But are they Jewish artists? I believe that to be an example of a bicultural person, one needs to have a degree of knowledge and respect for both cultures. Is it possible to draw any line that is not arbitrary?

A random selection will illustrate what a fool's errand it is. Spinoza was born Jewish. But he rejected Judaism and thought Christianity was the only true religion. Felix Mendelssohn's parents converted to Christianity; so did Karl Marx's. In contrast, I would argue that Kafka and Freud would be examples of cultural icons born Jewish, with no faith, but who contributed enormously to Western literature and thought. And they both tried in different ways to articulate an interest in and a commitment to Judaism in its widest sense—something that the others mentioned above did not.

Husserl was a philosopher who had a profound influence on me, but he says nothing of significance about Judaism or Jewish thought. On the other hand, Emile Fackenheim and Levinas in particular come to mind as Jewish philosophers. I should confess that Levinas's philosophy does not resonate with me. Perhaps because he was French (but then I do like Sartre). However, he certainly combined the rational with a use of Talmudic themes and narratives. On the other hand, I can find nothing Jewish in Derrida at all.

If I were to look for an example of a Jew who said something innovative about Judaism and contributed to mainstream of Western culture, Martin Buber comes to mind. Indeed, him aside, I cannot think of a modern Jewish philosopher who, regardless of other talents and contributions, has come up with any really innovative idea since. Those I have read might be good apologists or commentators, but they are either derivative or still use Maimonides as their starting point (which is like trying to fly with an Aristotelian cannonball attached to one's foot). Harold Pinter would be an example of a Jew who repudiated anything Jewish, and the great American triumvirate of Bellow, Malamud, and Roth were Jewish only in reaction. Noam Chomsky of course is an archetypal non-Jewish Jew.

These thoughts on biculturalism have been occasioned by reading *Western Art and Jewish Presence in the work of Paul Celan* by Esther Cameron. He and she deserve to be more widely known and read. Her book is an exciting discourse on the interaction of Western culture with Jewish experience. Where does Paul Celan fit into my matrix? He was born into a deeply Jewish German Yiddish-speaking town of Czernowitz. The Nazis murdered his parents and the rest of his family. He survived. After the war he moved to France and turned his back on Jewish life.

He chose to write in the German language, the one used by the most evil and debased of peoples, as they murdered and tortured while at the same time they professed commitment to Western culture. It was Celan's way of engaging directly with them, confronting them in their own language. His repeated refrain is *Damen und Herren*, "ladies and gentlemen," addressed to those who are not. Just as the Orthodox world has defied Hitler by refusing to disappear and reproduces in greater numbers, so Celan faces his audiences in German and defies them with his very voice and existence.

His Jewishness is unavoidable throughout his work. In one of his poems he mentions Vitebsk, the Star of David, the letters *aleph* and *yud,* the ghetto, and Eden. His range is incredible. But the real power of his poetry is his anger and pain. His howl of agony against the Almighty reflects the ancient Jewish struggle with God and the cruelty and incomprehensibility of life. He rejects the concept of resurrection for humans or humanity and anything that offers false comfort or hope. He struggles with everything around him and tries like Coleridge's ancient mariner to engage his audience in his odyssey of agony.

I do not understand why, after the war, he chose to visit Heidegger, that Nazi-sympathizing anti-Semite. Esther Cameron suggests a comparison with Jacob's struggle with the angel who stands in for Esau as the emblem of the eternal hatred that Jews have and always will have to contend with. That is our fate.

This is not an easy book to read. But it is worth the struggle. It pays tribute to a tragic but brilliant multicultured Jew whose life was intertwined with his love of ideas and of culture despite the failure of so many to rise to the moral standards that they were called to. Their failure might have been too much for him to bear, but his legacy remains.

PART 5

FESTIVALS

OBLIGATIONS

For many Jews, Rosh Hashanah (the new year, or more accurately the head of the year) is not a great spiritual experience. It is a burden. Some turn up at synagogue on sufferance (because someone in the family insists) or out of guilt (if most of the year they have nothing to do with the Jewish community, at least a token appearance is a sop to the conscience). Either way the services they encounter are long, boring, and very rarely inspire them or help bring them back to their roots.

It could be argued that the role of the synagogue is not to inspire religiously so much as to act as a sort of social center to give one a sense of belonging and community. And that may well be one of its functions. But if one feels alienated by what goes on there, its impact is likely to be negative. Is the synagogue a place for prayer and study, or is it as it originated in Babylon, just a place to get together? I would say that too often, and with exceptions of course, it is both, but I would also say it fails on both levels too.

There are various reasons why so many Jews feel alienated in synagogue. Inevitably, if one doesn't understand the language, the poetry, the sounds, and the conventions, then it's like the village idiot going to the opera!

But it is not just the liturgy. After all most people do not understand Italian but they can still enjoy opera. Sounds can also convey emotions. The case for the prosecution begins with the attitudes of religious authorities. Too often they say nothing that sounds relevant to the modern mind. There is no point in castigating those who do come, for the absence of others. Hectoring the apathetic will not encourage them to return. Jingoistic appeals for national solidarity will not engage with those who feel no such deep emotion.

There is no point in preaching to intelligent, thinking people ideas that manifestly contradict their experience of the world they live in. I am not talking about mysticism or matters of faith, because although they are not subject to scientific analysis, neither do they actually contradict scientific evidence. They just do not compete. Or they ought not to at any rate. However, arguing in support of a fundamentalist worldview, for example, that refuses to engage with science if it contradicts a simplistic reading of ancient texts certainly does. I know that scientific theories are also given to error and change. But they are at least open to question. Emotion is very important in one's life, and it is not usually subject to logic. However, neither does it contradict it. Simple faith is well and good for those capable of it, but to many it is not enough.

Lots of young and not so young Jews have no interest in religion whatsoever. Most have had no Jewish education beyond childish levels and no positive experience of living a Jewish life beyond parental foibles and occasional encounters with an alien tradition. Some have been to Jewish schools and turned off badly by the poor quality of a lot of Jewish studies, teaching, and antediluvian attitudes. Some were educated in Israel in a society that is ideologically opposed to religion, made worse by the inept behavior of many state rabbis and religious politicians. Talking about something they have no sympathy with will not help.

The version of Judaism that has dominated in Western Europe for the past two hundred years has been a dry, pseudo rationalist imitation of many Christian attitudes. For example, the idea of getting married in a synagogue is so alien to tradition where under the sky is preferred, that for a while most religious authorities actually rejected the practice on the grounds that it was Christian. The exclusion of mysticism and ecstasy (no, I'm not talking about the pill) has left a dry, formalistic, uninspiring experience that is incapable of enthusing or inspiring.

The very fact that ersatz mystical alternatives are proving popular nowadays and often attract lost souls is an indication that there is a desire for something more. The attraction of Chasidic services and communities attests to what warmth, enthusiasm, and informality can achieve (and I don't underestimate the value of a good kiddush afterward as an added attraction). Clearly some models work better than others. Too much creativity and innovation can take a community away from its core structures and links to tradition, but too little will simply allow the grape to wither on the vine.

So if things are so terrible, how come, if one takes an overall view, synagogues that appeal to traditional Jews have never been fuller? It is true that some areas have declined while others have mushroomed. But our religious life has never been richer, and our Jewish world has never been better informed or educated in Jewish learning. I guess it proves that our religion is greater than the sum of its parts, and somehow or other the voice of spirituality can be heard above the noise of the chatter that most of us will hear this Rosh Hashanah in shul.

Nevertheless the saddest of all is the fact that the vast majority of the Jewish people are, if not lost, at least alienated from their tradition. Does it matter? I believe it does. Objectively having a period of ten days a year in which we judge ourselves and compile an honest account of our past year's performance is a very healthy human exercise. I agree that many committed Jews don't really do it as it should be done but go through the form. Yet as an important contribution to the mental and moral health of society, this seems to me to be an invaluable process.

The anthropologist Mary Douglas points out how so much of ancient custom is built on the idea of displacement, of bodily fluids, animals, and humans out of their normal context. "In context" means "balance" between God and human society. Out of context is dissonance or alienation. Dirt is only dirt when it leaves the cabbage patch and gets in your eye! Sex in one context is good, but when it interferes with other relationships is not. Feeling at home in a Jewish atmosphere, whatever one chooses to derive from it, indicates a certain state of balance and reconciliation to one's position in the world and one's culture.

Rosh Hashanah as a festival is designed to restore balance between the mundane and the spiritual. The "clear" sound of the shofar contrasts with the bombardment of constant sound waves, of witch doctors' rattles, the hubbub of the crowd, the pressures of normal society. Rosh Hashanah only works on a therapeutic level as opposed to a social level, if it works on the individual to achieve a degree of improvement, however small.

A healthy community needs healthy members. In the end it is the essential human relationship with life and its forces that transcends the social function of the synagogue, important as it might be in its own way. As the Talmud says, "God wants your heart" much more than "bums on seats." Thank God for God!

PAIN OR PLEASURE?

The Torah tells us very little about Rosh Hashanah. Even its name as recorded in the Bible is not given as "the New Year." The three harvest and pilgrim festivals are named Pesach, Shavuot, and Sukkot. These were the main focal points of national Jewish life in biblical times, when as many as possible gathered in Jerusalem and attended temple ceremonies. The Torah keeps on reiterating how they are supposed to be happy occasions, time to eat, drink, be merry, and share. Yom Kippur, the Day of Atonements, is the single biblical holiday devoted to personal introspection, a serious and painful experience, physically and spiritually, a day for "constricting your souls."

But when it comes to Rosh Hashanah, all we have to describe it is "the first day of the seventh month is a Sabbath of remembering and blowing (the shofar)" (Leviticus 23 and Numbers 29). It is up to the oral law to clarify. The name we use universally nowadays, the new or rather the head of the year, came into Judaism much later than the Bible.

So I wonder, where does Rosh Hashanah fit in on the scale of pain and pleasure? Is it a happy, joyful festival like the other three, or is it painful and serious like Yom Kippur? Is it a self-analytical moment in which our very existence is examined and justified, or is it a mystical occasion when we should try, through ecstasy and experience, to get as close to heaven as we can? Is it a case of "turn from evil and do good" or "do good and turn from evil"?

There is an alternative option, that it is a mixture of both. Just like good chocolate, it has salt as well as sugar. Throughout the history of human intellectual civilization, we have always been expected to choose, to decide which one is right. Should we be happy or sad? Should we be enjoying life or suppressing and disciplining? Should we be rational or emotional? Should we be individuals or a community? Perhaps they are both right and necessary.

The Western philosophical tradition likes to be precise. It has no time for fuzzy combinations. Either you are a Stoic or an Epicurean, an Aristotelian or Platonist, a Greek or a Roman, a Christian or a Muslim, a rationalist or a mystic, a capitalist or a socialist, a Freudian or a Jungian, a person who wants to have fun or a killjoy. But surely we are a mixture of different ideas, opinions, experiences, and feelings. So is Judaism. That's why we can never agree on anything. Do we have to be scholars or populists, legalists or fabulists, have analytical minds or great memories, prefer Gemarah or Midrash, be Chasidim or Mitnagdim, Sefardi or Ashkenazi, strict or lenient? Why can't we combine lots of different elements and move in and out of different moods and situations?

History plays a part, of course. Zechariah, two and a half thousand years ago, was ready to scrap all the sad fast days and turn them into joyful celebrations. But then came years of oppression and suffering and exile. The number of negative days increased. Once we were exiled from Jerusalem, our liturgy overflowed with sadness, alienation, loss, and woe. Now we have penthouses overlooking the Old City, with swimming pools and saunas. Once Ashkenazi and Sefardi prayed in different worlds; now we are next door and often visit each other, pray with each other and dance with each other, and even marry each other. Once Lithuanians placed bans on Chasidim; now they imitate them. Rav Ovadya Yosef implored his followers to stop dressing in black Ashkenazi gear; now his sons looks like nineteenth-century Viennese doctors despite his Egyptian oriental origins. You might argue that blurring the lines can be good. We should embrace it.

So historically we refer to the first ten days of the month of Tishrei as Yamim Noraim, Awesome Days, serious days, or the Ten Days of Repentance. Heavy days with much longer services than normal, lots of additional poems, much breast-beating and tears of contrition, and the expectation that being found unworthy, we will be condemned in ten days to heavenly punishment. Yet there is another side. Rosh Hashanah is two days when we sit down to huge banquets. Our tables are laden with goodies. We dip apples into honey and wish each other a sweet year. We get hold of as many exotic fruits as we can to symbolize good things, and to be able to thank God "who has kept us alive and enabled us to enjoy this moment." We buy new things and wear our best clothes. And we are treated to the sounds of the shofar, and we go down to the water to remark on our never stepping into the same river twice (I bet you never thought of that association with tashlich).

We can be happy one moment and reflective the next. That, according to the Talmud, is why we break glasses at weddings. It is why we thank God for the bad as well as the good, and vice versa. It is why we celebrate life and we record death. It is why we work but also rest, why we eat but also refrain. The more we do, the richer our lives. But the more we overindulge, the less rewarding and enjoyable they become. Unless you add salt, the chocolate cloys. Unless you enjoy life and look on its bright side and remember your good fortune, however modest, each moment becomes less significant.

Rosh Hashanah has no biblical name because it stands in between (metaphorically) the extremes of the delightful pleasures of harvests and the self-denial of Yom Kippur. It stands for the golden mean between them, the best of both harvest festivals and serious self-analysis. Pain or pleasure? Yes. We all experience both when we look back at our lives, let alone the past year. There are things we did that give us a sense of success and satisfaction. And there are things we did that we regret, wish we had done differently or better, that cause us pain. It's precisely that combination of the two that Rosh Hashanah reminds us of.

REPENTANCE

People are often surprised when I say there is no actual command in the Torah to repent. You might compare it to the afterlife. It is something that was so obvious on a spiritual level and so universally accepted by every civilization at that time that it did not need to be stipulated in a book concerned with living life in the present. But still, repentance is such a crucial part of our tradition, and at this time of the year it is such an omnipresent theme that it is worth examining where it comes from and what it conveys.

There are words in the Torah for doing the wrong thing, for confessing, for making reparation, for atoning, and you might think that one cannot do all that without a change of heart. But there is no specific command to have a change of heart. Perhaps this is because you cannot command people to change their hearts. You cannot know if they are sincere or not. You can only judge by actions.

I always like to start by going back to language and the origin of words. The Hebrew word *shav* ("to return") is the root of the word most commonly used for repentance, *teshuvah*. Throughout the Torah it simply means returning property, position, or status to the situation before, to a given moment in the past. It is like land returning to its original owner during the Jubilee. The only time it is used outside of the legislative part of the Torah is when it talks about the rift between the children of Israel and God. There it is as much about God returning to humans as about humans returning to God. In other words, it is not repentance, as such, but rather reconciliation. And since reconciliation is a two-way process, it cannot be legislated for in terms of a single party.

A similar word to *teshuvah* that the Torah uses is *lenachem*. It is used anthropomorphically of God regretting such things as giving humans the freedom to disobey Him, to behave in a corrupt manner (Genesis 6.6 or Exodus 32.14). But the very same word means to be comforted (Genesis 24.67 and 38.12) or to reconcile. It is another example of words in biblical Hebrew sometimes meaning opposites. One might say that the very things that cause alienation and fracture are the means of reconciliation and healing. That part of the human brain that distances mankind from God and good is the very feature that brings humans closer to God and to good.

The fact is that such terms are metaphors. We don't actually come back or return, because most of us were never there in the first place. There's an interesting term used in the Talmud to describe someone who never, ever experienced Jewish life. He or she is called "a child captured and brought up by non-Jews." Or, to use the Hebrew, a *tinok shenishba bein hagoyim*. Since the breaking down of the physical and cultural barriers of the ghetto, this term has been applied to those born Jews who have assimilated, never knowing what it was they were assimilating from. I believe it was first used this way by the "Chafetz Chayim," the pen name of a scholarly and saintly rabbi of the nineteenth century. He was and is known for his commentary on parts of the essential legal commentary on the Shulchan Aruch known as the Mishnah Berura, and for his books against gossip and telling tales.

This principle has been used by recent and current authorities because, in this world of massive assimilation, if someone has never known better because the nominally Jewish home they came from had no Jewish content, he or she cannot be punished or blamed for disobeying Jewish law. Such a person does not become a returnee, a *baal teshuvah*, the equivalent to "born again." Somebody who comes to Torah for the first time is conceptually closer to a convert.

It seems to me that the very notion of repentance is really a metaphor for a relationship, any relationship. Most people have some sort of idea of God, however vague and ill defined. Such relationships are often taken for granted and ignored until a crisis brings them to the fore. Indeed like all relationships, associations, and pathways through the brain, they need to be reinforced, repeated, worked upon, and nurtured before they become part of one's mental makeup.

It is for precisely this that Yom Kippur exists. It is to reinforce a certain kind of relationship. It is not the festive, fun, pleasurable experiences of other festivals. It's the hard and painful exercise that all relationships need if they are to survive. It is not that there are no festivals celebrating the pleasurable, positive, and even fun side of our relationship. They are in the majority. But sadly, the occasional visitor to a synagogue usually comes on the sadder or more serious occasions. We need both the happy and the serious.

The *teshuva* we emphasize on Yom Kippur, what we call repentance, really means to come closer. It is not a formulaic ritual of performing a mitzvah, a command, as such. It is rather the process through which both parties remember each other, remember what needs to be done, and devote time to nurturing that relationship.

We anthropomorphize God all the time, in our liturgy and in the Talmud. God is happy, sad, angry, and, yes, misses us. He yearns for us as much as we for Him. He is disappointed and alienated as we are and sometimes even hides from us. Yet we can and do come together. That is what *teshuvah* really is. Relationships vary in kind and intensity, but they all share the need for the parties to be reminded of one another.

WATER

Whatever can be said about the festival of Sukkot, the fact is that water is the most significant subtext. All plants need water, as do humans and all other living things. But the four "kinds of plants" we take and wave are all associated specifically with water, whether natural rainfall, irrigation, or oases. Sitting in the sukkah is our farewell to the dry season in areas where for thousands of years Jews mainly lived. The important postbiblical traditions of *Nisuch Hamayim*, pouring water over the altar as part of the prayers for rain, and the massive public celebrations of *Simchat Beit HaShoeva*, the rejoicing over the well house in Jerusalem, prove the point that water is at the core of this festival.

Universally we associate water with physical cleanliness. In addition, Jewish tradition looks at water as essential to symbolic purification, both physical and spiritual. As with all the ancient "elements," it bridges the gap between the physical and the spiritual, the mundane and the sacred. And prayers for rain and dew appear in the liturgy throughout the year, where they also remind us of the Holy Land and its dependence on rain as opposed to river water. But the festival of Sukkot is in a league of its own.

Water of course is not the only theme to the festival. In ancient times Sukkot was also the major communal reunion of the Jewish people. The hard work had been done. The harvests were over. One was feeling good and successful. Now it was time for the community, the nation. On the second day, everyone gathered to hear the Torah (or parts of it) read in public. It was a huge public exercise in mass education that included women and children as well as men. Then much later, Simchat Torah emerged as the happiest festival of the year, to record the conclusion of the annual cycle of reading the Torah in synagogues. The festival ends with new prayers for the rainy season, which were in part held off until the pilgrims from Babylon and the west could get home before the deluge made roads impassable.

During the early years of my life, no one seemed to make too much out of the issues of water and rain in general, or indeed ecology; no concerns then about climate change. The prayers for rain in the synagogue were regarded as a hangover from our agrarian past, something relevant only to the Land of Israel, not wet Manchester. But now the rising temperatures, the shortage of water, and the political tensions over its availability have all brought the issue of water and rain to the forefront. It's as if Moses and the rabbis of the past really could look into the future. Now nothing is more important on earth.

The Greek philosopher Thales thought that everything was derived from water, one way or another. He lost out to the popular theory that it was a combination of water, air, fire, and earth. That theory lasted until modern times. Even Maimonides believed it. In medieval times water was so dangerously contaminated that people drank beer and wine instead. No wonder they called it the Dark Ages. We do not seek such simplistic solutions nowadays, but we do know how important drinkable water is; indeed, almost any water is important to irrigate crops and facilitate industry.

The hot baths of Tiberius figure prominently in the Jewish tradition, but the famous Caracalla baths in Rome, built around 212 CE, provided baths and recreation for the Roman population, and the whole system of transporting water to the city was a wonder of the world. Like the circuses, it was a way of keeping the voters and the masses happy. They were unique and exceptional. It would take well over a thousand years before sanitation, sewage, and water became the norm in human society, and still they elude the vast majority. China's water crisis costs 2 percent of its gross domestic product annually, and it has had to spend over $100 billion on the Yangtze Canal project to bring water to more of its population.

In the rich world, everyone is aware of the need for hydration. We spend vast sums on bottled water that is rarely superior to ordinary tap water. But in most of the world, pure, potable (why the heck use that foreign word instead of simply "drinkable"?) tap water is still unavailable to too many. The facts are disturbing. I am no fan of the UN, but it does occasionally produce something of value. The UN World Water Development Report (WWDR, 2003) from the World Water Assessment Program, indicates that in the next twenty years the quantity of water available to everyone is predicted to decrease by 30 percent. Forty percent of the world's inhabitants currently have insufficient fresh water for minimal hygiene. In 2000, more than 2.2 million people died from waterborne diseases related to the consumption of contaminated water or from drought. I might add the sad statistic that in the industrial West 40 percent of the water is wasted each year through decaying infrastructure, leaking pipes, and poor management.

Increasingly, conflicts around the world relate to water. We are replaying Abraham's conflicts with the Philistines over wells. We know the problems in the Middle East over the feeding rivers into the Jordan, the diminishing aquifers in the Judean hills, and the shrinking Dead Sea. This while swimming pools expand alongside villages where the wells have dried up. At least Israel is now investing so much in desalination that it is able to satisfy most of its water needs this way. Israel does not get enough credit (because it's not political enough) for how much Israeli universities are investing in joint projects with Palestinians to deal with the water problem. The Israeli Government over the years has made incredible concessions to Jordan and Syria over water supplies. But as we see millions of refugees trek across deserts to safety, the urgent need for water and its availability is growing by the day. It's a sad state of affairs that too many states spend more on arms than they do on ensuring safe, accessible drinkable water for their citizens.

So when we celebrate Sukkot, we are indeed celebrating water and how lucky we are to have it. Literally, *lechayim*, for life.

INNOVATION

You won't find Simchat Torah, the festival that celebrates completing the annual cycle of the Torah reading, mentioned anywhere in the Torah or indeed in the Talmud. Yet it has become one of the most popular of Jewish festivals, an occasion for plenty of drink, doing a "knees up," and having a wild time. You may be aware of the fact that the English diarist Samuel Pepys visited a synagogue (Creechurch Lane in London, 1663) on Simchat Torah this day and no one had told him what to expect. He looked at the proceedings and thought the Jews were a bunch of primitive lunatics (looking at communal politics, you realize nothing has changed!). Simchat Torah, however, is a complete rabbinic innovation.

The Torah says quite explicitly that one should blow the shofar on Rosh Hashanah. But sometimes, if Rosh Hashanah falls on a Shabbat, you will not hear the shofar. The rabbis of the Talmud decided that, as people might carry the shofars in the public domain, they had the right to overrule the Torah. And the Torah says that on the first day of Sukkot, one should wave the *Arbah Minim* (the four plants specified in Leviticus 23). But on some years, the only waving done on the first day of Sukkot will be the assignations arranged by semaphore from down below up to the gallery or over the *mechitzah*, the division separating men and women, with the ladies. The rabbis had no compunction about cancelling a direct command from the Torah! All because according to the Mishna, everyone used to bring their *Arbah Minim* to the Temple the day before the festival. The officials laid them out on a platform, and the following day everyone came to pick theirs up. The officials, as all officials, soon got fed up trying to pair up the owners with their sets and simply threw the lot at the crowds. They all started fighting to get the best ones. Great fun religion—you don't need football matches for a punch-up. The injuries mounted, so the rabbis said, "Stop! No more!"

It was Ezra, the great scholar of the Persian Empire who helped rebuild the Jewish community in the Land of Israel two and a half thousand years ago, who first insisted on reading the Torah every Shabbat. This led in different communities to completing the cycle every three or seven years. Then the authorities in Israel reduced it to one and turned the last day of Sukkot into the celebration of Simchat Torah, the rejoicing of the law when one annual cycle ended and the next began. It was not until the period of the geonim in what we now call Iraq a thousand years ago that everyone adopted the annual cycle. We all accept this even if it is an innovation, although sometimes I wish we could revert to the triennial.

So if rabbis two thousand years ago could be so creative, how did we get to the point nowadays where there are no innovative rabbis in the traditional world? What happened? Some say it was simply an inferiority complex that prevented later rabbis from feeling they were neither learned enough or arrogant enough to overrule earlier authorities. But the fact was that rabbis in the past were sometimes bullied by their hosts, the Christians and the Muslims, or thought it wise to modify laws their hosts found offensive.

A classic example is Rabbeinu Gershon (960–1040) of Troyes who banned polygamy in the West, where Christian clerics did not like the idea of one wife, let alone more. He also banned reading other people's letters! Then Reb Yaakov Ben Meir, Rabbeinu Tam (110–1171), in France decided some eight hundred years ago we shouldn't force husbands to give divorces in a world where divorce was forbidden anyway. Reb Shlomo Aderet, the Rashba of Barcelona (1235–1310), decided we shouldn't annul any more marriages (or study philosophy).

These were examples of innovative rabbinic decision making, even if they were negative and influenced by external pressure. Much later in a mood of counterreformation in more ways than one, the Chatam Sofer (Pressburg, 1763–1839) decided that anything new was forbidden. Thank goodness he didn't extend this to commerce, otherwise we'd be like the Amish whom parts of the Charedi world resemble in lots of ways already. As a result they try to ban computers and the Internet (except for work)! "Honest, Rebbe, my property company needs to see which are the most popular Internet sites are for purely commercial reasons!"

It all reminds me of the Francis Bacon story of monks arguing about how many teeth are in a horse's mouth. They looked in all the holy books but couldn't find the answer. A young novice suggested they go out, get a horse, and count its teeth. They threw him out of the monastery because they insisted on relying only on what could be found in holy texts, whereas he had the temerity to suggest that they actually look at the evidence. A perfect example of the refusal to change even in the face of verifying the facts.

Simchat Torah is a wonderful example of how a tradition does in fact adapt and innovate to meet changing circumstances. There are many examples of how the rabbis dealt with biblical laws they felt no longer ought to apply. Some were forced on them by circumstances. If you don't have a temple anymore, you can't very well sacrifice. If you can no longer identify Canaanite tribes, you can hardly apply biblical laws that mention them. And others were changed because rabbis felt that they were no longer appropriate, such as allowing a husband who suspected his wife of adultery to be hauled before the priest, especially if he was not such a shining example of fidelity.

The fact is that biblical Judaism was very different from the way Jews in Babylon lived their lives. Later rabbinic Judaism completely transformed Judaism after the Roman destruction from a religion of sanctuary to one focussed more on the home and the study hall. Medieval Judaism was very different in so many ways from Talmudic Judaism. And I doubt that medieval rabbis would recognize a great deal of Judaism today. The main constitution, the primary laws, may be the same, but so much else—innovative laws, different customs, and ways of interpreting—has completely changed. Sephardi and Ashkenazi Jews share the same Torah and legal system but still have many different customs and styles, and the same goes for Chasidim.

Simchat Torah's origins remind us of this innovative streak that our religion has all but lost nowadays as we seem to be interested only in adding restrictions and refusing to deal with examples of discrimination and bias.

MACCABEES

Why is Judah Maccabee not mentioned in the Talmud? There are all sorts of reasons suggested. Some academics argue that it's really two quite separate stories merged into one, a rebellion against the Syrians and the rise of a dynasty. Others say it was just a fictionalized account of the rivalry between the Sadducees and the Pharisees. The earliest sources are the books of the Maccabees (not included in the Jewish canon) and then Josephus. But no one would argue that either could be regarded as objective.

We do know from all sources that the later Maccabee dynasty was strongly anti rabbinic. The great exception was the remarkable Queen Shlomzion (Salome Alexandra) possibly the greatest monarch of post-Biblical Judaism. One in the eye for the male chauvinists. Her apart the dynasty came to identify itself with the rich Sadducee aristocracy, rather than the poorer Pharisee populace, whose leadership came to dominate post-destruction Judaism. We can leave out the Dead Sea sects who didn't like anyone.

Thanks to the Roman assaults on Judea, one might not be so inclined to regard Judah Maccabee favorably. He it was who sent envoys to Rome asking for an alliance, which was Rome's excuse for interfering and led directly to Jewish subjugation. And the dynasty was identified by then with Herod, who killed just about every member of his family and thought that by paying vast sums to redecorate the Temple, he could buy off public opinion and God.

The achievements of Judah and his brothers from 165 BCE onward, significant as they were, in fact amounted to little more than guerrilla campaigns. The Syrian Greek armed forces had far more important issues to deal with at home and only sent secondary forces to deal with what they saw as a minor local disturbance. Indeed, a Syrian garrison remained in the fortress in Jerusalem throughout Judah's life and beyond, until final settlement with Simon. Only in the next generation was John Hyrcanus a really successful military commander. But what started off as a pious rural priestly family's stand against Antiochus, and indeed against assimilatory high priests in Jerusalem, soon became an example of how power corrupts. Nevertheless, nothing can take away from Judah's achievement of regaining control of the Temple, purifying and rededicating it.

The Chanukah story as an idea is emblematic of the Jewish people. They are always divided between religious and not so, between sect and sect, rich and poor, nationalists and internationalists, idealists and pragmatists. Indeed, every Jew sees Chanukah through his or her own eyes and personal agenda. Rabbinic emphasis on the spiritual rather than the military is surely a reaction to the disempowerment of Jewish life under Roman and successive regimes as a result of thinking violence could overcome the Roman threat. The emphasis on leaving it to God to fight our battles is a classical Diaspora response to the loss of our land and exile.

And of course in our own era, the different emphases abound. Physically robust secular Zionism saw Judah as its military hero, standing up to the enemy, unlike the Jews of the ghettos, who were seen as cowards walking like lambs to the slaughter. Of course it was not universally like that in Europe. But even if it were, overwhelming firepower and military superiority would give one very little option. The possibility that acceptance of divine will, with dignity and an awareness of life beyond this world, may have created spiritual heroes simply could not have occurred to a generation of Jews more influenced by secular, socialist material values.

The countermyth that Matityahu, Judah's father who started off the resistance, was a sort of Rosh Yeshiva, and his family sat in kollel studying Gemara all day and emerged only occasionally to waste good study time fighting the

Greeks is not only an anachronism but equally off the mark. It is proof that we all reinvent our own heroes in our own image.

The irony of a materialist viewpoint in which this should be seen as the oppressed workers or peasants rising up against the rich bosses is that it claims to redress the balance in favor of the masses but in practice elsewhere has always led to abuse and excess. Think of what happened after the French Revolution, after the Russian Revolution, after Maoism in China or Pol Pot in Cambodia. Their abuses could not illustrate this better.

The sad transformation of Israel from the idealist state I recall of the 1950s to its relatively corrupt decadence of today is only a natural consequence of a society that dismissed or relegated spiritual values. The result has been a collapse of ideals. But then I believe that Jewish religious life in its organizational and hierarchical manifestations has become corrupt too. Power and money decide more than justice and spirituality. The poverty and deprivation that characterized most of the very Orthodox world fifty years ago produced a generation of men determined to make money at almost any cost, legal or otherwise. Those who have risen out of poverty have gone overboard with material excess, as the conspicuous consumption on display at many Charedi weddings, airport lounges, or vacation watering spots illustrates. Officially, Charedi society worships its rebbes and the great rabbis. Unofficially, it worships the *gvirim*, the rich ones, and their money. I do not wish for one minute to suggest there is no more idealism in secular Israel, any more than in the religious world. There are good, honest, caring people in both societies. But the time when the idealists were the elite is long past. Mammon rules everywhere, both in the Jewish and the non-Jewish world.

It is only when we have economic crises that often turn heroes into villains that we realize that those whose only criteria for success was money have failed by the very standard they wanted to be judged by. It is only then that they begin to consider that other values might be preferable, that teachers and social workers might be making a more important contribution to humanity than bankers and dealers. Sadly, most humans cannot see beyond their immediate material needs, and only a very few within religion and beyond genuinely aspire to the various degrees of authentic saintliness. Even rabbis nowadays are more often associated with amassing money in various ways, or selling indulgences, than heavenly values.

The rabbis of the Talmud never spoke out against wealth per se, but that was because they always emphasized other, more important values that were ends in themselves. Money was always only a means. If they downplayed Judah Maccabee and focused instead almost exclusively on the miracle of the oil lasting longer than it should have, it was because they wanted to downplay materialism and emphasize light, enlightenment, and the flame of spirit.

CARNIVAL

The great "carnivales" of the Catholic world have always coincided with the period preceding Lent, when the righteous avoid pleasures of the flesh and atone. You said good-bye (*vale*) to meat (*carne*), and you celebrated being forgiven your sins. Many Christian ascetics and killjoys objected strongly to the levity that came with carnivals. Indeed, in places like Venice they were occasions of mass debauchery. The tradition of wearing masks or dressing in disguise to preserve anonymity or to assist secret assignations came to be part and parcel of carnivals to this very day.

The Bible knows only too well the link between religion and sexual impropriety. The golden calf led to an orgy. In the pagan world in general, religious worship involved "giving of oneself" to the deity, or its willing priests and priestesses, whether sexually or with defecation. Biblical Judaism was not opposed to fun and pleasure. But it did emphasize self-control and restraint. Time and again, the Bible admonishes the children of Israel not to follow the corrupt religious rites of the peoples they were trying to dispossess.

Just as festivals of light were universal, and each religion found its own way of celebrating it, so too carnivals were universal. This does not mean that each culture did not have its own and original reasons for celebration. Either you did win a battle against the Greeks or you didn't. Either there was a plot to destroy you in the Persian Empire or there was not. But if the reason to celebrate varied from culture to culture, the carnivals came to resemble each other through the inevitable cross-fertilization that comes when different cultures share the same space.

You will find examples of lights for the dead or covering mirrors to keep out evil spirits throughout the ancient world, long before they appear as Jewish customs. You will find lighting flames as the depth of winter approaches long before Chanukah was celebrated. And you will find masks and fancy dress and getting drunk well before Purim.

The fact is that for all the drunken excesses and self-indulgence of Purim, it has never been known as a time when sexual misconduct was rampant (one or two historical exceptions notwithstanding). If it happened, it was not part of the culture. As the Talmud says, you can judge a person by how he drinks; so too I would argue you could judge a religion by what happens when you remove restraints.

Purim has come to be associated with masks, which normally means "to disguise" or "to cover." They have different usages, but the one thing they have in common is that when you are masked, you are not who you appear to be. No one was supposed to know who the Man in the Iron Mask really was! In a good person, disguise may be no more than a game, but in a bad person, such as a robber, you are covering your face to get up to monkey business. So it usually has been with carnival masks.

In general, masks and disguise have played an important role in religious ceremonies going back well to before the biblical period and all around the world. From Oceania to Africa and the Andes, they were and often still are used to control, to instill fear and obedience. Chiefs and witch doctors wear them to reinforce their authority. In Africa, to frighten and discipline the child, a mother will often paint a frightening face on the bottom of her water container. In many cultures judges wore masks to protect them from the fury of those they punished and their families. Disguise and uniforms are associated with authority and power. And of course masks are still used in war to frighten the enemy or ward off evil spirits.

In the Bible, masks only appear once, in Exodus 34:

> When Moses came down from Mount Sinai with the two tablets of Testimony in his hands, he did not realize that the skin of his face shone...When Aaron and all the people of Israel saw Moses and his face was so bright, they were afraid to come closer to him...So Moses put a mask/veil on his face. When he went in to speak with God he took the mask (or perhaps it was a veil) off, until he came out, and then he it on his face again until the next time he went in to speak to God.

This does seem strange. He was not wearing the mask to frighten anyone or to hide his identity. Quite the contrary. He was scarier without it. It seems he was wearing a mask in the way a disfigured person might, to make him appear less alien. In his encounter with God, something so powerful happened that his face changed in a way that other people might have found frightening. In his case the mask was making him more accessible. You might think that the process of religious inspiration itself was the scary part. Once you transmit it to ordinary people, it is less frightening, but it is also less pure; it has been modified to make it accessible. This is why Moses is the only one in the Bible who wears a mask. He was uniquely close to the source. It's a symbol of the degree of proximity and distance from the ideal. We all of us are somewhere along that line that runs from one extreme to the other.

Even if the custom of masks and disguises on Purim has come from somewhere else, it still finds a place in our tradition. Just as pagan harvest festivals have been adapted to a monotheistic purpose, so too masks and disguise. We can all be Hamans or Mordechais. Different potentials lurk beneath our surfaces. It is up to us to choose which one, which mask to wear, for better or worse.

HOME

What do we mean by a family? There are so many new definitions and variations. Too often people who, for circumstances beyond their control, cannot offer a conventional family life feel somehow inadequate. It needn't be that way. I take my clue from Pesach.

Pesach is special in the sense that it is the most home-centered of our festivals. The highlights of Rosh Hashanah and Yom Kippur are the services. But on Pesach the focal point is the Seder meal, at home. It is not just that as on Shabbat or other festivals the emphasis is on having a family meal. Here additional ritual, study, and involvement are required, along with, of course, the tradition of completely cleaning out and preparing the house for the festival, which involves lots of preparation beforehand.

It is true that in general Judaism gives us much more to do at home than in our places of worship. It commands all the laws and ceremonies that govern home life, from the kitchen to the dining room to the bedroom. But on Pesach the rituals include complex combinations of different foods and ways of eating them. There is the obligation of studying together, getting everyone involved in asking questions, in trying to understand the significance of the ceremony and our very existence as Jews. No other biblical festival involves the children, the whole of the family, in the readings and customs as does Pesach and the Seder night. But is it the family or the home that matters most?

At a time when we tend to talk about "family life" in all its varieties, it strikes me as significant that the Torah on Pesach talks mainly about the household, the *bayit*, rather than the family. Generally speaking, the language of the Torah describes the building blocks of a healthy moral society. We would expect it start with mishpacha, family. Then would come the *beit av*, the father's household or extended family. From there we expand to *shevet*, tribe, and finally arrive at *am*, people. The implication would be that if we build healthy parts, the sum of the parts will be a healthy one as well. There are, incidentally, some exceptions to this sequence notably in Devarim (Deuteronomy) 29.17 family comes after the individual: "A man or a woman or family or tribe."

Perhaps then it is not the family but the person that is the core. The relationship between individuals is the essential defining characteristic of family. If so, the conventional family is not the crucial building block of society. After all, there are plenty of unconventional families. There are single-parent families, couples of all varieties, families reduced by war, death, and sickness. What really matters is the nature of what goes on in those different structures and relationships. It is what goes on in the house, as a haven. The home is a place where there is security and love, an educational and moral laboratory. That is essential for healthy human development.

Passover is, after all, the first command that was given to the people as a whole. Exodus 12:13 says,

> On the tenth day of this month, every one of them shall take a lamb, according to each household of their fathers, a lamb per house. And if the household is too few for a lamb, let him and the neighbor near his house share it according to the number of the souls.

It is the household that seems to be the essential element here. They come together not by family, but by household, and most importantly, the souls within. Each household had to put blood on its doorposts so that the Almighty would pass over their homes and not kill their firstborn. That, of course, is where the festival gets its name. Passing over the homes. And it involves a positive act of identification. But again it is the home that is being identified as much as the individuals.

There is a tendency in religions to downplay the issue of individuality in favor of conformity to the community. But there is creative tension between them. We need both to be balanced. We tend to be self-centered. It is the individuals who make up the community, after all. That is why our tradition forces us into communal association, concern for the welfare of the community, charity in all its forms, and communal prayer to counterbalance the solipsism. But on the other hand, without an individual experiencing the beauty of the tradition, without a personal, existential pursuit of a connection with God, we would be left with empty routines and just social affiliations.

That is why we have developed the idea of *deveykut*, of reaching out to try to imagine we can touch and feel close to God. Our mystical tradition has called on us to preface each mitzvah with a meditation on it with the words *Hineni Muchan uMezuman*, "Here I am ready and prepared to perform this act." It is this personal commitment that lies at the core of our tradition, and it is this that is the essential building block, the atom of our structure.

That is why the Seder requires each one of us, as individuals, to imagine what it must have been like to be enslaved and then freed. But we cannot live only for ourselves, without a household or without a people. One is constantly assailed nowadays with the failure of families, abuse, cruelty, and violence. When relationships collapse, suffering ensues. And one wants to shake people and ask them if they fully appreciate the consequences of their actions. But we can rebuild in different ways.

I am redefining family here to mean something very different from the idea previous generations had of families. That earlier model that is family centered is all well and good, so long as the responsibility of caring human beings is preserved. But sadly we have seen a lot of abuse within families. It is the individual functioning appropriately and well within the family that is core, not the structure of family itself. In other words, no matter how we define families, what really matters is what is going on in the house, the home. Love and respect is what defines a good relationship. That is what children need, no matter what kind of home it is or who the loving caregiver is.

SHAVUOT

"Do not cook a kid in its mother's milk." This is a puzzling statement that is repeated three times in the Torah. Twice it is in connection with Shavuot, the summer first fruits and harvest festival. The third time is in the context of forbidden foods. Traditionally these texts have been taken to ban cooking, eating, and benefitting from milk and meat together.

There's a cute joke: Moses is up on Mount Sinai, and the Almighty is conveying the text of the Torah to him. They come to "Do not cook a kid in its mother's milk," and Moses looks up and says, "By this I assume you mean we should not eat meat and milk dishes at the same time."

"No," replies the Almighty, "I simply said, 'Do not cook a kid in its mother's milk.'"

"OK," says Moses. "So you mean we should have separate dishes for meat and milk."

"No," says the Master of the Universe, "I simply said, 'Do not cook a kid in its mother's milk.'"

"Fine," says Moses. "So you mean we should wait six hours after meat before we can eat milk?"

"All right, Moses," says the Holy One, "have it your way."

Maimonides, in his *Guide for the Perplexed*, hazards a guess that this was an ancient pagan harvest custom that the Israelites were forbidden to imitate. But there was no external support for this theory until 1929, when at a site in Syria called Ras Shamra, now known as Ugarit, a French archaeologist uncovered the first of more than a thousand cuneiform tablets from about the fourteenth century BCE.

One of these tablets, experts later claimed, describes a Canaanite religious ritual, part of the worship of their chief god, El, which included a command that was deciphered to read, "Cook a kid in milk." Out of this emerged the claim that the pagans did indeed have a practice of cooking a kid in its mother's milk. Given the repeated insistence in the Torah of not imitating local pagan worship, this would explain the biblical law. Maimonides's intuition seems to have been right. Even the great biblical scholar Umberto Cassuto of the Hebrew University was taken in. Unfortunately, it seems that this theory was based on a mistranslation. The Ugaritic said nothing of the sort. The Ugaritic word *gdy* doesn't mean "kid," and there was no mention of milk or of cooking.

Perhaps the prohibition was linked to the other biblical laws requiring humans to treat animals with consideration. Laws included not sacrificing a newly born animal until it has had a week with its mother (Exodus 22, Leviticus 22), taking care of lost animals or helping them when struggling under heavy loads (Exodus 23), not slaughtering a mother and child on the same day (Leviticus 22), sending away the mother bird if you want to take away the eggs or fledglings (Deuteronomy 22), not getting disparate animals to work under the same yoke (Deuteronomy 22), and not muzzling an ox while it threshes (Deuteronomy 25).

Philo of Alexandria suggested a more abstract idea, that "it is unacceptable that the very liquid that sustained the animal at birth should now be used in its death" (*De Virtute* 13). And this links to the idea of separation. The Israelites were told to separate themselves from the pagans, both morally and behaviorally. The idea of not mixing is found in the laws of *kilayim*, sowing different plants together, or crossing plants and animals (*shatnez*, wearing wool and flax), holy spaces and communal ones, permitted foods and forbidden foods, permitted unions and forbidden unions, God's time and human time, meat and blood. It's a recognition of difference, an awareness of everything that goes on around one in the natural world and the human world.

And that's where "babies in their mother's milk" comes in. It is a separation of life from death and an assertion that life is our primary concern on earth. Milk is the initial food of life. Protein is as well. One came to us through death, the other through life. Both sustain, but we need to set boundaries between sustenance from life and sustenance through death. Setting boundaries plays a very significant role in the Bible, boundaries on Mount Sinai, between the parts of the Tabernacle.

You might also apply this logic to priests and laymen and see the whole structure as a response to pagan priests and practices. And indeed it explains all the biblical laws that relate to blood of one sort or another. But as the Talmud says, the only biblical law with an explicit reason is the one in Deuteronomy, limiting the king in pursuit of horses (military power) sex and money for fear they might turn his heart. All were contravened by King Solomon precisely because he reasoned he was above temptation. Anything based on reason alone is risky.

But is it all really relevant? Is all this guesswork anything more than an intellectual exercise? We try to explain the laws of kashrut through medical or utilitarian theories, but none of them cover the entire subject. Like them, this seemingly obscure law is part and parcel of the whole system of Jewish lifestyle of modulating all human activity, from sex to food. The way to do that is through law and custom, regardless of origin. In effect, when one considers it this way, the rabbis were right to emphasize the practical, to expand on the poor little kid. Actions speak louder than words.

Why do I keep these laws? It certainly isn't because of archaeology or complicated associations of ideas. I keep them because they are part of an existing way of life I subscribe to and enjoy, part divine, part human. I like archaeology, and often it validates traditions, but that is not why I adhere to the rules. They reinforce all sorts of emotions. That is how most thinking religious people relate to their religious traditions. Does the critical Christian really believe the myths of the Gospels? Does the reflective Muslim really think that a warring, illiterate Bedouin was given a work of poetic genius in his sleep, or does a Mormon believe that Joseph Smith discovered golden tablets? Does an academic Hindu believe the panoply of gods is anything more than symbols and points of reference? And how many of us Jews now literally believe "the sun stood still in the valley of Ayalon" (Joshua 10.12)? We delude ourselves into thinking religion is primarily theological orthodoxy. It is concerned with narratives (some like to use the word "myths") and rituals that should lead to correct actions and appropriate thought. This should be the function of ritual of course, not just routine thoughtless behavior.

Does it matter where the custom of eating cheesecake on Shavuot came from, or how late the idea of Shavuot being the anniversary of the Sinai Revelation emerged, or whether the *tikkun*, the all-night study session, was an invention of seventeenth-century kabbalists? It is all interesting and worthy of study, of course, but it is not the reason we do it all. That lies deep in our human minds and in our mystical souls, as well as in the very basic physiological need for order, system, and a structure for facing the constant challenges and pressures of life.

FUZZY

Plato's theory of ideas and Aristotle's more empirical approach are the foundations of the Western intellectual tradition. The result of this patrimony has been the search for truth, even absolute truth, which I believe has tended to constrict our way of thinking and reflects the desire to find a specific answer to every problem, assuming there is one.

In our times we have at last realized that there are such phenomena as quantum physics, fuzzy logic and fuzzy mathematics, which are, to put it simply, more approximate, variable, and less definite. In a similar vein, what is called "chaos theory" offers a different way of looking at empirical data and discovering that there can be several answers. One might not need to choose one specific theory or solution.

I have always sensed an affinity to the fuzzy. I find consistency boring and often self-defeating. The Torah itself gives us conflicting models of management, the divinely appointed leader, the hereditary priesthood, and then the monarchy, the prophet, and the judge. Which is the ideal? There isn't one. Much later we adopted the idea of the rabbi and scholar. Perhaps the implication is that circumstances may require different models of leadership, and we should be open to such possibilities. There is no single simple answer. So it is with Shavuot.

Shavuot, the Festival of Weeks, Pentecost, is a perfect example of a religious institution that defies categorization. Is it a harvest festival, an extension of Passover, or the anniversary of the revelation of Torah on Mount Sinai?

It is all, and I suggest that which aspect we ourselves emphasize depends on circumstances, history, and personality. When it comes to understanding Shavuot, one can, as with other theological issues, embrace several approaches simultaneously and find satisfaction in some or all.

In the Torah, the festival is described first as Hag HaKatzir (Exodus 23:16), the harvest festival as well as the occasion for dedicating bikkurim, the first of the harvest (23:19). Then a few chapters later it is Hag Shavuot (Exodus 34:22), the Festival of Weeks together with the first of the harvest. In Leviticus (33:16–17), the festival is referred to only as the culmination of the forty-nine days of the Omer, although the term *bikkurim* is once again specified. In Bmidbar (28:26) again the name HaBikurim appears, but as *yom* (day) instead of *hag* (festival). And in Devarim (16:9) it is Hag HaShavuot, as in Exodus 34, but with the definite article.

Academics will suggest that this variation can explained from the different sources the Torah was originally based on. The theory (and it is after all a theory) has its limitations. It creates as many problems as it solves; not least is the obvious incompetence of the editor or editors. Or perhaps simply different assumptions as to how one dealt with texts. A passive collator might make more sense. But one can suggest other possibilities. The Talmud Gittin (60a) suggests that the text of the revelation was not written down immediately, but extended over a forty-year period. So just as our own vocabulary and usage varies over time, so too may have that of Moses. I do not suggest this solves the issues that the documentary hypothesis raises. But it highlights that there are options.

It is common for the Torah to repeat narratives and laws. Its context was very different from our modern scientific minimalist approach. Each repetition and variation adds an extra dimension. Rather like "remembering" and "keeping" the Shabbat. Two different words used in the Exodus and Deuteronomy text of the Ten Commandments that do not cancel each other out as much as add to one's understanding. This variation in the terminology of the festival in the Torah might simply mean that it had many functions, just as Passover is sometimes called Hag HaMatzot (the human proactive idea of baking matzot) and sometimes Hag HaPesach (divine protection). Sukkot too is also Hag HaAsif (Festival of gathering in, human activity) and Sukkot (divine protection again).

Postbiblically Shavuot became the anniversary of the revelation of the Torah, *Zeman Matan Torateynu.* There is no explicit mention of this connection at all in the text of the Torah. It is only implicit. One might well understand the shift in emphasis that the changes in Roman society, migration away from one's early Hebrew agricultural land-based roots (whether forced or by choice), and urbanization must have had. The harvest aspect would no longer have been primary, and as rabbinic emphasis shifted toward study as the acme of Jewish self-identification, the focus on Sinai and Torah would have made sense. So from the period of the geonim at the end of the first millennium and particularly during the height of the period of kabbalah, staying up all night to study Torah acquired much more significance than the harvest or first fruits.

But even here we have variations. The actual description of the Sinai theophany in the Torah contains inconsistencies, and indeed apparent contradictions between Exodus 19, Exodus 24:1–11, and Exodus 24:12–18. There are variations in the sequence, in the responses, and in what actually was received or given on Sinai. And there is the question of why the mountain is sometimes called Sinai and sometimes Horeb. In postbiblical literature, what happened at Sinai is sometimes referred to as *Matan Torah* (giving the Torah), *Torah MiSinai* (Torah from Sinai) and *Torah Min HaShamayim* (Torah from heaven). They signify the same concept, but may not mean or were not intended to mean exactly the same thing. We are left to make what sense or derive what significance we want to. And we might each come to different conclusions, which does not matter so long as we all come together to celebrate the occasion at the same time.

I used to think that the agricultural, like the prayers for rain, were out of date and out of touch with modernity. I now know much better. The accelerating dangers of climate change, shortage of water, droughts, and ecological tragedies such as deforestation have woken us up to the importance of emphasizing the agricultural and the natural. The circle has come round. Had the Torah only given one reason, we might have been left high and dry. But it consistently gives different names and significances. I find this amazing and empowering. That's why I like the flexibility of the fuzzy, and that's another reason I will celebrate Shavuot!

FASTING

Although the Torah does not mention one fast directly (Yom Kippur is only referred to as a day when one "afflicts one's soul"), we have accumulated over time a lot of fasts and periods of official mourning. Almost all of the postbiblical fasts are associated with disasters, either those inflicted on us from the outside or those we have brought upon ourselves. The question is whether the idea of fasting altogether occupies a central or a marginal position in our core tradition.

The prophet Zechariah, writing two and a half thousand years ago, said, "Thus says the Lord of hosts: The fast of the fourth month, and the fast of the fifth, and the fast of the seventh, and the fast of the tenth shall become times of joy and gladness, and cheerful feasts to the house of Judah; therefore love truth and peace" (8:19). So it seems that in Babylon fasting as a response to the loss of our land and exile already played a significant role. And yet the prophet wanted to see them removed.

The Torah mentions being happy and rejoicing in life far more often than it mentions sadness. Yet we have added the days of the Omer, the three weeks of mourning for the loss of the Temple and Jerusalem, as well as the fasts of Gedaliah, the tenth of Tevet, and the seventeenth of Tammuz. Less well known are the optional fasts that follow festivals, the Monday, Thursday, and Monday fasts, not to mention fasts for bad dreams.

There are people mentioned in the Talmud and indeed those today who say that the fast of Tisha B'Av is redundant and should be cancelled. Their argument is that we now are free to return to much of our ancestral homeland, and we have access to the Old City of Jerusalem. Jerusalem today is, if anything, overbuilt and certainly not desolate. We should no longer mourn its destruction. Others counterargue that we are still very much in a state of siege and danger and the Temple is now a mosque.

There is still a serious problem with the state of our Jewish souls. And some of our people put this down to the temptations of materialism and a failure to emphasize the importance of making our world a better and more equitable place.

The Talmud in Sotah 49b says, "In the lead up to the Messiah, arrogance will spread and honor decrease...among scholars there will be immorality and no one will dare to rebuke them. Wisdom will degenerate and good men will be despised. Truth will be rare...the face of the generation will be like that of a dog." Yes, like a dog. That's how I feel when I see rabbis carted off in handcuffs. Outwardly religious or simply overtly Jewish men arraigned for corruption, money laundering, and dishonesty. And it keeps on happening year after year, sect after sect, community after community, country after country, and there is no letup. It is embarrassing when men who should know better behave like dogs.

I only hope the Mishna will be right that this is indeed a sign that God will intervene, because frankly none of our religious leaders seems capable of stopping it. Oh yes, they will excoriate us for eating the wrong food, for wearing short sleeves, for using teabags on the Sabbath, or making the wrong blessing. They will ban the use of computers, cell phones, and television, but remain silent on corruption and deceit. Some will even argue that laws of the land are not sacrosanct, and they will praise and honor the criminals who subsequently pass on chunks of their illegal booty to religious institutions.

All this is why I fast on the ninth of Av. Because when I read the first chapter of Isaiah that is the haftarah on the Shabbat beforehand, and I read the words he used of his generation, I realize we have not changed in nearly three thousand years. His words still accurately and correctly apply to swaths of Jewish life today. Hardly a month goes by without rabbis being indicted for one felony or another. It makes no difference if corrupt politicians outnumber them. It is irrelevant if others are more corrupt than we are. Should we judge ourselves by scum or pure water? I fast for my inability to make our own world a better place. I fast for the desecration of God's name *we* are guilty of. I fast because we have not learnt. Because we make money our god, and because not one of the so-called great rabbis of our generation comes out publicly and condemns corruption the way they do any petty infringement of their own political and social standards.

Think of Sodom and Gomorrah. Indeed, Isaiah makes the comparison. The Torah in Genesis (13:13) says, "And the men of Sodom were evil sinners to God exceedingly." But if you look carefully at the traditional punctuation, there is a comma between "sinners" and "to God exceedingly." I wish I knew who first made the point that the verse, if read according to its punctuation, really says, "And the men of Sodom were evil sinners," take a deep breath, "[but with regard] to God [they were] exceedingly [pious]!" That is how it is nowadays. Too many of us are outwardly holy and pious, but inwardly rotten to the core.

There's another crucial line in the first chapter of Isaiah. "Had it not been for a tiny minority, we would be no better than Sodom and comparable to Gomorrah." Thank goodness for the tiny minority. But sadly, it is all but silent. And for as long as this is the situation, Tisha B'Av remains as relevant as ever. We are in danger of destroying ourselves once again, if not physically, then certainly morally.

So it is true our religion requires us to be happy and enjoy the heavenly gifts we have been fortunate enough to receive. But in every Garden of Eden there is a snake. The custom of breaking a glass at a wedding is a reminder that even in the happiest of places there can be sadness and tragedy. And by the same token, in the worst of conditions they can be hope.

NINTH OF AV

Tisha B'Av, the ninth day of the month of Av, is the second-most-important fast day in the Jewish calendar, after Yom Kippur. All other so-called "minor fasts" run from dawn to dusk, like Ramadan. Unlike Ramadan, which lasts for a month, we have many fewer fast days, but we also have these two in the year that run for longer, over twenty-four hours. I would be interested to see a study as to the comparative impact, physical and mental, of a month-long daytime fast as opposed to the four obligatory rabbinic fasts (leaving out the mystical and ascetic options).

I used not to understand how ordinary mortals could go about their daily business on minor fasts without the necessary fuel. I find it hard to concentrate when I fast. I feel weak. It's not the food I miss as much as the liquid. If I could drink, I'd have no problem. I wonder if it isn't the fact that they are normal working days that affects me psychologically. I am not a multitasker.

The spiritual function of fasts, I believe, is to encourage self-analysis. But if you are feeling physically weak, it's difficult, though you might argue that at least you cannot get easily caught up in your daily, demanding physical tasks as a distraction. Surely fasting merely as an endurance test has no spiritual value, any more than doing it to diet has. On the contrary, it seems to me it is more likely to cause delusion.

Yet the fact is that I am able to handle Yom Kippur without too much difficulty. Is it just that psychologically I know I have to, because it is so important religiously, whereas on the other days, because I know they are less important, my body tries persuading me I should not try or perhaps give up halfway through? Even if all the empirical evidence is that I *can* do it? Perhaps it's autosuggestion trying to undermine me.

I have no doubt that this is why the rabbis said (Eruvin 21b) that keeping a rabbinic command is even greater than keeping one from the Torah. One is inevitably inclined to want to treat what the rabbis say less strictly (they are, after all, only human) than something coming from a higher authority! What this indicates is a perfectly natural human tendency to seek the easy way out.

We who are religious seem much better at keeping the little things than we are at keeping the big ones. We are more inclined to bother about strictness in matters of food than we are in matters of personal relations. Yet if one were to weigh up the number of what we would call moral and ethical statements in the Torah, they by far outweigh the ritual ones (with the exception of two areas that are no longer applicable: sacrifice and priestly purity).

There are different traditions that seek to explain why Tisha B'Av is so significant. One is the destruction of the two temples, two Jewish states, and Jerusalem. One is the collapse of the moral order. This is what the prophets during the First Temple period focus on. The other is the collapse of the political order, and this emerges more from the destruction of the Second Temple in the Talmud in Gittin 55 and 56, which, by tradition, we study on Tisha B'Av. In both Temple periods, the actual rituals were being carried out all the time. But something fundamental, a moral compass, was missing. I suggest it was and is the inability or the reluctance we have to go beyond our comfort zones. Someone who is ritually particular and disciplined finds it difficult to know when to bend the law toward being sensitive to humanity. On the other hand, someone who focuses primarily on the broader human scheme of things finds it difficult to focus on the smaller, more mundane practices and community obligations.

This is typical of most humans. Many of us are weak, and we like immediate gratification. But if our vanity is at stake, it is a mighty strong factor in selecting the foods we know are better for us and minimizing those we know are not. It's vanity that may drive us to find time for hours in a gym or on a yoga mat. And we usually put the needs of self before the needs of others. It is vanity to focus on externality rather than internality. The function of religion is to offer a counterbalance in pursuit of the golden mean.

If Yom Kippur takes us out of our comfort zone for spiritual matters, I suggest Tisha B'Av should take us out of our comfort zone on political issues. So much suffering and death in almost every generation has come from making the wrong political decisions. This has been as true (dare I say it) of our greatest rabbis as it has of ordinary, simple folk. But unless we are prepared to step outside of ourselves every now and then, however difficult, we will never get a different perspective on our own limitations.

Yet there is a third element too, the irrational hatred that never goes away. This is one reason that many make Tisha B'Av their memorial day for the Holocaust. They do this in reaction against political decisions to record the catastrophe that are usually more political than spiritual. They follow the tradition of trying to roll as many reasons to feel sad into already existing established days of mourning. Many earlier special days that recorded catastrophes in Spain, northern Europe, and North Africa independently have fallen into abeyance. And since the Holocaust is part of the long history of venomous hatred we have suffered from, it is appropriate to link it.

But in the end each one of us finds his own reasons and justifications for fasting or not. Experience tells me we may enter a fast with the best of intentions. But by the end it, the good intentions and resolutions are largely dissipated in the rush to eat!

PART 6

POLITICS

KARL MARX

People seem to love lists and reducing human achievement to popular votes. The BBC conducted a poll to find out who was the greatest philosopher of all time!

Now I guess most people who know what philosophy is are familiar with only a couple of names like Socrates, Aristotle, or Plato from Greece, perhaps Aquinas and Augustine if you're Christian, or Maimonides if you are a Jew. Modern philosophy arguably begins with Descartes (1596–1650). But after Voltaire (1694–1791) the French fall away, and although some like to claim that Sartre was a philosopher, we rational Anglo-Saxons don't rate them. We go rather for our "empirical" practical giants: Hobbes (1588–1679), Locke (1632–1704), and Hume (1711–1776).

The Germans have a list of heavy hitters (actually there wasn't a Germany there yet, but I mean from that area). There was Liebnitz (1646–1716), Kant (1724–1804), and (again if you think he's a philosopher) Hegel (1770–1831). After them came Schopenhauer (1788-1860) and Neitzsche (1844-1900), although the latter was more fantasist than rigorous philosopher. Of the moderns I refuse to include the Nazi-loving Heidegger because on principle, a racist and admirer of a genocide simply doesn't merit the title. I am a great fan of the earlier Husserl (1859–1938). Wittgenstein (Anglo-Austrian) has been the biggest influence on my thinking, but he's long gone, and I have to say, in general, current philosophy sounds rather uninspiring and leaves me cold and uninterested.

Now not one of these giants headed the BBC poll. No, it is a man who, as far as I am concerned, was not a philosopher at all. If anything he was a social economist with some absolutely crackpot theories, a Jew who hated Jews, and the man indirectly responsible for more deaths than any other human being ever. I refer to Karl Marx. Which only goes to show that the BBC's audience, and by implication its political bias, is as far left short of communist as you can get.

Marx's best idea was his quasi-messianic dream of a perfect world devoid of oppression, domination, and inequalities, giving "each according to his need." It was a lovely dream that goes back in Judaism two and a half thousand years to our prophets. He didn't invent it. I confess I do agree with his choice of who was responsible for most of human suffering at the time that he wrote: the church and the rich. But really it is the evil alliance of human ego and power that does and has done most harm consistently over the millennia.

Religion was, according to Marx, "the opiate of the masses," a tool whereby the aristocracy, in league with the church (or whatever religion), conspired to hold the poor down, promising them "gravy tomorrow" while they indulged themselves in this world. The industrial revolution saw millions of men, women, and children enslaved under the cruel workhouse and factory systems, receiving a pittance to barely survive on, while the bourgeoisie were flourishing on the backs of "the toiling masses." Just think *Les Misérables* or Charles Dickens. Marx's analysis of the problem was correct. His suggestion as to why was half correct, but his solution was lunacy. As the English essayist George Orwell had it in his satire of Marxism, *Animal Farm*, "All animals are created equal, but some are more equal than others." The naïve slogan soon gets perverted.

The forced socialization that was carried out in his name across the world to make everyone equal and thus eradicate poverty, corruption, and exploitation merely replaced one awful system with a far worse and more dangerous one. For while the old system at least paid lip service to the sanctity of life, Marxism proclaimed the dispensability of humans and the right to destroy those who stood in the way of the greater good. The end justified the means, the untold millions who suffered in Russia, China, Cambodia, Cuba, and countless other failed experiments (not to mention the kibbutz movement in the list of failed ideals, though despite the emotional damage Bruno Bettelheim described, I don't think any died as a direct result!).

Thanks to Marx, the crimes committed in his name make the worst excesses of religion look positively benign. The end *never* justifies the means. Any politician, let alone thinker, who argues thus ought to be hanged, drawn, and quartered, slowly.

Yet why has Marxism so dominated the Western academic world? Why does it persist in any way at all? How do we explain the unholy alliance between a brilliant thinker like Noam Chomsky and a guttersnipe like George Galloway?

I agree that capitalism and the excessive gap between the rich and the poor is an offense, but getting rid of initiative will not necessarily level the playing field. Neither will government handouts that encourage dependency and sloth. I can sympathize with the Marxist critique of religion, particularly when it gets involved in politics. Indeed, I could bring plenty of examples from within Judaism to support their case that religion is often more concerned with power and keeping others under control than with making the world a better place for everyone. There is and has been a lot wrong with religion, but it does have some saving graces that Marxism does not. Hence the flight from Marxism the moment compulsion is removed.

But why do Marxist sympathizers, particularly BBC pundits such as John Pilger or Michael Rosen (no relation, thank goodness), express such antagonism to Judaism or Jews, specifically? Is it because we support a Jewish state? If they objected to all forms of nationalism because they'd rather see a benign universal government "of the people, by the people, and for the people" (no, Marx did not say that), then I could understand, even sympathize to some degree. But why single out Israel to hate while approving of splitting Yugoslavia into all those little statelets?

Why is Marx the man that most thinking, cultured Britons think is the greatest philosopher of all time? Because when you are a failed academic or politician or anything else, and you feel you are not getting your due while other, inferior beings are richer or appear to be doing better and enjoying themselves, you respond with hatred. We see this in disenfranchised or unemployed Muslims, neo-Nazis, drunken hooligans, underpaid academics, and even alienated Jews. Just as the destructive antiglobalization, anticapitalism movement appeals to Marxist rebels (or spoilt trust-fund kids looking for a cause), so anyone looking at any other group that survives and thrives and wins the battle for survival is filled with envy and bitterness.

The solution to poverty is industry and motivation (though to be fair it also requires bully nations to give the poor ones a fair chance if they're willing to try for it). Once upon a time, many intellectuals supported Marxism as the antidote to fascism. Then slowly they realized they are virtually the same evil with different names. The fact that Marx is still so popular shows how failing ideas are sustained by failing individuals who always blame others, look for scapegoats, and more often than not pick on the Jews. You can tell an ideology stinks when its proponents stink.

MARGARET THATCHER

The death and magnificent funeral of former prime minister of Britain Margaret Thatcher has reminded us of what a divisive figure she was. Obituaries ranged from panegyrics to abuse.

My only personal encounter with Margaret Thatcher was when, as minister of education, she was the guest of honor at the Carmel College graduation ceremony (we called it Speech Day) in 1971. I did not warm to her. She was hectoring and lacking in warmth. I admit I was biased. I was brought up in a family that considered voting Conservative a betrayal of one's intellectual and moral integrity. But that was at a time when Britain was still dominated and hobbled by class. The Conservative Party was regarded as the preserve of aristocratic, military, wealthy, male Britons (and their obedient ladies), and it barely tolerated those aspiring to upward mobility. Most Jews in my youth were still closer to the ethic of socialism and the Labour Party (despite the ghastly postwar anti-Semitic Ernest Bevin). It was much more pro-Jewish and had many more Jewish members of Parliament in those days.

Britain was polarized in my youth, far more than anyone can imagine nowadays. Class pervaded everything. In the Oxfordshire countryside where I grew up, the landed gentry lived on their own estates, and everything and everyone around them was kept at a discreet distance. In the village pubs there were two bars: the public bar for the working classes and the saloon bar for the genteel middle and upper classes. In the local town, Wallingford, there was one general store called Field and Hawkins for the upper classes, and a discreet square away was Petits for the rest. The wealthy went to private schools (ironically called "public schools"), and the middle and working classes went to state schools. There was an annual cricket game called Gentlemen v. Players. Gentlemen were upper-class amateurs. The Players were the working-class athletes who were paid to perform. Upper classes went horse racing at Royal Ascot. The poor went greyhound racing. The upper classes went to work with a bowler hat and furled umbrella, the workers in cloth caps.

During the sixties everything began to change, however slowly. West Indian immigration and the Beatles and Rolling Stones who appealed across the class divide all helped. But still, the historic grip of the royal family and its aristocracy was preserved. Those of aristocratic birth or ecclesiastical seniority rather than either merit or democracy dominated the House of Lords. It could interfere with or block the will of the freely elected House of Commons (don't the names themselves say it all). Women might have had a vote, but they were still regarded as the weaker sex. A woman was expected "to be seen and not heard."

The Conservative Party was dominated by "peers of the realm" and their relatives, and only Jews who emulated the upper crust were acceptable to the party. Into this atmosphere swept Margaret Thatcher, ably supported by her wealthy husband. I well remember the extent to which she was despised by her own party for being a woman with a mind of her own, and worse, for being the daughter of a grocer. That was the most damning insult the Tories could throw at anyone in those days.

Her own party begrudgingly allowed her promotion only because she fought for it, and most of them disliked her for dislodging the weak, anodyne Edward Heath. But she had the strength of character and will first to fight her ground, then to overcome, and finally to hector them into submission. It was only after a long reign that they were they able to turn on her and pay her back.

Inevitably, she was and is despised by the Left and adored by the Right. Her economic record is still a matter of dispute. But there is no doubt she was a catalyst for significant change in many areas. There were inevitably battles she lost or causes she got wrong. But she had guts. She took on the uncompromising coal miner leader Arthur Scargill and broke the back of union resistance. She fought against political correctness and turned Britain into a society where you could get things done and there were opportunities for rising out of dependency if only you were prepared to "get on your bike," as one of her ministers put it.

It would take another twenty years before the Labour Party broke the vice the unions still had on them. Tony Blair became electable precisely because he followed Thatcher's pragmatism and, surprisingly, his more feminine approach. Even so, neither she nor he could control the abuses and costs of welfare. She was fortunate that North Sea oil sustained her economically.

She was accused of being unenthusiastic about the European Economic Union. That was because she loathed lazy bureaucracy, incompetence, financial corruption, unnecessary subsidies, and decisions based on not upsetting anyone. Imagine, members of the European Parliament shuttling between two duplicating parliaments, one in Brussels and the other in Strasbourg, just to keep France sweet. She was right. The EU has shown itself administratively and financially to be a mess, even if culturally and as a market for goods it has been a success.

As for the Jews, she understood us better than any other prime minister. Her Finchley constituency was heavily Jewish. Her ideology was closer to biblical self-sufficiency than Anglican noblesse oblige. That was why she got on so well with Chief Rabbi Immanuel Jakobovits. She surrounded herself with more Jewish cabinet ministers than any previous PM, and don't think she wasn't resented for it.

In the Old World they don't like strong leaders who are unafraid to get tough. They prefer consensus. They look for compromise. The result is that they tend to either capitulate or awake too late to stop the inevitable. Thatcher was never afraid to speak her mind, to say it as she saw it. That was why the Americans always admired her more than the Brits did.

Whether it is politics or religion, boredom, consensus, or bureaucracy and vested interests, they all place a dead hand on creativity and innovation. The gutsy, radical, innovative thinkers lose out to competent, conforming self-servers. Maggie riled her civil servants and loathed her diplomats. The epithet "the Iron Lady" was originally intended as an insult. It became her badge of honor. She was tough. And "tough" is what we really need if we are ever to get things done. Give me a gutsy leader I disagree with rather than a weak one who will not take a stand.

RACE IN AMERICA

The challenge of racial discrimination still hangs over most human societies. The shooting of yet another young unarmed black man, this time in the town of Ferguson, Missouri, in August 2014 has ignited a firestorm in the United States over the treatment of blacks. The return of a grand jury decision that there was insufficient evidence and too many contradictory witness reports to charge the police officer has only made matters worse. And similarly the grand jury's decision in New York not to prosecute the white officer whose choke hold led to the death of Eric Garner gives the impression that there is one law for whites and another for blacks. Riots and looting in Baltimore too have underlined the feeling of most blacks that they are being victimized by the systems of law and order. Once again the argument is polarized between two sides that put all the blame wholly upon each other. Then there are those like me who see both angles.

In both cases the victim was not entirely blameless. Brown was wanted as a suspect in a petty robbery and behaved aggressively. Garner was doing something illegal and resisting arrest. Nevertheless, it cannot be stressed enough that none of these warrants taking a life. Clearly something is wrong with police tactics. But the juries focused on whether there was malign intent to kill and decided as in the case of Trayvon Martin that there was not. Was this racism? Did this mean that the jury thought it is OK to shoot blacks?

Let's tackle an incidental issue first, that of firearms. Regardless of what gun supporters claim, the prevalence of guns in American society means they are more likely to be used, and police officers likely to be feel more jittery about their being used against them. Almost every day on American streets, police officers shoot first and ask questions afterward. And equally policemen are shot dead simply for who they are. Eventually American society will have to decide what it prefers.

It is true that far more black men are shot by police officers than white. But this might reflect the reality of crime statistics on the one hand and that too few blacks graduate school and get into police forces as much as racism.

There are those who claim that this in itself is a hangover from the racism of slavery. The reality is that the overwhelming number of black deaths are caused by other blacks. If demonstrators really believe the issue is black deaths, why are they waving placards saying “Don’t Shoot” at white policemen when they should be waving them at other blacks, those who do most of the killing, who spread the message that black lives are cheap?

Although the crime rate in the United States has dropped significantly in general, specifically in certain big cities, the evidence shows the link between poverty and violent death. If one is raised in certain high-crime areas, one is more likely to become a criminal and more likely to get killed by same-race criminals. There is a whole substratum of alienated and violent young men and women, predominantly black but also Latino, and this was only underlined by the violence, looting, and wanton destruction that accompanied the demonstrations in Ferguson and Baltimore.

The question is whether this is about poverty, poor values, poor education, poor parenting, and desperation, or only about race. Are not gangs of poorly educated unemployed white youths just as intimidating? America has improved racially a great deal over the past fifty years. There are black Americans at every level and in every area of American social, economic, and political life. Clearly to rise is possible. Yet much of the black community is still held back. Who is to blame?

Some blame must be shouldered by the flawed American judicial system. Almost 90 percent of criminal cases are decided on the basis of plea-bargaining, where often innocent people admit to guilt to avoid the possibility of a much longer prison term. This means that bullying and coercion too often decide a person's guilt rather than merit.

The legal system has decided that nonviolent drug crimes are the biggest threat to society and deserve incarceration. Overwhelmingly, poorer Americans get caught up in this. The result is that 40 percent of the massive prison population is made up of blacks, even though they only make up 12 percent of the population. One in three blacks is likely to spend time in jail. Blacks are three times more likely to go to jail for the same offense as whites. And the three-strike laws in many states mean that for repeated nonviolent drug offenses a person could spend most of his life in prison.

The result of this is that hundreds of thousands of blacks come out from jail brutalized and unable to find employment and become responsible citizens. Family life is further eroded. Sixty-seven percent of all black children grow up in single-parent families. This affects education as well as stability. For most young poor blacks, if they cannot become sports stars, entertainers, drug dealers, or petty criminals, they have no way of making a living other than joining the army, which produces its own disastrous aftereffects. All this breeds desperation and hopelessness, which in turn increases violence.

Another cause of holding poor people back is the culture of dependency and expectation. Once it was a European disease to rely on welfare. Now in the United States, government employment is the sinecure that the poor have come to rely on. The massive growth in lotteries and gambling and the huge sums the poor spend proportionally on them also underline the reliance on salvation coming from somewhere else. In addition, a culture of blaming others and failing to take responsibility is reinforced by the culture of litigation. The career agitators, the Al Sharptons, are out in force, as are the lawyers looking for million-dollar paydays. Making a noise does not necessarily mean you are helping. Baltimore has had billions of state aid poured into it to seemingly little effect. Its political hierarchy is overwhelmingly black, but nothing is filtering down.

The media is to blame too for encouraging notoriety, instant fame, and excessive rewards for no talent other than self-promotion (usually through violence or pornography). The worse you behave, the better you do. But another factor is that black culture is indeed more exuberant, less constrained than white. Many blacks resent it that to do well in a white world they have to ape the white culture. But then this is the same problem women have accommodating themselves to a man's world and that all different or immigrant populations have to contend with wherever they are.

I also blame the Left as much as I excoriate the excessive greed of the Right. They love to simplify the enemy, to blame the other and look for any excuse to further their agenda. The proof is that at these current demonstrations one is seeing pro-Palestinian and anti-Israel placards. It is the same pathology. Too many ideologues focus on perpetuating problems by playing the blame game. And then for all their good intentions they end up supporting those who refuse to support themselves peacefully, because the victims are encouraged to look to others to get them out of their mess.

Finally, blame lies squarely in the teachers unions that perpetuate poor schooling by refusing to allow failing teachers to be fired, that resist any attempt to improve the quality of education, that seem concerned only with preserving the jobs of their members regardless. And they try their best to prevent any viable alternative.

These are all grave problems that must be addressed. There is blame on both sides, and changes are essential. There is some good news. The school dropout rate among the black population has fallen from 21 percent in 1972 to 9 percent in 2012. Education is slowly improving, if only because there are more alternatives, despite the opposition of the teachers unions. There is hope.

I believe it is right to demonstrate and show one's anger and concern. Where there are peaceful demonstrations, I believe all caring citizens ought to be joining them. If something is not just or right in the societies we live in, it is our religious and social obligation to protest and work toward a resolution.

But we should not perpetuate the problems by doing what most politicians love to do, by indulging, pandering, and pretending it is what it is not. That might win votes, but it does not solve anything.

FREE SPEECH

The Ramaz School in New York is one of the better Jewish schools in the Diaspora. One of its student societies invited the well-known Palestinian apologist Rashid Khalidi of Columbia University to speak to a closed meeting. When the school authorities became aware of the invitation, they cancelled it. In my opinion they were wrong. They sent a dangerous message that undermines our intellectual and moral integrity.

Intelligent, thinking students need to hear other opinions, other arguments, and other convictions. Knowing what the other side's arguments and emotions are, they can better make up their own minds about the issues of the day. One of the primary tasks of a good education is to present different ideas. Certainly where a school prides itself on the intellectual quality of its staff, its pupils, and its curriculum, there is all the greater responsibility to present conflicting points of view and intellectual challenges, even if they sometimes might be painful. Presenting different points of view is indeed the very difference between education and indoctrination.

This does not mean that a good school cannot promote its own particular favored position and ideology. It should and it must. But if you do not expose your charges to an opposing point of view, they will be totally unequipped to deal with the challenges they will face on the outside in situations when there may be no one there to consult or to give them another point of view. I assume Ramaz has on its staff or has access to people who are well enough prepared and capable enough debaters to respond either directly or through the curriculum to any argument that is false, biased, or offensive.

In my years in education, both at the high school and adult level, I was always ready to invite controversial speakers to present another point of view, even if I hated the opinion and the person who propagated it. Whether it was the Austrian neo-Nazi Joerg Haider or South African archbishop Desmond Tutu, or even an extreme left-wing Israeli opinion, which was often much more extreme and harder to take, I thought it important to actually listen to them in a context in which they could be challenged, both for their own good (though it rarely achieves that; hatred rarely tolerates a riposte), and in order to learn how to respond. Even, I might say, to listen with humility if there are strong arguments that are painful that should be taken to heart.

The process of dialectic, of classical philosophical debate, is an invaluable tool for young people to learn not only how to think for themselves but how to try to persuade others. Similarly, when it comes to religious issues, I have welcomed atheists to speak, such as Anthony Grayling. I think it essential that young Jews learn how to defend themselves. After all, even Pirkei Avot commands us to "know how to answer the heretic."

All this presupposes that in the audience and afterward there will be well-informed teachers who will be able to defend the other side. Sometimes this is not the case. But if it does happen, the school has every opportunity to make sure that this is rectified farther down the line with better-equipped experts brought in to ensure that other arguments are given and the nuances appreciated. Anyway, there are levels of commitment that go beyond logic: priorities of family, people, and nation, even if one has reservations or sees another point of view.

One of the sad features of political debate nowadays in general and the Israel-Palestinian issue in particular is that one side, invariably the Palestinian, in my experience, usually tries to shout down the other. In Europe Israel rarely gets an opportunity to present itself, and when it is given a platform, the other side and its amen choruses try their best to disrupt. This is happening on American campuses too. Fashion in academia is as insidious as in *Vogue*. More so, given the stakes. The illogicality of boycotting Israel over, say, China or Russia, simply defies logic or justice. Balanced and reasoned debate is increasingly rare. But this doesn't mean a well-organized school genuinely interested in education should be frightened of presenting both sides, even if universities do not.

Rashid Khalidi is indeed an apologist for the Palestinian cause, and a supporter of armed resistance. He is intelligent and articulate. I think it would have been very useful for Jewish students to hear his arguments. Besides, now that he has been denied a platform there, I have no doubt that many pupils will try to find out for themselves what his arguments are, outside the school. And the fact that he was denied access to them will only make him appear more credible. So what has been achieved? All that has happened is that some young, intelligent Jews now have the feeling that the community does not want to hear another, unpalatable point of view.

When, as a rabbi or headmaster, I did invite controversial speakers, the skies fell down around me, and all sorts of pressure was tried to get me to change my mind. Everyone who thought, or whom other people persuaded, that they could influence me, either because they were donors or communal bigwigs, weighed in on the matter and tried everything from threats to withdrawing financial aid. Interestingly, it transpired that those who fought hardest to stop freedom of speech invariably had dirty secrets of their own they wanted hushing up! That's Jewish life for you. Fortunately I was always in a position to ignore them, sometimes politely. Not everyone is.

It is a grave mistake to believe one can completely protect one's children intellectually, and even if you could, it would certainly not help if one wanted them to grow up to take their places in a competitive society. Ironically, I am more in favor of refusing to give our enemies a platform as adults within the established community than I am in schools, precisely because there the minds are more open and malleable.

Once again it is the season for anti-Israel campus events. The very terminology, such as apartheid, is proof of the intellectual ignorance and dishonesty of the campaigns. Yet left-wing academics rush into the fray all over the country. Not enough is being done to arm young Jewish students to fight back. Sadly, it too often has to be against other Jews who are as fanatically opposed to Israel as the blindest of jihadis. But their arguments and lies must be exposed, not avoided.

There are enough reasons to criticize Israel without lies and distortions, and equally there are enough good arguments to show that Palestinians themselves are the authors of their own sorry state of affairs. I wish it could be resolved amicably, or even not amicably. But the last thing we want to do is to descend to their level of dishonest debate, falsified history, and a culture of physical and mental dependency. Unless our youngsters actually hear the lies and learn how to answer them, they will not be prepared for university life or the moral challenges that face them.

PREJUDICE

I am prejudiced. No doubt about that. My level of prejudice, of course, varies. I am prejudiced against all loudmouthed, aggressive human beings who think that aggression wins arguments and violence solves problems. I am prejudiced against any faith or ideology in which a significant majority expresses anti-Jewish sentiments. I am prejudiced against people who think they just have to follow current fashions, who wear tattoos, or who feel that showing off conspicuous consumption is a necessary and positive attribute. I am prejudiced against fanatics and religious people who want to impose their religion on others. I am prejudiced against anyone who thinks that he or she is the sole possessor of the complete truth regardless of color, size, race, or religion. If I am on guard facing a black youth at midnight in Harlem, I am equally scared of a white supremacist at 1:00 a.m. in Montana, a white biker at 2:00 a.m. in California, or a hooded Ku Klux Klan member at 3:00 a.m. in Louisiana.

Even so, I try very hard to overcome prejudices when I meet someone regardless of appearance or loyalty because I know that one should not judge a book by its cover, a man by his dress (though Shakespeare's Polonius thinks I should), or a woman by her plastic surgeon. I have met more good, admirable people of all races than I have evil, nasty ones. Above all, I do not believe in being rude, unkind, and certainly not offensive or aggressive toward people I disagree with and may be prejudiced against. And it certainly makes no sense to me to harbor any resentment against anyone who has never done me any harm, regardless of religion, nationality or color. Despite my recognizing certain prejudices, I work hard to ensure they do not affect the way I interact with others (until more information either confirms or removes the preconceived mind-set).

Prejudice usually means something more than just feeling one wants to avoid certain people. Prejudice has come to involve not just hate crimes and abuse but preventing people getting jobs, renting homes, or even entering certain places. In free Western countries, the law bans such prejudicial actions and behavior. In some countries it reinforces them.

Laws, of course, cannot control people's thoughts or choices of company or where they choose to buy a house. And equally so, prejudice does not depend on where we live. Some of the most tolerant human beings I have met live in ghettos, and some of the most intolerant live in the wilds. We do not yet live in a world of thought police where we convict for thinking politically unacceptable ideas or for being cautious, whether with cause or without.

I do, however, draw a distinction too between prejudice based on race and prejudice based on people's actions. Prejudice against blacks simply because of a skin pigmentation is as ridiculous as prejudice against someone because he is ugly or her hair is red. On the other hand, prejudice against criminal gangs, be they white, black, or yellow, is just a protective mechanism. It is self-defense. Similarly, employers preferring graduates to school dropouts might not always make sense because there are always outliers. But it certainly does as a general rule.

There is a distinction between Europe and the United States as to whether hate speech is illegal. In the United States, it is not until it is translated into action. In Europe it is enough to be regarded as incitement. Throughout Europe, as with smoking weed, the police forces virtually never react to such incitement. So in practice it's the same. I am in favor of free speech even if it offends and hurts. I believe all authority needs to be challenged, including religious authority. Western society is predicated on such freedom, and we must resist those Muslims who attempt to prevent it. I dislike Pamela Geller and her supporters not for the principle they claim to uphold but simply for the crude, generalized, and careless language they use to buttress their case.

At this moment in time, many Jews feel that most Muslims are ill disposed toward them even if in the past many had good experiences with their Muslim neighbors. If it were just because of Israel's present actions against Palestinians, one would expect equal anger at Muslims killing Muslims. But one rarely sees this. Is it perhaps because Islam regards Jews as dhimmis, second-class citizens? But then one would expect equally negative attitudes toward Christians. Perhaps it is linked to the fact that until relatively recently Muslims were one of the most powerful groups, and they lived almost exclusively under Muslim rulers. Now they see the imperial West as humiliating them, and Israel is identified with the imperialists (regardless of the fact that most Israelis originated in Muslim lands and identify with Arab culture). The sad fact now is that Muslim anti-Semitism is the major single cause of anti-Semitism around the world. But fascism is not dead. Even so, shouldn't they know that not all Jews think and feel the same way?

The Jobbik party in Hungary is violently anti-Semitic. So are skinheads in Germany. And ironically, so too is the left. Which makes it all the stranger that it identifies with a fundamentalist, anti-humanist, antifeminist, and anti-egalitarian brand of religion. But then it was a principle in Marxism that you could ally yourself with anyone if it helped your cause, a principle that Hamas shares.

I grew up in a Britain where anti-Semitism was common. It was lurking beneath the surface, but it was never as overt and public as it is now. But as a child, whenever I went into the local town I knew I had to be aware, and self-protective. I am told now that I must not wear my head covering in many cities in Europe. So when I see a skinhead, or when I see a Muslim, should I not now assume the worst until I know differently? Should I not run for cover or cross over to the other side of the street? Or should I rather give humans the benefit of the doubt? And if I should, what is the tipping point? At what point am I simply endangering myself? And should I be afraid of wearing my kippah while everyone else campaigns to allow the hijab? Am I wrong, therefore, to assume that most Muslims hate me? Or should I refuse to generalize and simply say my prejudice is against anti-Semites of whatever kind?

The Jewish answer is that, although I must defend myself, I should judge each individual on his or her own merit. After all, on Rosh Hashanah we quote the Mishna that says that the Almighty evaluates every human being. Not all are found guilty! The Torah tells us to treat the stranger as one of us even though the environment in which this was said was one of pagan hostility and a clash of cultures. But it is true this only applied where the stranger was willing to accept us and our moral code, not when he wanted to kill us or impose his laws instead.

Some of my Muslim correspondents can no longer speak to me civilly. But others still do think rationally. Some have confessed that other Muslims such as ISIS or Assad are a far bigger danger than Israel, but they are reluctant to stand up against overwhelming public opinion. And others rely on the negative stereotypes in the Koran and the Hadit.

The sad fact is that we Jews have our full range of those for and those against, those in and those out. Large numbers of young Jews with no first-hand experience of intolerance, expulsion, or insecurity, or of religious commitment, no longer see the need for a Jewish state or its right to defend itself. So should I not be prejudiced against them too?

There are good people everywhere, and there are thinking, considerate humans even among those who we assume are our enemies. We must seek them out and try to make common cause with them, however few, frightened, or battered they may be. Prejudice toward "the other" seems almost to be an evolutionary natural state. The whole point of a religious morality is to combat "naturalism," the animal aspect of our nature, and to try one's best to elevate the better aspects. If others cannot, we must still try.

REFUGEES

In the United States, a debate rages over the thousands of refugees from Central America streaming across the porous southern border. The fact that in the past few months over fifty thousand of them have been unaccompanied minors makes the situation particularly emotional and complicated. In 2014 alone, some three hundred thousand immigrants have crossed illegally into the United States. Among them is a significant number of drug dealers and criminals, not just from Latin America, but from around the world. Some states and some cities actually need more immigration and want to encourage it. Others want to exclude immigrants.

The issue is humanitarian, wanting to assist those in trouble. In 2015 literally thousands of refugees have been drowned in the Mediterranean and East Asia seas trying to escape or simply to better themselves. It is also a need for new blood to replace an aging retired population with those who can and will work. But it is also an existential one. What happens when the flood of refugees threatens to radically change the character of the receiving nation? Is it relevant to distinguish between political, social, and simply economic refugees? And finally, there is a principle of whether breaking the law, coming into a country illegally, as so many do, should be rewarded.

This is now a problem that affects the free world everywhere. Countries that are blessed with freedom and at least a semblance of democracy are seen as places to run to when living at home is no longer congenial. If you have money or good qualifications, you will be welcomed. If you are poor, you will not be. And does it matter if you also have an agenda of replacing the culture of the host nation with your own?

The movement of millions of human beings from one country to another across the globe, these quasi-invasions, sounds almost like science fiction. It is a huge, illicit, corrupt business. Human trafficking has apparently overtaken drug smuggling in profitability. And of course, tragically, many die on the way. What can one do?

In Europe, thousands of refugees from violence, together with economic migrants, are smuggled or try to sail across the Mediterranean each month. Hundreds die in the process. The millions of North Africans now living in France have already changed the character of the nation. But now these new waves are going to radically alter many other European states. Already Jews feel uncomfortable in many parts of the continent and mobs attacked synagogues and assaulted Jews and encouraged hatred. Anti-Semitic marches are now regular features. The European Union has dithered and completely failed to deal with the issue. Its passivity means that with the dislocated from Iraq, Syria, and Afghanistan, hundreds of thousands are going to continue risking the journey to try to get into Europe.

In Israel, too, on a far smaller scale, thousands of refugees from Somalia and east Africa are heading through Egypt (where none of them want to stay even if they share the same religion) across Sinai toward Israel. They are often tortured, raped, and murdered on the way. If they do get in, Israel is not the most hospitable of destinations, given the security problem and Islam's antipathy to the Jewish state. If Israel welcomed millions of Muslim refugees, it would completely lose what often tenuous Jewish identity it has. Indeed, why would any country want to be swamped with desperate people, often unemployable, particularly if they belong to cultures and religions diametrically opposed to the values of the host society?

The simple answer is that there are laws and conventions that require countries to accept refugees. The Convention Relating to the Status of Refugees was formalized at a special United Nations conference in 1951, where certain rules were established to protect European refugees who had no state after the upheavals of the Second World War. The numbers were limited. Much later it was expanded to include anyone "fleeing their countries because their lives, safety or freedom have been threatened by generalized violence, foreign aggression, internal conflicts, massive violation of human rights or other circumstances which have seriously disturbed public order."

Originally the law required those seeking refugee status isisated that they stop and apoply in the first ciountry they arrived at after fleeing. But nowadays this is rarely adhered to as migrants land in one country and trhewn press on to the destinations they prewfer because welfare is more accessible. Both in Europe and the USA blind eyes are turned.

What started with a limited number of internal European refugees now applies to millions who can claim that living conditions in their countries of birth are insufferable. The world population has expanded from the less than a billion then, to seven billion today. What should one do?

There are those who say that one should simply accept the reality and let the chips fall as they may. But, as we have seen in the United States, this is also a matter of cost in welfare and housing. Many governors who in principle approve of welcoming genuine refugees do not want to have to house and fund them. Either one simply opens the floodgates to all and sundry, or one helps create this massive industry in human smuggling. It was the reasonable attempt to apply an amnesty to millions of illegal immigrants in the United States that has caused this massive influx of desperate Hondurans eager to escape a country with the highest murder rate in the world. So is Honduras to transfer its population en masse to the United States, leaving a few gangster oligarchs to enjoy what's left?

You might argue that rich countries should spend money trying to reform or prop up the failed regimes the refugees want to escape from. America has tried that and notably failed in the Middle East, South America, and Asia. Europe tried pouring money into North Africa to stem the outflow. Not only did it fail, but refugees are now pouring in from farther afield. Regime change can only come when enough of the current regime's own people insist on it. Australia has tried shipping its illegals off to island camps, with disastrous results. Logically, the answer is to ship them home. But due legal processes in democratic countries often prevent that. In Britain, no matter how foul or lethal new immigrant rabble-rousers are, they avoid being sent home by claiming they would be mistreated. And the courts usually agree.

If the original idea was to protect those without a state, and now millions are moving from states with passports, perhaps we should be taking action against the original states for creating the problem in the first place rather than against the "victims" of poor governance. It does seem ridiculous to help failed states by taking in the very people they want to drive out for political reasons. Because all that does is to reinforce the corrupt regimes that created the problem. Instead, by forcing people to stay (by not giving them refuge) they may act to change their evil rulers. Then we would be doing them a greater favor in the long run than by allowing our states to be overrun, diluted, and in due course become failed states themselves. But at what humanitarian cost?

Clearly the conventions on refugees are simply neither working nor any longer logical or practical. Even when refugees arrive somewhere, they are often treated as pariahs. It seems the only solution is for each state to determine for itself whether it wishes to commit cultural suicide or not and act accordingly. It is ironic thart for all the fear of immigration, many countries in Europe and the Americas desperately need cheap labor, a hard working body of those willing to do low paying jobs thar most indigenous citizens do not want to do. The migrants who seek a better life are needed! Love them , hate them or need them they may prove to be of benefit rather than harm.

Think of Russian Jews a hundred and fifty years ago who emigrated in their millions to escape pogroms and poverty. They benefitted and enriched other societies they went to. But they never intended to return to their countries of origin. Neither were they committed to a religious culture that wanted to change the societies they moved to. Perhaps in the long term, this generation of migrants will integrate and enrich the host societies. I hope so, because at the moment the picture does not look so hopeful. I fear it is too late and the new reality is just that.

We are socially doomed if we do and morally doomed if we do not.

DRUGS

I met an old pal recently who lives in a very, very tight, ultra-Orthodox enclave. He works in the property business and comes from a long line of rabbis. He told me that the only way he copes with the pressures of life is by smoking marijuana, not occasionally but all the time. He offered me a drag there and then, and I said I didn't smoke. "OK," he said. "I'll make you some brownies and send them round." Once upon a time that would have sounded terrible. But now that several states in the United States have legalized marijuana and others have decided not to prosecute personal users (as opposed to dealers), it seems that attitudes are changing. How far should we go?

I am strongly opposed to taking (nonmedical) drugs. It is beyond any Halachic doubt that Judaism forbids anything that may damage one's body or brain. The same system that requires us to treat the bodies of the dead with respect requires us to treat the bodies of the living with respect. That means not willfully doing anything that might cause damage. I also believe that those societies or sub societies that have used drugs regularly have been the failure stories of our world, not the success stories. Escapism, whatever drug or method is used, has a destructive effect on the human capacity to make correct decisions and to take responsibility.

There is of course a difference between drugs such as heroin, opiates, and mind-altering psychedelic poppers and food and alcohol. They in some quantities can be both beneficial and essential. Sure, with food, as with alcohol, excessive use or abuse can be lethal. Some might argue this way about pot, hash, and weed. They can help reduce pain. Morphine reduces pain, but it also kills. And there is growing evidence that marijuana, as well as helping one cope with pain, also causes damage and, in reducing alertness, causes accidents.

Having said this, I am strongly opposed to criminalizing drugs. No attempt to ban anything ever succeeds. Prohibition in America spawned the mafiosi empires of the 1920s. The lord chancellor's attempt to ban *Lady Chatterley's Lover* in England some forty years ago spelled the end of his office. Pornography survived Mary Whitehouse. Forbidding abortion merely drove it into the hands of dangerous back-street amateurs. The ban on drugs simply makes criminals rich.

We should decriminalize and tax them heavily as we do tobacco and alcohol (and use part of the money for clinics, rehabilitation, and palliative procedures). A free democratic society allows people to do what they want so long as they do not damage others. It leaves personal choices up to religious or other moral codes to regulate voluntarily. Personally I would not criminalize euthanasia or suicide for those citizens of free countries who choose those paths, despite my religious opposition to both, provided of course there were safeguards to prevent abuse.

In socialist societies where the health and welfare of citizens falls upon the state, it is necessary to recoup the cost of allowing people to smoke, drink, and take drugs and thus damage their health. In New York, Mayor Bloomberg banned smoking in all public places. After some agitation it has thankfully been accepted. I am grateful because I hate having to smell other people's breath at the best of times, and more so when it stinks of tobacco. So this comes under the category of something that does indeed affect other people involuntarily and should be allowed only in private. This is where heavy taxation helps. Tax the living daylights out of them all and earmark the money for cure and therapy. I know the poor will suffer most, but we might be doing them a favor.

Now if I rely on religious values to impose stricter standards than civil society, why is it that in the Orthodox Jewish world, which is so strict on so many laws and restrictions, drug use and tobacco smoking should be tolerated at all, anywhere? There is not one single Halachic authority who denies that smoking is against the law. But they tend to be tolerant of people "who cannot help it." You can't very well ban yeshiva students from smoking on Halachic grounds if half the teachers are addicted.

One might argue that in Halacha there are two important themes that support tolerance. First, the Talmud is against adding restrictions on the grounds that it is difficult enough to stick to the limits God has placed without adding to them. Second, the Talmud accepts that rabbinic laws that are simply too much for the masses to cope with can be annulled (hence the Talmudic ban on non-Jewish bread and oils had to be modified or simply cancelled altogether).

The trouble is that in almost every other area, Orthodoxy piles on extra and added restrictions regardless. So if the tolerance of smoking and drugs is based on the principle that religion should limit its negative impact or that some things are just asking too much of people, how come the general mood of Orthodoxy is to add restriction on restriction on restriction?

I suspect the answer is self-indulgence. On matters that offer concessions to males of a certain affiliation and conformity, their rabbinic leaders tend to be soft. But on matters that might make life easier for the average Jew or Jewess in the marketplace, this looks too much like giving in to secular influences and being too concessionary. In other words, there is one law for the god squad and another for the devil's gang. Does not this highlight an inconsistency?

The authorities in most countries have banned opiates. But then painkillers became the drug of choice and addiction. It's a never-ending cycle. The drug agencies keep running around like dogs chasing their tails. They spend more money, employ more agents, cause damage and ruin people's lives, and still make hardly a dent in the flow or use of the drugs they do not tax. Think of the money saved by scrapping wasteful agencies, by legalizing and taxing all drugs, by freeing up police to stop other, more serious social crimes, and then using all that money to make the world a better place. Those who insist on ruining their lives will do so with or without drugs. We haven't introduced laws against being bums. But we know common sense rarely wins.

RESIGN

In February 2013 Pope Benedict became the first Pope to resign in 600 years. His resignation sent an important message to our own religious leadership though they show no signs of taking it on board. Know when it's time to step down. What humility it takes for someone to realize that he does not have the strength or the capacity to lead such a significant movement. Most geriatric leaders hold on until the Almighty (or His agent) puts them out of their misery.

Religions have always faced the challenges of how to get the faithful to behave in practice according to the ideals and original visions of their founders. Haven't you noticed how they love to talk about peace and goodwill on earth and loving one's fellow human being, yet at the same time tend to disregard the feelings and sensitivities of others? They seem to believe that only the faithful deserve love and concern, and all the rest had better either agree with them or face the consequences. All religions now face the challenge of self-indulgent materialism, to which the overwhelming majority of humans on earth subscribe, regardless of faith. And all religions suffer from the abuses of power, of petty men and women seeking to control, bully, and fight their internecine battles as though this was what they were created for.

It is true that religions also have their saints and altruistic souls who toil and struggle to improve the human condition and to help individuals of all sorts cope with the pressures of life. They may actually be the majority. But on balance it's the abuses and misuses that get the publicity.

A public religious leader has to be strong and of saintly disposition; ideally a scholar, too. But if he heads an organization he has also to be a CEO controlling an unwieldy institution. He has to be a disciplinarian to rope in rogue clerics, a fighter to hold firm against the inroads of secularism and fanaticism, a warm and empathetic healer of souls and supporter of colleagues. Such a person doesn't exist. But to come close requires strength and energy.

Normally large organizations and parties promote up through the ranks, and the safe men of consensus tend to get the job. Think of the Russian Communist Party, but then think of the exception in Gorbachev. Similarly the papacy has had its exceptions like John XXIII and John Paul II.

The Catholic Church has been facing very serious internal issues of sexual abuse and financial corruption. The very size of the papal bureaucracy, with its rival departments, interests, and theologians, has been compounding its difficulties. In Europe the church is in serious decline. The largest Catholic communities are in the Americas; yet there too it is shrinking and facing the growing popularity of Pentecostal churches. And in the Middle East, Pakistan, and China, the Catholic Church is actually under serious assault. The last seriously reforming pope was John XXIII, but those who have followed him have tended toward caution and conservatism even where they have been charismatic. They have fought to preserve a hard-line orthodoxy that in fact has proven to be an ineffective response to the challenges they face.

The single most notable change in the Catholic Church in my lifetime has been its attitude toward the Jews. The history of the papacy has been one of persecution. The norm was to attack Jews and Judaism. Only rare exceptions extended any sort of sympathy. Pope Pius IX, who died in 1878, supported baptizing and kidnapping a Jewish child, Edgardo Mortara, and refusing to ever hand him back to his parents. Pope Pius XII was accused of not condemning Hitler's treatment of the Jews, and although he may have turned a blind eye to sheltering some Jewish victims, many in his church stood in the way of returning Jewish children who were rescued by Christians.

We owe a tremendous debt to John XXIII for beginning the process of reconciliation that Benedict XVI has so formidably championed. From a Jewish point of view, the last two popes have both been influenced by the Holocaust and have been the most positive and supportive of Jews and Israel. From being the branch of Christianity least well disposed toward the Jews, it has now overtaken by far most of the established Protestant churches that are now solidly, sadly, in the thrall of anti-Israelism. Even so, reformers have faced opposition within their own house. The church is not monolithic. Parts of it remain anti-Semitic. But the choice of Francis as the new pope, a humane, saintly man who had excellent relations with Jews, marks a new positive phase in the papacy.

All this reminds me of why we should take a leaf out of the pope's book. Who are the leaders of the Jewish religious world today? One thinks of the late Rav Shach, Rav Elyashiv, and Rav Ovadia Yosef, as well as Rav Shteinman, still alive today, to mention only the most prominent. They are a gerontocracy of men who, in their nineties, might still have amazing brains, honed on years of study and analysis. They might also be the most pious of men. Yet it is also clear that they are tired and weak and out of touch with the world around them. Rav Shteinman refuses to make any compromise on allowing those Charedi young men who do not want to sit and study to go into the army. Some rabbis call Naftali Bennett worse than a non-Jew, a Nazi, because he refuses to abide by Charedi authority. Those are not the words of spiritual leadership.

Because of their infirmity, elderly rabbis are surrounded by warring family heirs, political fixers, gatekeepers, and secretaries who shelter them and filter through only what they want to let the great man see and hear. Unfortunately the next generation of rabbis is riven with rivalry and ambition. It is not a hopeful picture.

The challenges Judaism faces in Israel and in the diaspora are enormous. More conferences will not make a jot of difference. But new leadership just might. Yet the present reactions of its leadership are akin to paralysis. There is no sense of the need for new perspectives and new ways of dealing with the challenges. Orthodoxy, like the Catholic Church, has its scandals. It thinks it can deal with them itself when clearly it is not. When this happens, it is time for either a peaceful change or a revolution. I feel we are thriving despite our leadership, not because of it.

WEALTH

Thomas Piketty is a French economist. His book *Capital in the Twenty-First Century* has taken the left-wing intellectual world by storm. Reviews are everywhere, and if you want to be up to date in the salon or the pub, you'll need to read up on his major points. The truth is that it's not the essence of his message that has made his book such a topic of conversation and worth reading, but rather the impressive way he has marshalled his facts, research, history, and broad cultural analysis to make his point. The book is worth reading even if it is long, dense and you think his prescriptions and parts of his analysis are arguable.

The increasing gap between the very wealthy and everyone else has now become a cliché of the "1 percent." There has throughout history always been excessive inequality. Piketty argues that it is getting significantly worse than it has been for a long time. His touchstone is the Belle Époque (associated with France in the fifty or so years before the First World War and the period of the massively wealthy US robber barons and bankers). Such periods end either in revolution or in an extended period of recession, slow growth, or stagnation. Which is what he thinks will happen unless, among other things, we tax the rich more to reduce the gap.

There is much debate between those who think one should spend one's way out of it by encouraging job creation and letting the rich keep as much as possible in the hope that it will trickle down, and others who believe the less fortunate need more help and the rich should be taxed to provide it. The welfare element of the US budget is rocketing to the point where it is beginning to look as though the United States is indeed becoming a welfare state. Government increasingly is the employment safety net of the disadvantaged. At the same time, the very rich have many means of avoiding taxation not available to middle-class wage earners.

Piketty makes the point that once wages were the route to upward mobility and financial self-improvement. But increasingly the gap is in capital, mainly inherited, that provides the 1 percent with its wealth. Old forms of employment are increasingly obsolete. Whole swaths of the population will be left in the cold as many simple human tasks are more cheaply done abroad. This means that, with exceptions, the American dream of upward mobility is becoming less and less realistic. It is very difficult to rise on the basis of employment, which means that, as in Jane Austen's era, if you care about such things, you either inherit money or marry into it.

All this might be so, but there are other scenarios. Nowadays brainpower is the gold dust of success. After all, a brainy (and hardworking) child will win scholarships to good universities, regardless of capital. There are many who use their brains and flair to create Internet fortunes every bit as big as those of the old industries. And many of the richest of the new billionaires now, as in previous years, plan to leave most of their fortunes to their charities. Sure, the majority remain scrooge-like, selfish, egotistic accumulators.

Humanity has always been the good, the bad, and the ugly. At the same time, most of humanity is rising faster out of poverty and hunger than ever before, and world health is improving by leaps and bounds. So I am not as pessimistic as Piketty can sound. Revolutions come not when the rich have too much, but when the poor have too little. But then Plato said that in *The Republic* over two thousand years ago.

Humans have always been different, some more successful than others. People will always be unequal (though of course they should be treated equally under the law). Some are brainier, stronger, and better looking, and some try harder. Give me the ugly grafter any time. Oligarchies and aristocracies, regardless of whether they have been praiseworthy or revolting, have always tried to preserve their wealth. They have done this through military expansion, theft, and strategic marriages. The 1 percent of Rome, medieval Europe, American Robber Barons, or colonial imperialism all accumulated massive wealth on the backs of conquest, the subdued, serfs, and slaves. In the end they did all collapse, but was it just because of financial inequality, and are we witnessing the beginning of the end of the American empire?

Historians, philosophers, and economists have always disagreed on fundamentals, on statistics, on which system of capital is preferable, whether markets can or cannot monitor themselves, whether government intervention is always good or always bad. The great economists of the past all claimed to have the answer. Now we know they didn't, and we still don't have it. The best academics analyze. The worst prescribe!

That is why I find the Jewish approach so wise and validating. The Torah recognizes there will always be differences. It does not assert that money is necessarily the root of all evil or that accumulation is wrong. The Torah prescribes no specific or doctrinaire economic policy. It simply advocates and stresses honesty and charity. No matter what the economic or the political system, "the poor will never cease," says the Bible. And in dealing with the problem, the Torah insists that in addition to the obligation to give, justice should be fair and blind.

We have always had our fat cats: the Bible mentions Korach, the Talmud Ben Kalba Savua and Rebbi Yochanan ben Zakkai. Spain had Shmuel HaNagid, the Ottoman Empire the duke of Naxos, Europe gave us Rothschild and Montefiore, and now our Jewish billionaires are mainly American but there are plenty of Israelis too. Most of them have all tended to donate generously to charities while living way above the average standard. Still, the vast majority of our people have always struggled. We have an enviable record of helping the poor. The amount of charity that the Orthodox, in particular, dispense is unbelievable (and much of it is kosher).

Our theological position is clear. First of all, financial is not the only form of wealth. Secondly, if you are fortunate to have it, share it. If God or nature or chance has bequeathed you billions, it is up to you as the custodian and the agent to ensure that you help those in pain, poverty, and oppression. Systems come and go like fashions. I do not know who is right. But I do know that if there's someone I can help, help them I must. That is my religion. That is Judaism.

ISRAELI PREJUDICE

The riot of Ethiopian Jews in Israel this year of 2015 protesting against racism is a sad reflection on Israeli society. It must not be exaggerated, but it should come as no surprise. There has always been a disconnect between the ideals of Israel's state institutions and the petty prejudice and fighting against and between its minority communities. There has always been a distinction, in countries as well as people, between the theory and the practice.

Israel, as a matter of policy, has always taken pride in the fact that Judaism is colorblind. Unfortunately, too many of its citizens have not been. Israel always voted against apartheid in the United Nations. But when it needed to protect itself, it entered into covert negotiations with racist South Africa. Israel took great pride in welcoming thousands of black Jews from Africa, and many of them have risen to positions of prominence in Israeli society. But at the same time they have, as a community, suffered from both religious and secular prejudice. The poor Ethiopian soldier who was beaten was both black and religious. In some quarters in Israel that is a double whammy.

Israel has always been a complex, conflicted, and confused society. Originally the pioneer Zionists came into direct conflict with old-time religious settlers in the Holy Land who had been coming to live there for a thousand years before Zionism ever existed as a movement. The newcomers treated the old ones with contempt and ridicule. As Zionism grew in strength and numbers, it came into conflict with Arab nationalism. The succeeding riots and wars only exacerbated tensions between them. Within the Zionist movement itself, left-wing ideologues fought with right-wing pragmatists. They struggled and even killed each other.

The eastern European left-wing secular Jewish pioneers of the early years despised the more cultured and sophisticated central European refugees, who came in response to Nazism. Together they combined to discriminate against the Oriental Jews who came in droves after the state was declared and they were expelled from Arab countries. The conditions they lived in and the disadvantages they labored under simply beggar belief but then State of Israel was new, poor, under constant attack, ideologically divided and barely organized. It took thirty years before the Sefardi communities reached parity in power and social standing. Even then, Moroccans, Yemenites, Bene Israel from India, Karaites, and sundry exotic scattered tribes brought home all had to fight legal and social discrimination. There was even a Black Panther movement in Israel of Oriental Jews fighting against prejudice and disadvantage. Once the Department of Statistics used separate categories for Oriental and Occidental Jews. Now no longer, because they are so intermarried. Yet still there is discrimination, particularly in the Charedi world, where the Ashkenazi rabbinic elite feel the Oriental Jews are neither as religious nor as socially acceptable as other Ashkenazis are.

The Russian Jews who came later were discriminated against too. The women were all supposed to be hookers and the men all gangsters, until their intellectual contribution to Israeli life proved their value and equality. Then came the Ethiopians, who were welcomed (although their religious status was challenged by the Ashkenazi rabbinate). They were given a far better life than the one they had before, but then they were discriminated against because, like any immigrants, they needed more help to overcome their disadvantages.

The sad fact is that Israel, like a high school where the newcomers are made to pay by the top classes for the hazing and bullying they suffered as freshmen, has always given the new "pupils" a rough time. This doesn't excuse it, but it is a sad reflection on human nature. Yet no country anywhere in the world has succeeded in absorbing so many disproportionately large and different cultures into one society with only marginal and occasional ruptures. Certainly the army plays a crucial equalizing role.

There is of course another form of discrimination: the economic one. Usually racial minorities are the ones who suffer disproportionally from this, if they come from societies with poor education. The economic issues in Israel were highlighted by the public protests in Tel Aviv. They went beyond any racial lines and focused purely on the gap between the rich and the poor. The Ethiopians suffer twice.

This is an issue throughout the world. In the United States, spontaneous and organized violence has erupted in Ferguson and in Baltimore over police brutality, which is as much a problem as are poverty, unemployment, and disrupted family structure. Just as emblematic of the challenges are the demonstrations against Wall Street and the "one percenters." In the United States, as in Israel, the gap between the rich and the poor exacerbates the sense of insecurity and alienation. These issues must be addressed. Every politician says so. Yet the fact is that in the end political dysfunction gets in the way of finding solutions. So do ideologically different and conflicting approaches to the problems. Actually, as the Torah says, "The poor will never cease," so thinking that soaking the rich will solve the problem is misguided. Creating jobs is an important step. But still it assumes young poor people will necessarily want them.

The only truly effective answer (once legislation against discrimination is legally enforced) is the slow but inevitable intermingling of different racial and social communities. We have actually seen this happen in Israel over time. But it takes time, and it takes education and opportunity to succeed.

Israeli leadership is responding well in public to the latest eruption. They are going out of their way to express solidarity and to bring rogue cops to justice, as indeed is the United States. But the social issues will continue to be a challenge until time and the better human qualities of our nature get round to realizing that we are, as the Talmud says, all the children of one God and all equal under the law.

SALONICA

Wondering about Jews living in Europe under difficult conditions reminded me of the Jews of Salonica. Once it was one of the most bustling and creative of Jewish communities. Now it is gone. Most of them were carted off to Auschwitz.

Several years ago I reviewed Mark Mazower's excellent *Salonica, City of Ghosts*, which covers the rise and fall of a major Jewish community from 1430 to 1950 and records its changing fortunes under different conquerors and occupiers. They were rarely completely safe. Neither Greek nor Turk (and certainly not Nazi) comes away with much honor. Of all of them, the Turks were the ones who treated the Jewish population the least inhumanely.

Most Ashkenazi Jews are sadly unaware of the richness of Salonica's long Jewish history and the important part played by the Ottoman Empire in welcoming Jews fleeing from Spain after the expulsion of 1492. Whereas Yiddish is now thriving as the lingua franca of ultra-Orthodox Judaism around the world, the number speaking Ladino, the Sephardi equivalent, is sadly small and diminishing. However, more and more books are now bringing its rich heritage to light.

Salonica was not just a city of Sephardi Jews. There were Ashkenazi communities too, attracted by trade and the tolerant conditions that were far more attractive than most eastern European communities. The Ottoman Empire in the early nineteenth century was still threatening central Europe, and both Russia and the western European powers were meddling in Ottoman affairs. It was only by the end of the century that the Ottoman Empire was described as the "Sick Man of Europe." Nevertheless, the writing was on the wall. Society was fracturing. Extremists were spreading their malignant aggressions. Western and central Europe were in the ascendancy as the industrial revolution swung the balance of power away from religious control, and the slow decline of Islamic power in the Middle East began.

I have just read a moving short memoir written in Ladino and translated into English: *A Jewish Voice from Ottoman Salonica: The Ladino Memoir of Sa'adi Besalel a-Levi*, published through the generosity of Joe Dwek.

Sa'adi a-Levi's memoir covers this period of transition in the early nineteenth century. It starts with a community controlled by its rich men and its rabbis exercising power through the millet system, in which each religion in the empire ran its own affairs with absolute authority, subject only to the administrative oversight of the Ottoman government and its agents. Within a society that was dominated by religious authority, and before the Enlightenment began to weaken the grip of the pious, rabbis, imams, and priests could make use of the death penalty, corporal punishment in the form of the bastinado (lashing the bare soles of a victim's feet with canes), and the ban or excommunication that effectively excluded someone from the benefits, support, and protection of the community. At a time when there was no governmental social security, health care, or unemployment benefits, communities played an essential role in people's lives. Exclusion meant destitution, and the only option was to convert to another religion. The authorities exercised enormous power buttressed by a culture of gossip, malicious slander, and, above all, incredible superstition. The ordinary Jew, Christian, or Muslim was at the mercy of his or her religious authorities.

Sa'adi inherited a modest printing business and had to eke out a living for himself and his orphaned siblings by becoming a successful musician and singer, able to perform both Jewish and Turkish music at weddings and community celebrations. But he was constantly being threatened by his own religious authorities who disapproved of his non-Jewish music and by competitors who used underhanded methods to destroy his livelihood and attack his family. Sa'adi himself was outspoken in his criticism of the methods used by rabbis to control the community, of the unfair financial impositions that made kosher food very expensive, and of the way the rabbis fought among themselves and supported their favorites to make life difficult for those who opposed their abuses. Things haven't changed!

Sa'adi describes how, in his own case, his only protection was to find some important member of the community, one of the rich men, the *gevirim*, to support him. He struggled in his early years. But as Western powers began to exercise an influence on Salonican Jews, this led to the opening up of the community. The arrival of the French Alliance Israélite Universelle spread secular education and ideas. This divided the community between those who wanted to preserve the old ways and those who welcomed progress. The absolute authority of the rabbinate began to wane.

This situation applied just as much to the Ashkenazi communities of Europe. They too had been controlled by this usually unholy alliance of the wealthy and the rabbinate, where control and conformity were the tools of social cohesion. Superstition, the fear of curses, and exclusion were used freely to coerce and subdue. All this is still effective nowadays in certain circles.

We are inclined to forget how significant the Enlightenment was in challenging this religious monopoly. The freedoms we have are overwhelmingly due to the separation of state and religion and the limitations imposed on religious authority that developed during the nineteenth century. But every movement produces a reaction. As religious authority lost its grip, materialism, La Belle Époque, lack of any restraint, and the abuses of freedom began to gnaw away at the security that closed communities offered.

In the West, these polarizing forces usually coexist and accommodate. Much of the Muslim world continues to regress. The very forces that led to the collapse of the Ottoman Empire drove its fragments back to the dark ages. This is where much of the Middle East finds itself today, with its executions, amputations, rape, and slavery that so many refuse to recognize or condemn.

It is ironic that in the Middle East now, only Israel is able to accommodate both secular values and extreme religious ones.

Sa'adi reminds us of what we have escaped. But his memoir stands as a warning of what we might return to if we allow religion too much control. Personal choices and freedoms are essential. Equally, the right to live an extreme religious life must also be preserved. But if we do not limit extremism to its own backyard, we too will be dragged back to the primitive, cruel, and fanatical medievalism that he survived.

18663251R00196

Printed in Great Britain
by Amazon